MILES COLLEGE

A Journey into Academic Excellence

■ ■ ■

Sarah C. Johnson, Editor
Miles College

KENDALL/HUNT PUBLISHING COMPANY
4050 Westmark Drive   Dubuque, Iowa 52002

CONTENTS

ACKNOWLEDGMENTS

I acknowledge with much appreciation the contributions of the following administrators, faculty members and staff members in development of this volume:

Albert J. H. Sloan, II, President
Hattie G. Lamar, Academic Dean
Carolyn Ray, Dean of Students
Emma Sloan, Orientation Instructor and Counselor
Edgar Lamar, Orientation Instructor and Counselor
Rick Owens, Photographer

I wish to extend special thanks to the Academic Dean, Hattie G. Lamar, for her support and encouragement in development of this textbook. Special recognition is extended to Mrs. Emma Sloan for her creation of the book's title: *A Journey into Academic Excellence.*

Sarah C. Johnson

PREFACE

or most students the freshman year is one of tremendous change and adjustment. Some students leave home for the first time to attend college in a strange city and environment. For others the freshman year represents a re-entry into the educational arena after several years in the work force. Still others enter college in their own city, but find that they too must make adjustments as they encounter new instructors, classmates, and meet the challenge of academic requirements and expectations that differ from high school.

While we recognize that the freshman year is characterized by change and adjustment, we hope that the changes and adjustments that are part of the first year experience will be transforming for each of you. We hope that the freshman experience at Miles College will be so very inspiring that you will develop the study skills, thirst for knowledge and cultural awareness that will propel you to the day of graduation, and help you realize your potential personally and professionally.

Miles College: A Journey into Academic Excellence represents our combined effort to create a collection of materials that we believe will be useful as you embark upon your college career. Through careful study of the materials that have been compiled in this text, we believe that you will acquire the essentials for success as a college student.

Since successful college performance is based upon one's understanding of requirements and services, Chapters 2 and 3 cover general campus regulations and a description of student services.

Chapter 4 begins with a well written piece by the Academic Dean, Dr. Hattie Lamar, regarding student deportment. Dr. Lamar presents the classroom behaviors and expectations for students at Miles, and challenges students to become serious and focused as they study and strive to achieve their personal and academic goals. Practical suggestions and study tips are presented along with point by point descriptions of the ideal Miles College man and woman.

Student Support Services Counselors, Mrs. Emma Sloan and Mr. Edgar Lamar, introduce Chapter 5 by presenting helpful suggestions for students regarding the role of the academic advisor and the importance of critical thinking as academic survival skills. Practical information and tips are presented throughout the chapter regarding time management, note taking, test taking, writing skills, listening skills and more.

Information is provided in Chapter 6 on relationships and communication. This information has been included because we consider social well being most critical to one's success in college. The friends we choose and the associations we make can sometimes determine success or failure.

In Chapter 7 of the text, information is provided regarding student health. We trust that you will find this information helpful as you strive to acquire good health habits and maintain a healthy life style during your stay at Miles.

Study carefully each chapter presented in this text, and strive to execute the suggestions and recommendations that have been presented for your consideration as a freshman at Miles. Then go on to become another great Miles College graduate.

Sarah C. Johnson

PRESIDENT'S MESSAGE

During the founding years of this great Institution, our forefathers' vision was to make Miles College worthy of the patronage of all classes. Men of vision accepted this challenge, and over the years, a rich legacy was created. For more than ninety-four years, students, faculty, staff, administrators, alumni and trustees have worked diligently to develop navigational aids that have guided our journey to excellence. We are the heirs to this illustrious heritage, from which we draw academic sustenance and fuel for many other endeavors.

We stand on the shoulders of the giants who preceded us. However, colleges possess a continuity that links the past and the future to the present. It is important for Miles to focus upon maintaining its traditions, while envisioning and acting upon those things that will make a difference in the future by continually improving the college's quality. Internally, we challenge each other to "Leave it better than you found it." It is because the Miles College Family has responded to this challenge in past years that the Institution has witnessed improvements and gains.

Over the past five years a metamorphosis has taken place at Miles College. Advances in enrollment and academic achievement have been matched by advances in the Institution's increased financial stability. With a strong financial base, and achievements resulting from hard work, Miles is poised to become an even greater center of learning in higher education. One obvious component of the college's evolution is the improvement in our physical plant. Within the last two years, Miles has committed over $600,000 in capital improvements, through which we have renovated the Humanities Building, Erskine Ramsay Hall, and the Knox-Windham Gymnasium.

Further, April, 1998, marked the beginning of construction of a new $4.7 million dollar residence hall, an upgrading of the athletic field, and renovations of the Taggart Science Building, and Williams Hall (the increase in enrollment necessitated the renovation of Williams into a residence hall for men). With the construction of the new residence hall, Williams Hall will be returned to the status of a much-needed classroom and office building.

Construction is exciting, especially as it is indicative of the extensive improvements the college is making. However, the true beauty of Miles College is not in its buildings, or its enrollment statistics, or its academic offerings. The true beauty of Miles College is in each of us. It is in the spirit of sensitivity and hunger for quality through which we support our daily work and long-range plans. As with our Founding Fathers, we too, commit to making Miles College an institution for which we can all be proud . . . an institution on the move, seeking new levels of excellence through continuous improvement . . . **preparing leaders for the twenty-first century.**

Albert J. H. Sloan, II

OFFICE OF ACADEMIC AFFAIRS

Dear Learners,

Because of your recent enrollment at Miles College, you are now a new Milean. Please take PRIDE in being a Milean and participate fully in both the intellectually challenging course work that will be offered you and in the numerous, enriching *extra-class* learnings that will be available to you. Your total involvement in the Miles experience will contribute greatly to your becoming the Miles College Man or the Miles College Woman that you are poised to become.

Welcome to Miles College. We have great expectations for your growth. You should have great expectations that we provide you with higher literacy, broad and specific subject matter knowledge, technological competence, spiritual values, and leadership skills to assist your total involvement in the opportunities that we provide. Successful teaching happens through the participation of eager learners.

Welcome to the Miles College teaching-learning connection.

Sincerely,

Hattie G. Lamar
Dean of Academic Affairs

THE COUNSELING AND TESTING CENTER

Dear Freshman Student:

Staff members of the Counseling and Testing Center are actively involved in a variety of campus-wide programs, and participate along with students in extracurricular activities. Such a collaborative climate is vital in helping students prepare for the life-long experience that is expected from a liberal arts education. Personal and group counseling sessions provide opportunities that help students stay on track socially, academically and emotionally, thus fostering a spirit of achievement that assists them in reaching their goals.

Counselors assist students in adjusting to the college environment immediately upon enrollment through the following services: assisting with interpersonal conflicts and stressful situations; redirecting emotional concerns; and redirecting uncertainties that interfere with the learning process. As students utilize the varied services offered through the Counseling Center, we believe that they develop a positive attitude; renew their strengths and share voluntarily in the excitement of their social and academic experiences at the college.

The Counseling Center continues to fulfill the diverse needs of students by (1) assisting them in effective problem-solving techniques and (2) aiding them in developing workable strategies for functioning productively in the college environment and in society at-large.

Enjoy your Miles College experience and know that trained and caring professionals will be available to you throughout your academic preparation.

Sincerely,

Joyce Dugan Wood, M.Ed., J.D.
Director

A Member of the United Negro College Fund

CHAPTER 1
About Miles College:
A Brief History

■ Historical Sketch

Miles College is a four-year, accredited, liberal arts College that enrolls more than 1200 students. It is located in Fairfield, Alabama, six miles west of the downtown Birmingham area.

Miles is a church-related college, founded in 1905 by the Colored Methodist Episcopal Church, now the Christian Methodist Episcopal Church. The College is still supported by and affiliated with the C.M.E. Church, although the faculty and student body represent many different denominations. The curriculum is formally and informally undergirded by attention to morality and ethics and to the perpetuation of Christian values.

Miles College began with efforts dating back to 1898 by the Colored Methodist Episcopal Church in Alabama to establish an educational institution. At that time, there were only two conferences in the state, the Alabama and the North Alabama Conferences. Each conference made an effort to build an institution, and for some years each of these conferences operated separate schools, one at Thomasville, established in 1898, and the other at Booker City (now Docena), established in 1902. The college is generally considered to have developed from the high school operated at Booker City by the North Alabama Conference. However, it may be considered a merger of the two schools, for the Thomasville High School served as a feeder to Miles College for several years.

In the spring of 1907, the Board of Trustees decided to expand the scope of the school's curriculum. Acting on this decision, it exchanged the site of Booker City for the present site and erected a large brick building along with one or more frame buildings. The work of the institution as a college was begun in the fall of 1907.

In 1908, the organization of the school was completed, and it was chartered under the laws of the State of Alabama as Miles Memorial College, in honor of Bishop William H. Miles. In 1941, the Trustees voted to change the name of the Institution to "Miles College."

The College has had the following Presidents:

James A. Bray, 1907–1912
William A. Bell, 1912–1913 (First Term)
John Wesley Gilbert, 1913–1914
George A. Payne, 1914–1918
Robert T. Brown, 1918–1922
George L. Word, 1922–1926
Mack P. Burley, 1926–1931
Brooks Dickens, 1931–1936
William A. Bell, 1936–January, 1961
Lucius H. Pitts, 1961–1971
W. Clyde Williams, 1971–1986
Leroy Johnson, 1986–1989
Albert J. H. Sloan, II, 1989–Present

Miles College has a particular responsibility to work for the welfare of all people, especially those in the Black Community, and, as a consequence, has been responsible for introducing into the community Headstart and Upward Bound programs, Manpower Training, and teacher institutes in English, history, mathematics and elementary education. Currently the college offers extended day classes and several community outreach programs.

Miles College has a cooperative, interinstitutional enrollment policy with the University of Alabama at Birmingham which allows students of either college to enroll for credit in courses of the other. Miles also has arrangements with Alabama A & M University for students who begin their work at Miles College to finish programs in Engineering and Physics. Too, the college has articulation agreements with Lawson State Community College and Bishop State Junior College. Miles College's participation in the Honors Program Consortium and the Birmingham Area Consortium for Higher Education (BACHE) expands the availability of course offerings by providing additional opportunities for Miles students to take special courses at Birmingham Southern College, Samford University, or the University of Alabama at Birmingham, though enrolled at Miles College. An Asian Studies program is available to Miles students through BACHE.

Miles College remains open to all qualified persons regardless of race, religion, or national origin. For most of its years of service, Miles has been the principal four-year collegiate institution open to Black students in the metropolitan area of Birmingham. As a consequence, the College has a proud record of achievement in preparing teachers, ministers, and business and professional men and women to serve the community. A high percentage of the Black educational and political leaders in the Birmingham area are graduates of Miles College.

Miles College is a fully accredited member of the Commission on Colleges, Southern Association of Colleges and Schools for the award of baccalaureate degrees and is a member of the United Negro College Fund.

Miles offers Bachelor Degree programs with majors in Accounting, Asian Studies, Biology, Biology Education, Business Administration, Chemistry, Chemistry Education, Communications, Elementary Education, English, Environmental Science, Language Arts Education, Mathematics, Mathematics Education, Political Science, Social Science Education, and Social Work. In addition courses in art, French, Spanish, philosophy, religion, dance, theatre, and computer science are offered. Graduates who complete approved teacher education programs qualify for the State of Alabama Class "B" Professional Certificate in Elementary and High School Education. The College also offers extended day classes for working students to begin study towards a degree.

■ College Mission Statement

Miles College is a Christian Methodist Episcopal Church-related, historically Black, four-year liberal arts institution founded in 1905 to provide leadership to the Black Community. This mission has been expanded to include an emphasis on the personal development of all individuals, regardless of race, who, upon graduation from Miles, will possess an understanding of their own mission in a global society. Accreditation by the Southern Association of Colleges and Schools attests to the college's ability to provide a strong educational program for its students.

The college aims to utilize the best of its rich heritage in providing an environment that is both Christian and intellectual. The College recruits students from diverse academic, social, economic, and racial backgrounds who manifest potential for academic achieve-

ment in an institution of higher education. Additionally, the College maintains an open-door admissions policy that allows promising underachieving students the opportunity to enroll in developmental courses with specialized learning laboratories and tutorial opportunities. Students must successfully complete all developmental courses with a grade of "C" before enrolling in a major division. Moreover, students are urged not to drop or withdraw from pre-college developmental or orientation courses—as an indication of determination to develop their potential for college work.

The college provides an Honors Program for the academically accelerated student who has been awarded an academic scholarship to Miles and who wishes to continue stimulating study through a specified number of advanced courses.

Teaching is undergirded by a strong advisement system and student-centered approaches to learning. Also, instruction is provided by a caring faculty that is committed to nurturing students' self-esteem, creativity, and humanistic nature.

Not only does the College strive to produce students who possess critical and ethical perspectives about a global and pluralistic society, it also dedicates its energies to sponsoring community programs and providing leadership opportunities. Relatedly, faculty and students are encouraged to engage in activities for the purpose of heightening consciousness of current societal issues.

To fulfill its mission, Miles College seeks to graduate students with the following attributes, expressed as

Expected Educational Outcomes:

1. Proficiency in standard communication skills—speaking, writing, reading, and listening;

2. Skill in critical and creative thinking;

3. Skill in problem solving;

4. Capacity to appreciate the arts;

5. Knowledge of various career areas that influence intelligent choices and productive membership in society;

6. Sensitivity to cultural differences in such areas as history, language, and customs;

7. Respect for religious creeds in general and for Christian ethics in particular;

8. Competence in at least one major field of study;

9. Capacity for lifelong learning; and

10. Computer and technological literacy.

The faculty and staff are serious about their commitment to the college's mission. Thus, all of the college's activities have a direct relationship to the personal development of individual students.

CHAPTER 2
General Campus Regulations

Appearance and Dress Code

A
s an academic institution, Miles College engages students in pre-professional, academic, and social learning experiences. It stimulates the student's awareness and appreciation of accepted societal expectations with regard to professional and personal preparation, appearance, and judgment.

In accordance with the goals and objectives of Miles College, to prepare students to competitively compete in the professional work force upon graduation, the College sets forth the following Policies which govern appearance and dress for all associations in the Miles College Community.

Undergarments may not be worn as fashion statements on campus. All undergarments must be covered by appropriate outer clothing at all times.

Slacks, jeans and shorts may be worn with appropriate fittings, belts, suspenders, etc. Baggy or loose fitting slacks, jeans, and shorts which hang from the hips and buttocks are never described as professional and are therefore unacceptable.

Shorts, skirts and dresses of varied lengths may be worn. To determine appropriate length, one must consider appearance when sitting or standing. Shorts, skirts, and/or dresses, should never expose the upper thighs or lower buttocks. Length of the shorts, skirts, and dresses can be determined by extending the arm down toward the knee. No hem line must be shorter than your fingertips when your arm is extended.

Splits in skirts and dresses may be worn. The appropriate length of the split will meet the fingertip when extended down the body.

Biking shorts, spandex clothing and biking pants should not be worn except while participating in related sports activities.

Hats and caps should never be worn by males or females while in an academic or residential building. Ladies may wear hats during appropriate formal occasions. Hats and caps may be worn during athletic events.

All **shirts, tops, and blouses** must fully cover the upper body. **Half shirts, tube tops, halter tops, and muscle shirts** may not be worn. **Blouses and dresses** may be cut in the neckline areas. Necklines, however, which expose cleavage and/or bust lines may not be worn.

No clothing may be worn which has cutouts or holes.

Clothing which displays messages or illustrations of a profane or violent nature—or which has sexual connotations, or which advertise or suggest statements concerning drugs, alcohol, illegal substances, and weapons, may not be worn.

The President of the college, and the Administration, have final authority with respect to the interpretation of this policy.

■ Sexual Harassment Policy

Miles College affirms its policy to maintain a working and learning environment free from sexual harassment of faculty, staff and students. Sexual harassment at Miles is not simply inappropriate behavior, it is a violation of federal and state laws. Title IX of the Education Amendments of 1972 states:

"No person in the United States shall, on the ground of race, color, national origin, age, or handicap, be excluded from participation in, be denied the benefits of, or be subjected to discrimination under any program or activity receiving Federal financial assistance, or be so treated on the basis of sex under most education programs or activities receiving Federal assistance."

Because of the seriousness of this matter, sexual harassment in any form is forbidden. Miles College is required by law to take steps necessary to prevent sexual harassment. These steps include informing individuals of their rights and responsibilities, and developing sanctions against sexual harassment.

Definition: Sexual harassment is defined as verbal or physical conduct of a sexual nature, imposed on the basis of sex, by an employee or agent of a recipient that denies, limits, provides different, or conditions the provision of aid, benefits, services or treatment protected under Title IX.

Sexual harassment can cause serious physical or psychological damage to faculty, staff or students; affecting grades, attendance, performance and pride in one's work.

Sexual harassment includes:

- Unwelcome sexual advances, requests for sexual favors and other verbal or physical conduct of a sexual nature carried out by someone in the workplace or educational setting.
- Such behavior may offend the recipient, cause discomfort or humiliation, or interfere with job or school performance.
- Sexual harassment may carry the explicit or implicit message that if the victim does not comply with the harasser's demands, there may be retaliation.
- Sexual harassment may include: inappropriate personal attention by an instructor, administrator, fellow student or a person with power or authority over another, inappropriate touching, personal questions or comments of a sexual nature; pressure for dates or sexual activity; attempted sexual relations, sexual relations, generally offensive cartoons or posters, and sexual jokes or comments.

Hearing/Grievance Procedure

Miles College has a legal responsibility to respond to allegations of sexual harassment. The College will take appropriate steps necessary to prevent sexual harassment from occurring by: raising campus awareness; identifying actions which may constitute sexual harassment; outlining responsibilities for preventing sexual harassment; explaining and making conspicuous procedures for dealing with harassment; and providing information on Institutional Policies and Practices for filing sexual harassment complaints.

Title IX mandates that all sexual harassment complaints be investigated and resolved in a "prompt and equitable" manner. Awareness of a sensitivity to the potentially negative effect on the lives and careers of both parties involved is of great importance in handling an investigation: therefore, **Miles College will assure confidentiality when dealing with a sexual harassment charge.**

Informal Complaint

Whenever possible, complaints should be resolved informally. Students may wish to report instances of sexual harassment in writing to the Counseling Center. Faculty and Staff members may informally report incidents in writing to the immediate supervisor and/or Department Head. If informal steps prove unsuccessful, the matter should be further pursued via the formal complaint/grievance procedure.

Formal Complaint Procedure

1. Complainant must submit the complaint or grievance in writing to the Counseling Center specifying the form of redress desired:

   a. A complainant is defined as any administrator, faculty/certified staff, other professional staff (non-teaching), non-professional/classified staff, or student, who has instigated prosecution or who refers an accusation against a suspected person.

   b. A determination of sexual harassment must consider two (2) factors:

      (1) the conduct itself; and

      (2) the context in which it occurred.

2. The written complaint should include the name, address and daytime telephone number of complainant, and provide the date(s) of, and sufficient information about, the alleged incident(s) so that the College can understand the nature of the complaint.

3. The complaint should be filed within 90 calendar days from the last date of the alleged incident.

4. Persons needing assistance in initiating or writing a formal grievance may contact the Counseling Center.

In the event the Institution's Internal Grievance Procedure proves unsuccessful, the complainant has 180 calendar days from the last date of the alleged discrimination to file a complaint with the U.S. Department of Education, Office of Civil Rights. The time for filing may be extended upon approval by the Department of Education.

Due Process requires that all persons involved in the grievance—both the grievant and the respondent (the party alleged to have violated Title IX requirements)—be provided equal opportunity to present their case and to receive a fair hearing.

Grievance Process

A. It is the intent of the college to provide individuals with a variety of sources of initial, confidential and informal consultation concerning incidents of sexual harassment without committing the individual to the formal act of filing a complaint with its required subsequent investigation and resolution. Following informal consultation, an individual could then decide whether to:

   ■ do nothing;

   ■ take personal action (such as a letter to the harasser);

   ■ request informal third-party mediation (for students, informing the Counseling Center; for faculty or staff members, informing the immediate supervisor and/or Department Head); or

   ■ file a grievance with the Counseling Center, which initiates formal investigation and resolution of a complaint.

B. Steps of Processing a Formal Grievance/Complaint:

Step 1—**College Level**

Authority: Grievance Committee consisting of a faculty member, staff member, and administrator.

Step 2—**Administrative Level**

Authority: President and Administrative Cabinet

Step 3—**Governance Level**

Authority: The Board of Trustees (either in its entirety or represented by designated members).

Each step of the grievance process will provide an opportunity for actual grievance resolution. Only those persons with authority to mandate action to correct or remedy any discrimination identified should be involved in decision making at these grievance steps.

C. When the complainant files a written formal complaint within the specified time, the following actions must be taken by the College:

1. Respondent must be notified immediately (within 2 days of receipt of complaint), of the allegations against him/her.

2. A hearing must be held by the Grievance Committee no later than five (5) calendar days after respondent has been notified.

3. Due process will be afforded all parties involved (both parties must have an opportunity to be heard).

4. Upon written notification of the date, time, and place of the hearing, both parties will be notified of their rights to:

   ■ have present at the hearing an individual or individuals to speak on his or her behalf;

   ■ have counsel of his or her own choosing during the hearing. This counsel may act only in an advisory capacity.

   ■ receive a copy of the names of witnesses, including a brief statement of their expected testimony; and a right to cross-examine the witnesses.

5. Hearings shall generally be closed to the public.

6. Formal rules of evidence and procedure shall not be followed.

7. A written record of the hearing shall be maintained. In addition, the college reserves the right to tape record and/or videotape the hearing.

8. After a decision has been made at any stage of the grievance process, all parties should be notified, within five (5) calendar days of the decision, and the grievant should be notified of his/her right to appeal the decision to the next level of processing.

■ Traditions and Events

ORIENTATION FOR NEW STUDENTS: At the beginning of each semester, the upper class students, staff, faculty, administration and all facets of the college engage in a variety of informative, religious, cultural, personal/social, career and recreational activities. The primary purpose of this week is to acquaint new members of the Miles Family to the Campus, curriculum, customs/traditions and programs, as well as assisting them to adjust to their new home.

THE CORONATION OF MISS MILES COLLEGE: Each year a young woman is chosen by the student body to represent the institution as "Miss Miles." Her court consists of the first and second runners-up, Miss Senior, Miss Junior, Miss Sophomore, and Miss Freshman. Other campus queens are presented during the Coronation Ceremony.

FOUNDERS' DAY: Annually, the College Family rededicates itself to the fundamental purposes for which the institution was founded.

THE CORONATION OF MISS UNITED NEGRO COLLEGE FUND (UNCF PRE-ALUMNI COUNCIL): Each year a young woman from the student population is chosen to serve as Miss UNCF. Selection is based on the amount of funds raised for the National UNCF Campaign.

HOMECOMING: The alumni are formally welcomed to campus for a weekend during the football season. A parade in downtown with campus decorations, the game and the homecoming dance are the highlights of this week-long event.

RELIGIOUS EMPHASIS WEEK: Each year, one week is set aside for the College Community to engage in deep religious thought and rededicate its life to God. Outstanding local, state, regional and national religious leaders address and counsel the Miles Family.

CAREER AWARENESS SEMINARS: Sometimes referred to as "Career Days," career conferences and seminars are activities conducted in a group setting that bring persons representing various employer organizations to the College Campus for interaction with all students, as well as with faculty and alumni to provide career information and insight into the world of work.

ALL SPORTS BANQUET: In the spring of each year, at the end of the sports season, the Athletic Department honors its athletes with an Athletic Banquet.

SPRING ARTS FESTIVAL: A Miles College Tradition sponsored by the Humanities Division. This activity familiarizes students with the Arts and Classicals.

BLACK HISTORY MONTH: A month-long activity which focuses on the accomplishments of African-Americans.

COMMENCEMENT: All college faculty, staff, and graduates are required to participate in this activity.

■ Expectations

In addition to the above traditional events, Miles College observes the following customs:

1. The staff, faculty and all employees of Miles are expected to assist students in becoming all they are capable of becoming mentally, physically, and spiritually. We are proud of you and we want you to be proud of MILES.

2. The audience stands when ever and where ever the Alma Mater is played. Respect is shown for another institution's Alma Mater by doing the same.

3. Regular, prompt attendance of all classes is required. Most instructors include in the course grade a grade for prompt attendance and participation in class activities.

   A student who misses, for any reason, 20% of the classes in a course may be dropped from the course with a grade of "F."

4. Every student must score at least 70% on the College English Proficiency Examination (EPE) in order to graduate from Miles College. This exam is usually given as the final exam for English 102. In addition, it is offered at least once per semester. Students may attend the Computer Lab (McKenzie Hall) for specific assistance on the EPE and any assistance needed for term papers, etc.

5. Twelve hours credit per semester are required to receive full financial aid, and a "C" average must be maintained to continue receiving such aid. Scholarship recipients are required to successfully pass no less than 15 hours each semester and to maintain a cumulative grade-point average as required by the specific scholarship.

6. Regular religious attendance is strongly encouraged to insure spiritual growth and maturity of faith. Every effort is made to provide for the religious needs of all students. Chapel forums are held Monday and Wednesday of each week, and attendance is mandatory.

7. Students should be polite and well-mannered and should always welcome campus visitors.

8. Students are expected to dress appropriately for all special occasions (i.e., special assemblies, cultural events, church, etc.). Formal attire is required for the Coronations of Miss Miles College and Miss UNCF.

9. As good citizens, Miles College students do not litter the campus with trash. They use sidewalks in order to preserve the beauty of the grass. Men always remove their hats when entering buildings.

CHAPTER 3
Student Life

Student Activities and Organizations

Miles College sponsors a number of extracurricular student activities and organizations across several fields of interest and concern—Student Government Association, fraternities and sororities, clubs associated with professional or artistic interests, publications, and religious organizations.

ELIGIBILITY: In order to participate in a college sponsored social activity, a student must maintain a minimum 2.0 cumulative grade point average.

Activities

STUDENT GOVERNMENT ASSOCIATION: Officers and Student Senate members elected by the students are responsible for representing student views and complaints to the College Administration. The student body, through the SGA, is responsible for conducting such campus-wide festivities as Homecoming in the fall, Miles (M) Day in the spring, and campus dances and entertainment during the college year. Through editors elected by the students, the SGA is also responsible for the publication of the *Columns* and the *Milean*, the campus newspaper and the college yearbook.

INTERCOLLEGIATE ATHLETICS: The Miles College Athletic Program is a member of the Southern Intercollegiate Athletic Conference (SIAC) and the National Collegiate

Athletic Association (NCAA), Division II. Participation in any of the intercollegiate sports is based upon eligibility guidelines established by these Associations. Miles offers the following intercollegiate sports: football, basketball (men and women), volleyball (women), track and field (men and women), cross-country (men and women), and baseball (men).

INTRAMURAL ATHLETIC PROGRAM: Miles College has a broad intramural program in which all students are encouraged to participate. The program enhances students' development in recreation, competition, cooperation, team work, and physical fitness.

COLLEGE CHOIR: Membership is open to any student who can meet the audition requirements. The choir performs for campus convocations and assemblies and presents a Christmas and a Spring Concert. All regular participants receive one academic credit hour per semester.

Clubs and Organizations

GREEK LETTER ORGANIZATIONS: These are selective membership organizations, each establishing its own pattern of selection. At present Miles College has chapters of the following societies: Gamma Kappa Chapter of Alpha Phi Alpha, Eta Epsilon Chapter of Omega Psi Phi, Sigma Chapter of Phi Beta Sigma, Delta Tau Chapter of Kappa Alpha Psi, Delta Eta Chapter of Sigma Gamma Rho; Alpha Chapter of Rho Nu Tau; Eta Nu Chapter of Delta Sigma Theta; Gamma Pi Chapter of Alpha Kappa Alpha; and Iota Chapter of Zeta Phi Beta. "Students must have accumulated 24 semester hours, 12 of which must be earned at Miles College, with a 2.5 cumulative grade-point average to be eligible for membership."

Other organizations are: Hospitality Social Service Club and Alpha Pi Chi. Students must have a 2.0 cumulative average to be eligible for membership.

MARCHING/CONCERT BANDS: Membership into these activities is open to all students enrolled at Miles who express the desire and the musical ability to perform with the Band. The Marching Band supports the athletic programs and performs half-time entertainment. The Concert Band performs benefit dates, community service activities, and performs for formal college events.

All band members are required to audition for individual parts and seating. Continued band membership is contingent upon the maintenance of a 2.0 cumulative grade-point average.

KAPPA KAPPA PSI FRATERNITY/TAU BETA SIGMA SORORITY: Kappa Kappa Psi Fraternity and Tau Beta Sigma Sorority are fraternal societies for college and university band members. The purpose of Kappa Kappa Psi and Tau Beta Sigma is to provide leadership, service, support, and assistance to the band director and the sponsoring institution.

Kappa Kappa Psi and Tau Beta Sigma provide for the student:

An opportunity to serve the band in a special way;
Experience in leadership, organization, and cooperation for a common cause; and

An opportunity to develop life long friendships through music;

(1) A social experience with wholesome fun and fellowship; and an opportunity to be a part of an organized NATIONAL effort that promotes college bands.

Kappa Kappa Psi and Tau Beta Sigma are open to the Miles College Band members who are academically qualified (2.2 GPA); who possess qualities of leadership, achievement, musicianship; and who possess appreciation of the best in music.

ALPHA KAPPA MU (HONOR SOCIETY): The National Academic Honor Society is open to juniors and seniors with outstanding scholastic records in college. The Miles Chapter is Alpha Sigma. The purpose of the Miles College Honor Society is to: (1) create an enthusiasm for scholarship among the Miles College student body; (2) recognize intellectual attainment; (3) stimulate a desire to render service as an essential to good citizenship; (4) develop character; and (5) promote leadership.

To be eligible for active membership, a student must be recommended to membership by a member of the society or by a faculty member, subject to the approval of two-thirds of the active membership and the approval of two-thirds of the faculty voting at regular session. The Honor Society consists of members having a scholastic average of "B+" or better each semester for three consecutive semesters at Miles College. In addition to having a good scholastic record, members must show evidence of a reputable character and exhibit active leadership and worthy service.

MATHEMATICS CLUB: The purpose of this club is to bring together natural sciences majors to exchange ideas and information, to keep up-to-date on the field of mathematics, and in general to give thought to career planning.

THE PRE-ALUMNI COUNCIL: The Pre-Alumni Council is an affiliate of the National Pre-Alumni Council of the United Negro College Fund. The Council engages in fund raising projects and in efforts to promote a collegiate spirit and unity among private black colleges throughout the United States. Membership is open to all Miles College students.

THE EDUCATION CLUB: The Education Club is an organization of college students interested in the teaching profession and in education. All majors in the Education Division are required to maintain active membership in the Education Club throughout their tenure as education majors of Miles College.

The organization involves itself in current issues in education through discussion, debate, analysis, and action programs. Each year college-wide programs are presented during American Education Week.

In addition, students are encouraged to join the Student National Education Association (SNEA) which is affiliated with the Alabama Education Association and the National Education Association. By joining SNEA, the student becomes affiliated with AEA and NEA and is thus entitled to participate in special conferences and workshops and to receive certain benefits of group insurance, educational travel allowances, and financial and legal assistance when professional, civil, or human rights are violated or jeopardized.

DRAMA CLUB: This club is composed of students who have an interest in drama. The club functions under the sponsorship of the Director of the Miles College Theater. It presents several plays on and off campus each year.

ENGLISH CLUB: A club of interest to English majors and minors but is open to all students interested in literature and language arts.

HUMANITIES CLUB: A club open to all students interested in the arts and humanities.

INTERNSHIP: A program that allows English majors to obtain on-the-job experience and academic credit.

INTERDENOMINATIONAL MINISTERIAL ASSOCIATION: This organization is composed of young ministers dedicated to a united fellowship. It is designed to bring together leaders and potential leaders of different denominations for the express purpose of joining forces in order to stimulate a more spiritual atmosphere and to render Christian service to Miles College.

THE INTERNATIONAL INTERCULTURAL ASSOCIATION: An organization comprised of foreign and domestic students of Miles College, the purpose of the organization is to acquaint students with cultures other than their own and to broaden their knowledge of the world and its people through seminars, international visitors, travel, and planned international, cultural events.

BUSINESS CLUB: The Business Club has the general objective of strengthening the Division of Business and offerings to students by planning and conducting business research and seminars, tutorials, field trips, used book outlets, social gatherings, projects, and professional activities. All business students are encouraged to participate in the activities of the club. A Phi Beta Lambda Chapter has been established in the Division to involve business students in developing leadership. Students with a 2.5 grade point average or above are encouraged to participate.

Phi Beta Lambda is a national business society created to enrich the academic and social environment of students majoring in Business.

HEALTH CAREERS CLUB: This club includes all students interested in pursuing careers in medicine or related health professions. The purpose of the club is to obtain and disseminate information on health careers among the students and to create interest in the health careers professions.

CLUB DE POLI SCI (THE POLITICAL SCIENCE CLUB): Club De Poli Sci is a club which seeks to promote scholarly interests and endeavors in the Social and Behavioral Sciences. It is open to all students who have demonstrated a capacity for and promise of excellence in all scholastic endeavors, especially in political science.

Any sophomore, junior, or senior student majoring or minoring in Political Science with an average of 2.5 or above in the social sciences in general is eligible for membership in the club pending a two-thirds (2/3) vote of the active members of the club.

THE PRESS CLUB: The Press Club is an organization of students interested in pursuing careers in the field of Communications—television, radio, newspaper, advertising, and public relations. The purpose of this club is to give students an opportunity to engage in extracurricular activities and experiences that will help them understand and appreciate the field of Communications.

STUDENT LIBRARY ACTION COMMITTEE (SLAC): Membership in the Student Library Action Committee (SLAC) is open to any student who believes in and wishes to fulfill its purposes which are:

1. To promote a strong sense of appreciation for the library, its facilities and resources, and its personnel;

2. To promote throughout the College community a genuine interest in the library and what it has to offer;

3. To serve as a liaison between the library and the College community;

4. To benefit the College community by sponsoring educational workshops; and

5. To strive to achieve the goals and objectives of the College.

THE STUDENT SUPPORT SERVICES CLUB: The Student Support Services Club is composed of students in the Student Support Services Program. This club endeavors to stimulate scholastic excellence, develop leadership, and encourage achievement. The specific objective of this club is to facilitate student growth and development through cultural and educational activities.

Student Publications

The *Milean* is a student publication issued quarterly during the school year. The *Milean* accepts articles from any member of the student body or faculty. The paper is sponsored by SGA, and the editor is elected by the student body.

Housing Program

STAFF: The housing program at Miles is designed to promote living-learning centers where emphasis is placed on enhancing the academic pursuits of the residents. Professionals, para-professionals, and students constitute the housing staff. Each staff person is selected on the basis of his/her ability to aid students as well as to manage the living units.

RESIDENCE HALL GOVERNMENT: In accordance with the philosophy of providing maximum opportunities for living and learning, the College places marked emphasis on acceptable conduct, social and orderly behavior, cleanliness, and/or basic concern for the individual rights of others as well as for the integrity of the institution.

Each residential unit has a governing body which is organized to develop a cohesive bond among the students who bring to the residential units diversified backgrounds and geographical and cultural differences. This organization provides opportunities for interest and attitudinal expression through student initiated activities.

COLLEGE HOUSING: Miles College maintains residence for approximately 380 students. This includes two dormitories for men and one for women.

HOUSING FACILITIES: The residence halls are equipped with recreation rooms, TV's, study areas, and refreshment machines located in the recreation area. All rooms are furnished and designed to house two students, and are equipped for individual telephone service. Residents must supply twin size sheets, a twin size mattress cover, pillows, pillowcases, toiletries, blankets, bedspreads, rugs, and towels. Laundry facilities are located in the basement of each dormitory.

Students desiring accommodations in college housing must submit an application for housing and remit a non-refundable room reservation fee of $50.00 upon acceptance for admission. Residence hall space is allocated in the order of receipt of room reservation fees. Admission to the College does not imply a guarantee of space in a College residence hall. A damage deposit fee of $50.00 is required and is refundable, less any charges for damages. When the room is released or if the student applies for campus housing in the subsequent term, the reservation fee is applied toward that application. A $15.00 refundable key deposit is required. The College reserves the right to change the room assignment of students whenever such change is deemed advisable.

The residence halls are closed when classes are not in session, and the College reserves the right to use rooms for conferences or conventions during vacation periods.

FOOD SERVICE: On a required meal plan based on a four-year phase system, all students living in the dormitories are issued meal contracts. Meal tickets are not transferable or exchangeable.

■ Financial Aid

Financial aid at Miles College is granted primarily to assist needy students in financing their college education. The college strongly believes that a student should not be denied an opportunity to receive a quality education simply due to a lack of funds. Need is, therefore, the major point considered in selecting students to receive financial aid.

General Information

All continuing and prospective students seeking financial assistance, including scholarships, through the college are required to submit a Free Application for Federal Student Aid (FAFSA).

All continuing and prospective students must apply for the Federal Pell Grant and submit to the Financial Aid Office a Student Aid Report (SAR) prior to being considered for any other aid through the College. Students who are residents of the State of Alabama are encouraged to complete an Alabama Student Grant Program Application.

In awarding financial aid to students, all sources available are considered in determining the financial aid award package through the college. Students are not awarded financial aid in excess of the amount needed to cover tuition, room and board, books and supplies, personal expenses, and other indirect educational expenses as determined by the college. In compliance with Federal regulations, no student can be overawarded.

The maximum amount of any scholarship awarded by the college does not exceed the amount specified above in combination with other forms of financial aid such as the Federal Pell Grant, Alabama Student Grant, private scholarships, and other sources of financial aid available to students.

Students selected for verification, a process by which the college must check the accuracy of the information which the applicants and their families report on the application for federal aid, are required to complete the verification process, including providing required documentation before receiving payment under any of the Title IV Federal Student Aid Programs or having a Student Loan certified by the College.

■ Financial Aid Programs Available at Miles College

Scholarships

Scholarships are distinct from all other forms of financial assistance in that they are generally granted to students with high academic promise and achievement. Scholarship awards vary and cover educational expenses as outlined in the scholarship description except as indicated in the previous general information of expenses section. All students who apply for or hold academic scholarships must maintain the cumulative averages as stated except where scholarships are donated which allow less than a "B" average by the donor. Scholarships are not redeemable as cash awards, but are offered by the college for the specific purpose of application toward the student's direct educational costs.

The Miles College Institutional Scholarships are awarded as supplementary funds applied to the student's indebtedness after all other assistance has been determined. All Institutional Scholarship funds that are in excess of the student's direct academic expenses will revert to the College's Institutional Scholarship Fund for allocation to other needy students.

Miles College Institutional Scholarships

President's Scholarship

Students who qualify must have a cumulative GPA of 3.70 to 4.0 and a SAT score of 1000 or ACT Composite of at least 22. This award covers tuition, comprehensive and lab fees, and room and board for residential students. The amount of this award may vary depending on the student's aid from other sources. This scholarship is renewable for three years with the maintenance of a 3.70 cumulative GPA and a minimum of 15 hours per semester.

Dean's Scholarship—A

Students must have a 3.10–3.69 cumulative GPA and a minimum SAT score of 950 or an ACT of 20/21. This award is for $2,000 and is renewable for three years with the maintenance of a 3.5 cumulative GPA and a minimum of 15 hours per semester. The amount of this award may vary depending on the student's aid from other sources.

Dean's Scholarship—B

Students must have a 3.0 cumulative GPA and a SAT score of 850 or an ACT of 18/19. This award is for $1,000 and is renewable for three years with the maintenance of a 3.0 cumulative GPA and a minimum of 15 hours per semester. The amount of this award may vary depending on the student's aid from other sources.

Athletic Scholarship

Miles College offers Scholarship/Grant-in-Aid for the students who are selected and are eligible to participate in the intercollegiate athletic program. The amount of this award may vary depending on the student's aid from other sources. Recommendations for this scholarship are made by the Athletic Director and/or Head Coach. Based on the rules and regulations of the NCAA, SIAC guidelines, and the student's performance in athletic competition, athletes may be considered for scholarship renewal yearly. For further information, please contact the Athletics Department, Miles College, Post Office Box 3800, Birmingham, Alabama 35208 or call (205) 929-1615.

Music Scholarship

Several scholarships are available for students whose training or ability will enable them to function effectively in the College band.

The Bishop Henry C. Bunton Scholarship

This scholarship is awarded through an Endowment Fund to ministerial students who are of good character, of African-American ancestry, and members of the Christian Methodist Episcopal Church. Preference is given to students who have a grade-point average of 2.0 or above.

The Edith Valentine Bass Memorial Scholarship

This memorial scholarship is available to members of the Christian Methodist Episcopal Church who, if continuing college students, must have a 3.0 grade-point average or above. High school applicants must graduate with a "B" average.

The Addie Cannon-Sloan Memorial Emergency Fund

This Emergency Loan Fund is available in memory of Mrs. Addie Cannon-Sloan, a retired teacher, civic and religious leader, and late mother of President Albert J. H. Sloan, II. Donated by the Cannon Family, this loan fund is available to students who have a valid emergency and are in need of a short-term loan.

The Delta Sigma Theta Sorority Scholarship

The Birmingham Alumnae Chapter of Delta Sigma Theta Sorority, Inc., gives, in alternative years, scholarships of up to $3,000 to worthy students who have demonstrated character, scholarship, talent, and need for financial assistance. Recommendations for the awards are made by the Scholarship Committee and faculty members who are Deltas.

The Helena B. Cobb Scholarship Fund

Scholarships from this fund are awarded to members of the Christian Methodist Episcopal Church who are seeking higher education. Applicants are selected by the General Conference Missionary Society and awarded through their respective conference.

United Negro College Fund Scholarship

This is the largest scholarship fund available to prospective and continuing students at Miles College. All recipients of scholarships through this source must have a 2.5 GPA or above and must have a demonstrated need. Names of eligible recipients are submitted annually by the Financial Aid Official to the United Negro College Fund (UNCF) Headquarters for consideration of scholarship assistance. Selection at the UNCF office is done by a random process. Many of the scholarships offered are renewable.

New students applying for such scholarships must submit an application for admission, their academic transcripts, and SAT or ACT scores to the College. In addition, each new as well as continuing applicant must complete and submit a Free Application for Federal Student Aid listing Miles College as a recipient of a copy of the report. Applicants must complete a scholarship application form which may be obtained by writing the Miles College Admissions Director.

Army and Air Force ROTC College Scholarships

Scholarships are available to students enrolled in the AROTC and AFROTC programs through a cross-registration with the University of Alabama in Birmingham and Samford University respectively. These scholarships are awarded based on academic ability and leadership potential and pay full tuition, laboratory and incidental fees, reimbursement for textbooks and a $100 tax-free subsistence allowance each month while on scholarship. Special scholarship opportunities are available for pre-med students that will assume all educational expenses from the sophomore year through medical school.

The Barber Dairies Scholarship

Barber Dairies awards a $2,500 academic scholarship each year to a junior or senior majoring in Business Administration. The candidate must have a grade-point average of 3.0 or better. Barber Dairies interviews the candidate for selection.

The Urban Bankers Scholarship

The Urban Bankers Association awards a $500 scholarship each year to a junior or senior majoring in Business Administration. The candidate must have a grade-point average of 3.0 or better and also must submit a Free Application for Federal Student Aid.

Institute of Management Accountants (IMA)—Birmingham Chapter

The Birmingham Chapter of the Institute of Management Accountants gives a $500 scholarship each year to a junior or senior majoring in Accounting. The candidate must have a grade-point average of 3.0 or better and must also submit a Free Application for Federal Student Aid.

The Miles College Birmingham Alumni Association Scholarship Fund

This scholarship fund, varying in amounts from $3,000 to $5,000, is a general scholarship offered to Alabama residents. This scholarship may be awarded to any student in dire need of financial assistance who possesses desirable qualities of character, fortitude, moral values, and good citizenship. At least four individuals may receive assistance through this fund.

The Miles College Detroit Alumni Association Scholarship Fund

This scholarship fund, varying in amounts from $1,000 to $3,000, is a general scholarship offered to one Michigan resident. This scholarship is offered on the basis of financial need, scholarship, and potential for academic excellence.

The Johnny Morrow Memorial Book Scholarship

This book scholarship is donated by the Morrow family in memory of their late brother, Johnny Morrow, a Miles College graduate. The scholarship is given annually to two students who have a demonstrated financial need for the purchase of textbooks.

The Strode Scholarship

The Strode Scholarship was established by members of the Strode Family who are graduates of Miles College. This $1,000 scholarship is given annually to either a full-time Education or a full-time Business Major with a 3.0 average or better. High school students selected must have an ACT score of 18 or an SAT score of 700. The recipient must be a resident of the Birmingham/Jefferson County area, be of good moral character, and have financial need. The applicant chosen may be considered for renewal.

The Alabama Alliance for Science, Engineering, Mathematics and Science Education (ASEMSE)

This scholarship is awarded annually to entering freshmen who major in the Natural Sciences and/or Mathematics or to students certifying in the area of Science Education. This scholarship is sponsored by the National Science Foundation.

Four (4) scholarships, each amounting to $2,500, are awarded annually and are paid each year for four academic years. The following are the criteria for receiving an ASEMSE Scholarship:

1. Cumulative 3.0 average on a 4.0 scale or better in a college preparatory curriculum.

2. SAT score of 800 or more/ACT score of 20 or higher.

3. Placement in the upper 10% of his/her class.

4. Proof of high school graduation (final transcript).

5. Interview with the Committee on Admissions, Recruitment, and Financial Aid.

6. An autobiographical essay.

7. Recommendation.

In addition, the following endowed and annually contributed scholarships have been made available for students by friends of the College:

The Juanita Lee Memorial Scholarship
The Miles College Alumni Club of Cleveland Scholarship
Bertha Little-Dilworth Education Scholarship

Miles College Class of 1942 Scholarship
Edith Patton Scholarship
The Mayor Richard Arrington Scholarship
The Ruth Strong Scholarship
The Foster Foundation Scholarship
The David Martin Scholarship
The John T. Stapler Chemistry Memorial Scholarship
The Sixth Avenue Baptist Church Scholarship
The Greater Birmingham Foundation Scholarship
The Epps Scholarship
The Fairfield Industrial High School Alumni Association Scholarship
The Johnnie Mae Glenn-Webb Education Scholarship

Grants

Federal Pell Grant Program

The largest student aid program is the Federal Pell Grant Program. It is awarded to help undergraduates pay for their education after high school. For many students, the Federal Pell Grant provides a "foundation" of financial aid to which aid from other Federal and non-Federal sources may be added. Unlike loans, grants do not have to be repaid.

All applicants applying for scholarship/aid from the College must apply for the Federal Pell Grant (See Financial Aid application procedures).

Federal Supplemental Educational Opportunity Grants (FSEOG)

Federal Supplemental Educational Opportunity Grants are "campus-based" federal assistance that is available to undergraduate students who have demonstrated financial need. A Federal SEOG is a gift of assistance to help pay for post-secondary education. This grant ranges from $100 to $4,000 depending on need, the availability of Federal SEOG funds at the College, and the amount of other aid offered.

Alabama Student Grant Program (ASGP)

The Alabama Student Grant Program is a State student assistance program established in 1978 by the Legislature of the State of Alabama for undergraduate non-sectarian, secular education at independent, non-profit, post-secondary institutions of higher learning located within the State of Alabama. All students from the State of Alabama are required to apply for this Grant. Applications for this Grant may be obtained from the Miles College Financial Aid Office.

Alabama Student Assistance Program (ASAP)

This is a "need-based program" that provides assistance on a limited basis to Alabama residents who demonstrate financial need and who are enrolled at Miles College.

Loans

FEDERAL PERKINS LOAN (FORMERLY NDSL)—The Federal Perkins Loan Program provides low-interest long-term loans to assist needy students in the financing of their education. These loans are awarded through the Financial Aid Office. Interest does not accumulate until the student graduates or leaves school. Such loans must be repaid to Miles College.

THE WILLIAM D. FORD DIRECT LOAN PROGRAM is a low-interest loan made to a student by the Office of Education to help the student pay for his/her education after high school. Undergraduate loans range from $2,625 for freshmen, $3,500 for sophomores, to $5,500 for juniors and seniors based on demonstrated need. A student must first apply for a Federal Pell Grant and have his/her eligibility or ineligibility for such a grant determined before the Direct Loan can be certified.

THE WILLIAM D. FORD PLUS LOAN PROGRAM—This loan program makes long-term loans to parents of dependent students to pay for the cost of study at post-secondary schools.

Applications and instructions for the William D. Ford Plus Loan Program may be obtained from the Financial Aid Office upon request.

Employment

FEDERAL WORK-STUDY PROGRAM (FWSP)—The Federal Work-Study Program provides work experiences for students who have a demonstrated need while earning a part of their educational expenses. A student may work up to 15 hours per week while school is in session. Students are not permitted to work when classes are not in session. Students are compensated, at least, at the minimum wage rate and are paid once a month for work performed.

■ Satisfactory Academic Progress

Every student must maintain satisfactory progress as one of the criteria for receiving financial aid. The requirements for making satisfactory progress are:

(a) A student who has attempted 31 or fewer hours at the end of two semesters of study must earn a cumulative grade-point average of 1.60.

(b) A student who has attempted 32 semester hours but fewer than 64 hours must earn a cumulative grade-point average of 1.80 at the end of four semesters of study.

(c) Juniors and seniors must earn a cumulative grade-point average of 2.0 at the end of each semester.

In addition to the cumulative grade-point average requirements indicated above, a full-time or part-time student is expected to have completed 75% of the hours for which he has enrolled.

If a student fails to maintain satisfactory academic progress as defined above, the student may be awarded assistance for one additional payment period to re-establish "satisfactory progress." A student who fails to complete successfully a minimum course load (12 hours) during this period will remain ineligible for any additional assistance during subsequent semesters unless: (1) the student, while ineligible, successfully completes the minimum requirements for one payment period at Miles College or (2) the student presents to the Office of Financial Aid evidence of unusual circumstances which are deemed by the Financial Aid Committee to be sufficient to justify an exception to this policy.

All transfer and re-admit students must meet the minimum grade-point standards indicated above in order to be eligible for financial aid.

An incomplete grade ("I") does not count toward course work completed, but does count as courses attempted; therefore, it negatively impacts the incremental measurement of progress. A GRADE OF "I"—INCOMPLETE—IS COUNTED IN HOURS ATTEMPTED. An "I" grade is intended to be only an interim course mark. It is to be used only if a student has satisfactorily completed at least 75% of the course requirements, and there is an excusable and acceptable reason for his/her not having completed all requirements prior to grade reporting time.

With the awarding of the "I," the instructor must include information as to the specific requirements for changing the "I" to a permanent grade. A grade of "I" must be changed by the end of the next semester in which the student is enrolled.

Remedial courses are counted in the hours attempted.

If a student officially withdraws before the last two weeks of the semester, he/she will receive a "W" grade (WD, WP, or WF).

A GRADE OF "W" IS COUNTED AS A GRADE OF "O" and is not COUNTED IN HOURS ATTEMPTED OR EARNED.

FULL-TIME students are to be allowed SIX years or TWELVE semesters to complete their programs (HALF-TIME students are allowed TWELVE years or TWENTY-FOUR semesters) and are eligible to receive financial aid.

Any student who feels that he/she is unable to maintain satisfactory progress due to extraordinary circumstances beyond his/her control, i.e., personal illness, death in the immediate family or some hardship, should contact the Financial Aid Director to request an appeal. The student must be prepared to provide documentation to substantiate his/her situation.

Financial aid is cancelled when a student is on suspension or dismissed. Upon reinstatement to the college, a student may reapply for aid.

Residents of the State of Alabama who are recipients of Alabama Student Grants are ineligible to receive such grants when the total number of hours which they have attempted exceeds by more than twenty-five percent (25%), five years for a four-year program, the number of hours required for the individual student's course of study.

■ Federal Refund and Repayment Policies

REFUNDS—Federal regulations require that if a student receiving Federal financial aid (Title IV Programs) received a refund from his/her school because of either withdrawal, drop out, or expulsion, a portion or all of the refund must be returned to the Title IV aid programs. The following formula shall be used to determine the portion of the refund to be returned to Student Financial Assistance (SFA) Program(s).

$$\text{School refund} \times \frac{\text{Total SFA funds*}}{\text{Total Aid*}} = \frac{\text{Amount to be returned to}}{\text{SFA Programs}}$$

SFA refunds, resulting from the above formula shall be returned to the SFA funds, to the extent that such refunds allocated to a program does not exceed the amount a student received from that program. Funds cannot be returned to a program from which

*Wages paid under the College Work-Study Program are excluded from both the refund and repayment calculations because they have been earned by the student for work performed.

no funds were received by the student. Priority for such SFA refunds shall be made in the following order:

First—FDirect Loan   Fifth—FSEOG
Second—FPLUS   Sixth—SSIG
Third—FPerkins Loan   Seventh—Other State, Private or Institutional Aid
Fourth—Pell Grant   Eighth—The Student

A pro-rata refund calculation is required by Federal Regulations for all first-time students who fail to complete at least 60% of the semester in which be enrolls.

Any portion of a refund that the College allocates to the Direct Loan Programs must be returned to the Office of Education.

REPAYMENTS—Federal regulations require that an institution develop a policy which determines whether a student owes a payment of a portion of a cash disbursement made to cover living expenses if the student withdraws, drops out, or is expelled. If the College finds that the student's living expenses incurred up to the time of withdrawal, exceeds the amount of cash disbursed, the student has not been overpaid. However, if the cash disbursement was greater than the student's living expenses up to the withdrawal date, the excess amount is an overpayment.

The College will not count any aid from the FWS, Direct Loan or PLUS programs in the cash disbursement when figuring the amount of the overpayment, since aid from these programs is excluded from the repayment formula.*

In determining the amount of the overpayment to be returned to the SFA programs that were part of the student's aid package, the aid administrator uses the following formula:

$$\text{School refund} \times \frac{\text{Total SFA funds*}}{\text{Total Aid*}} = \frac{\text{Amount to be returned to}}{\text{SFA Programs}}$$

SFA repayments resulting from the above formula shall be returned to the SFA funds to the extent that such repayment allocated to a program does not exceed the amount a student received from that program. Money cannot be returned to an account from which no funds were received by the student. Priority for such SFA repayments shall be made in the following order.

First—FPerkins Loan   Fourth—SSIG
Second—FPell   Fifth—Other State, Private or Institutional Aid
Third—FSEOG

Note: Refund Policy subject to change based upon Federal Regulations.

The College must withhold and promptly return to the Office of Education any Direct Loan proceeds that would otherwise create an "over award."

Borrowers under the William D. Ford Direct Loan Programs must be aware that they are obligated to repay the full amount of the loan even if the borrower does not complete the program, is unable to obtain employment upon completion, or is otherwise dissatisfied with or does not receive the educational or other services that the borrower purchased from the school.

■ Financial Aid Application Procedures

All continuing students or prospective students applying for financial aid from the college must submit a Free Application for Federal Student Aid (FAFSA) to the Central Processor listing Miles College to receive a copy. The FAFSA may be obtained from the student's high school or by requesting a form from the Financial Aid Office at the address specified in this section.

The Financial Aid delivery system at Miles College has been enhanced to include the electronic processing of financial aid applications, awards, corrections, and adjustments. All applicants applying for financial aid from the College are required to apply for the Federal Pell Grant. Within six weeks after applying for the Federal Pell Grant, the applicant should receive a Student Aid Report (SAR).

All students who are legal residents of the State of Alabama must apply for the Alabama Student Grant. Applications for this Grant may be obtained from the Financial Aid Office.

For priority consideration, the Financial Aid report should be received in the Financial Aid Office at Miles College on or before April 15 for the Fall Semester and November 15 for the Spring Semester. Summer School aid applications should be received by March 15. The FAFSA should be filed approximately six weeks prior to the above deadlines to ensure that a report reaches the Financial Aid Office by the above dates. Applications received after the above dates will be acted upon to the extent that funds are available at the time the completed application is received.

Students must re-submit financial aid applications each school year in order to be considered for financial aid. The address of the Financial Aid Office is as follows:

Financial Aid Office
Miles College
Post Office Box 3800
Birmingham, Alabama 35208-0937

Other Sources of Aid

Veterans Benefits

There are monthly benefits and/or tuition scholarships available to many veterans and to the dependents of disabled or deceased veterans.

If a student is a veteran or a dependent of a disabled/deceased veteran, he/she should contact the Financial Aid Office for further information.

THE VOCATIONAL REHABILITATION PROGRAM provides educational assistance for individuals with physical or mental disabilities. They are requested to please contact the State Vocational Rehabilitation Service Office nearest them for further information.

Other Sources of Assistance

Many places of employment, as well as labor unions, have programs to help pay the cost of education after high school for employees or members (or for their children). Those interested should check foundations, fraternities or sororities, and town or city clubs. They should include their State Agency, community organizations and civic groups, such as the American Legion, YMCA, 4-H clubs, Kiwanis, Jaycees, Chamber of Commerce, and the Girl or Boy Scouts as possible sources of aid.

Refund and Repayment Policy

All withdrawals from the College must be cleared through the Office of the Registrar. If a student withdraws during the semester or summer session, a portion of his/her fees is refunded in accordance with the following schedule:

Fall and Winter Semesters

Withdrawal within the First Week 75%
Withdrawal within the Second Week 50%
Withdrawal within the Third Week 25%
Withdrawal after the Third Week 0%

Summer Session

Withdrawal within the First Week 25%
Withdrawal within the Second Week 10%
Withdrawal after the Second Week 0%

The first day of class is considered the first day of the term.

If a refund is due the student under the Institution's refund policy and the student received financial aid under the Title IV Student Financial Aid Program, other than the Federal Work-Study Program, a portion of the refund shall be refunded to the Title IV Student assistance program(s) in the following manner: Direct Loan Programs will be refunded first. Any remaining monies will be refunded second to the Federal Perkins Loan fund (formerly NDSL); third, to the Federal Pell Grant fund; and fourth, to the Federal SEOG fund. The amount of refund to each Title IV Program will not exceed the amount disbursed to the student.

The College's refund policy is subject to change to conform with the United States Department of Education Refund Regulations.

Revision and Cancellation of Financial Aid

Miles College reserves the right to review, revise, or cancel a financial aid award at any time due to changes in financial or academic status, or one's failure to comply with applicable federal and/or state laws and/or regulations or College policies. In addition, a financial aid award is subject to revision should the annual allocation of funds from the Federal government be reduced below the anticipated funding level for a program(s), or should budget limitations be placed upon funds which are intended for student financial aid purposes. In no instance will a student receive need-based assistance in excess of his/her determined financial need.

Student Health Services

The Student Health Service is coordinated by the Office of the Dean of Students. A College nurse maintains daily office hours on weekdays in an office located in Pitts Hall. The nurse is available for emergency first aid and for health counseling.

Student hospitalization and accident insurance is available at low premiums to all students who are enrolled at the College for a minimum program of nine credit hours per semester. Medical Insurance, either through the College or through a personal policy, is required for all students residing in the residence halls. Proof of personal coverage must be submitted at registration.

The college provides a medical examination form which must be completed by the family physician certifying the general health and medical history of each student. This completed form is required before the student's initial admission to the College is complete.

Norton Student Union Building

The Student Center houses the faculty and staff dining room, the students' cafeteria, and a snack bar on the first floor.

On the second floor, the Center houses the Office of the Director of Student Activities, the Student Government Association Office, the Publication Office, a lounge, and a recreation area for social functions. The Center is equipped with cable television, pool tables, ping-pong tables, video machines, and a variety of table-top games.

The College Center's objectives revolve around four (4) basic ideas:

1. The Center is the community center of the College for all members of the College family, students, faculty, administrators, alumni, and guests. It is not just a building; it is also an organization and a program.

2. As the living room of the College, the Center provides for the services, conveniences, and amenities that the members of the College family need in their daily lives on the campus and for getting to know and understand one another through informal associations outside the classroom.

3. The Student Center is a part of the educational program of the College. As the center of College community life, it serves as a laboratory of citizenship, training students in social responsibility and leadership.

4. The Center serves as a unifying force in the life of the college, cultivating enduring regard for and loyalty to the College.

Residency Requirement

All students who seek a degree from Miles College must complete the last twelve (12) hours of their curriculum at Miles College. Any exceptions to this policy must be approved by the Dean of Academic Affairs.

Learning Resources Center

This facility opened for service on February 13, 1978 and was officially dedicated on October 17, 1978. The Learning Resources Center is named in honor of Bishop Chester Arthur Kirkendoll, then presiding Bishop of the Fifth Episcopal District of the Christian Methodist Episcopal Church and Chairman of the Board of Trustees of Miles College. The Center embodies the concept of integrated support services and enrichment to the instructional program of the College by providing information in a variety of styles and formats.

The automated air-conditioned facility is comprised of four levels, located on the west side of the campus in close proximity to student housing and classrooms. The first level houses a centralized pool of educational media and instructional services for all divisions of the College. Areas included are those for television, graphic preparation, photography, film previewing, instructional materials, classrooms, staff and faculty lounge, Board room, and a computer laboratory.

The second level is devoted to general library services: circulation, reference, periodicals, card catalog, library administrative offices, and technical services. Loan service is extended to all students, faculty, and staff who wish to use books and media materials for research, recreation, or other purposes.

The third level contains the College and CME Church archives, African-American materials, and stack and study areas including nine closed carrels for individual study. The African-American Materials Center in the Learning Resources Center is a growing collection of books, periodicals, recordings, films, video and film strips on Black culture. This center is open for the use of the community and visiting scholars. The LRC also has an intercultural and interracial area.

The fourth level continues with study and stack areas, four group study rooms, nine closed study carrels, a seminar room, and lounge areas.

The collection numbers more than 90,000 volumes including books, bound periodicals and a growing collection of multimedia materials and equipment. The facility has the capability of housing more than 200,000 volumes and seating more than 750.

To facilitate effective use of the LRC, personal assistance and guidance are also provided by the staff to faculty and students any time the LRC is open. The LRC HANDBOOK, available at all service desks, should be referred to for a more detailed description of LRC services and regulations.

Library Hours

Monday–Thursday	8:00 a.m.–9:00 p.m.
Friday	8:00 a.m.–5:00 p.m.
Saturday	1:00 a.m.–6:00 p.m.
Sunday	3:00 p.m.–9:00 p.m.

CHAPTER 4
Academic Life at Miles College

by Hattie G. Lamar, Academic Dean

Classroom Deportment for the Real Student

There are real students and there are pretend students, and each type of student has the personal power to *deport* him/herself accordingly. Because you have presented yourself here at Miles College and registered for classes, you will, inevitably, become one such type of student. You will be a real student or a pretend student. Half-stepping is not likely. Following is a definition of each type of student as well as other definitions that are intended to motivate you to think seriously about your responsibility for directing your own academic growth. This is your beginning, and it should be a productive time. As you read the definitions, determine which truly appeal to you. Decide which type of student you must become and the *deportment* that you will embrace now to increase your chances of reaching the personal and career goals that are within your grasp.

Definition #1—Student

At its simplest, a student is a person who studies. You will notice that the words <u>student</u> and <u>study</u> look alike, obviously belonging to the same word family. Further, *World Book Dictionary* asserts that a student applies himself or herself to learning. The definition is extended via a quote by Harold Taylor: "A student is a person who is learning to fulfill his powers and to find ways of using them in the service of mankind." Taylor's definition suggests an active process of acquiring knowledge. Too, it suggests that learning provides highly personal, visible, and satisfying growth for the learner, inspiring the learner to want to do something with what he/she knows, and to apply what he/she knows to improve life, to enhance existence. This definition suggests that the student continually creates opportunities to apply the knowledge that is being acquired (in English, math, history, literature, science, sociology, education) in practical ways.

Definition #2—The Real Student

Yes, you guessed it! The real student has already been defined in definition #1. However, because so many impostors have been coming into classrooms and calling themselves students, it has become necessary to add adjectives such as *real* and *pretend* in an attempt to distinguish those who have come into the classroom to learn. Therefore, the real student is (1) a person who likes to go to class for the learning opportunities that are possible, (2) a person who seeks knowledge and understanding, (3) a learner who tries to relate the knowledge he/she is acquiring to other learning in other classes, to things that are happening in his/her life, to things that are occurring in the world and to what he/she is thinking and feeling. (4) The real student enjoys learning and studying although he/she does not always find doing so to be easy; nonetheless, she/he has learned to enjoy the challenge that studying offers. (5) The real student has decided that she/he does not have time to work at Burger King or other jobs that do not help improve the mind and spirit. The real student has thought and decided that he/she will work outside the home only if it is *essential* to the basic livelihood of the family. (He/she does not work to make others rich by buying expensive tennis shoes, jackets, etc.) The real student knows that *learning* is his *real* job. The real student positively *deports* him/herself as a *learner*.

Definition #3—The Pretend Student

If you are reading this selection with honesty, and the voice deep within you is beginning to hint that you may be a pretend student, then listen to the voice. Please do not pretend that you are not guilty as charged. Understand that at *any time* you can stop the make-believe and demonstrate the behavior of real students. *You can definitely know that you are a pretend student if you*

1. think that teachers *must* entertain you to prevent boredom;

2. do not really like attending classes but think you may pass the class simply because you did attend with some frequency;

3. think that the knowledge you acquire through the course has nothing to do with your real life and is to be only memorized, remembered for the teacher's quizzes and tests and then forgotten;

4. look for excuses not to perform learning tasks, refusing to try, feeling satisfied with saying, "I've never done that; I don't like to; I don't have time, if . . ."

5. expect to be given good grades either for trying to learn or saying that you are trying, even when the results are negligible.

6. attend classes to sullenly *resist* learning or to be the class clown;

7. if you have the unmitigated gall to challenge, intimidate, and denounce teachers who dare to give you the poor grades that negative classroom *deportment* earned for you; and

8. if you cut classes, refuse to study, will not prepare homework with top effort that results in both learning and earning a good grade, yet demand an A, B, C, or D of the teacher.

Definition #4—The Classroom

Classrooms are not places to

- chew gum
- sigh in boredom
- eat
- slouch
- sleep
- pop knuckles
- daydream
- wear hats
- clown
- vegetate
- discuss matters unrelated to the course topic or
- disrespect others for any reason.

Rather, a classroom is defined in the *American Heritage Dictionary* as "a room in which classes are conducted in a school or college." Relatedly, a class is a "group of students meeting to study the same subject." These definitions carry the following implications:

1. A classroom is a place for real students.

2. Students are persons who seek learning; and they come to classes for that purpose ONLY, often working together to acquire common knowledge about a specific subject.

3. Classrooms are learning laboratories that become alive and interesting to the degree that they are able to attract *real* students. They become moribund when flooded with pretend students.

Definition #5—Deportment

According to *World Book Dictionary*, deportment is "the way a person acts: behavior, conduct." You have been in classrooms in which fake students deported themselves badly, so as to disrupt and interfere with learning. Too, you have been told for years how *not* to act in class. But has anyone delineated or outlined what real students should *do* in class? Obviously, real students behave in ways that allow them to acquire maximum learning in and out of class. Below are some behaviors Miles would like for you to demand of yourself—daily—as you move from class to class. The purpose of these notes is to inspire you to deport yourself as a *real student*.

Definition #6—Positive Classroom Deportment: How to Be a Real Student

1. Report for class two–five minutes early:

   ■ Dress to support your image as a student. Does your dress (your clothes) suggest that you are trying to make a studious impression?

   ■ Rid yourself of gum and food. Gum and food have no place in the classroom. They compete with the teacher for your attention.

   ■ Greet persons who are present when you arrive. If you talk further, let it be about the last or today's assignment. Get ready to learn, by quietly reviewing—*again*.

   ■ Take out your notebook and writing tools. Review the notes from the immediately preceding class period, relating them to the new assignment. When the instructor begins class, you are already in the mood to listen critically for what is said, for what is meant, and to grasp the extent to which it relates and applies to specific, previous learning.

2. Take a seat as close to the front of the room as possible. In the past, African-Americans *had* to sit in the back, away from comfort and relevance. Always sit in the front to show that you are *interested*

   ■ in hearing; for paraphrased note taking;

   ■ in being known by the teacher as a real student;

   ■ in being available to answer questions and to ask questions;

   ■ in protecting yourself from distractions promoted by pretend students;

   ■ in being called on to *do* . . .;

   ■ in listening to follow the *structure* of the teacher's lecture, and in organizing information as follows:

      □ What is the *main* topic?

      □ What are the major parts or divisions of the topic? (Leave space for explanations.)

      □ What explanatory and descriptive details clarify and support each part?

      □ What are the key concepts and vocabulary entries for the day? Write these under a separate heading, including a brief context to assist usage. Use the words daily, for the week, aloud or silently.

      □ Think as you listen. Mentally restate in your own words what you think is being communicated. Think of a "for instance." If you need to, ask for or give examples of what is being discussed. Voluntarily share a connection that you see between an important point in the lecture and something observed or learned previously (or share something that is the total opposite or antithesis) and justify the reference.

      □ Date your notes.

3. Clearly understand the assignment before leaving class. Are you to study or do homework? (Know that homework is a specific learning activity, but it does not substitute for continuous study.) You will study and review even when there is no homework. Read to (a) paraphrase, (b) raise questions of meaning, (c) diagram and/or supply examples, (d) consider "what if . . .?" (e) classify or categorize, (f) go to the next class session with one or two sincere questions or a thoughtful comment or opinion about what you studied. These behaviors will (a) help to in-

vigorate the class and (b) help you to grow in understanding. Form a regular study group with two other *real* students, and have a study *plan*.

4. Feel that you have a responsibility to contribute meaningfully to class discussion—voluntarily, with premeditation. The classroom is a place to risk being right (for good feelings and self-confidence) and wrong (to correct, to know, to grow in clarity). Locate supplementary material from the library at least once a week.

5. As you leave class, initiate conversation with a classmate about some *specific* information from the lecture. You may paraphrase, relate, infer, apply, etc.

6. Evaluate your own performance daily, or at least weekly. Never be surprised by a teacher's evaluation of you.

7. Schedule a minimum of two hours study for each class session. Make usable notes. Summarize chapters in your own words, relating the content to the chapter title. When you begin to practice positive classroom deportment routinely, you will find that there is no time for clowning and displaying negative attitudes that interfere with your learning and that of others.

   Your learning is personal and is your responsibility. Teachers are present to motivate, guide, and serve as one type of resource. Only *you* can decide if you will avail yourself of their services. And *why* should you? Because you are an American of African descent. Your ancestral genes produced the first human beings and the potential "civilized," modern Homo Sapien man more than 200,000 years ago. The ingenuity of your people gave to civilization the tools of survival: language, science, math. Surely, you too must make your contribution, by at least being a productive student.

8. Look at more than the grades or papers that are returned. What problems must you avoid in the future? Do you *understand* how to correct them? Is tutoring necessary?

9. Evaluate your own academic behavior *continually*.

10. Matriculate to graduate.

The Miles College Man . . .

- Appreciates women and encourages their self-improvement and contribution to his own growth.
- Believes that a "man" is responsible, respectful, resourceful, reliable, and relevant—academically, socially, and personally.
- Participates willingly in campus seminars, advisement sessions, learning laboratories, and extra-class activities designed to develop him fully.
- Studies, as an exercise in self-respect and resents the thought that he might be given a grade—unethically.

The Miles College Woman . . .

- Appreciates men and encourages their development as she pursues her own.
- Believes that a "woman" respects her body and mind, viewing them as amazing, wondrous vessels that must be treated with utmost care.
- Desires to be a whole, fully-functioning woman who is informed and ready for positive challenge.
- Attends all campus seminars and advisement sessions and uses all available learning resources.
- Studies in and outside of classes to earn decent grades and to *demonstrate* learning.

■ The Miles College Man and Woman

Both the Miles College Man and Woman have:

1. A respect for self that is manifested in behavior that uplifts;

2. A respect for others as an extension of self-respect;

3. A respect for Miles College: its physical plant (grounds, classrooms, dorms, etc.), its mission, and its students, staff, faculty, and administration;

4. A respect for learning as self-enhancement and career preparation;

5. A desire to lead productive lives that benefit themselves, their families, and the communities with which they have association;

6. They both believe that their college education is a valued investment which requires their study, critical evaluation, desire for capital, and continuous reinvestment; and

7. Desire to graduate from Miles College in very good standing and to become an active member of its Alumni Association.

CHAPTER 5
Academic Survival Skills

Academic Survival and Your Advisor

by Emma Sloan

Each freshman student is assigned an academic advisor by the Director of the Counseling Center. All full time faculty members, counselors and department heads can serve as advisors.

The duties and responsibilities of the advisor are to help students develop plans for completing their academic program. Advisors help students with clarification of what program the student would like to enter, and they help students develop strategies for completing their academic programs. The advisor guides the student with curriculum and academic planning, which includes clarification of a major and any other issues related to academic success. However, the student is ultimately responsible for meeting the requirements of his/her academic program. The advisor does not make decisions for students, but rather refers students to the proper sources.

When a student is assigned to a particular advisor, the student is notified and provided with the name and location of the advisor. It is the student's responsibility to contact the advisor and schedule an appointment. The office hours of the advisor should be posted on the faculty member's office door. If not, students may contact the department chair for information concerning the office hours of the advisor.

During a conference, the advisor will keep a record of the meeting and will keep all records and information pertaining to a student confidential.

Students will normally remain with an assigned freshman advisor until the student has completed the general education course requirements. If a student has completed all courses successfully, the student will then be eligible to transfer into a major at the college. The following are the steps for transferring into a major at Miles College:

Step I—Students must successfully pass all of the general education course requirements. If a student has completed all courses successfully with the exception of one or two requirements, they may be eligible for conditional admittance to their major area of study.

Step II—Students must make application for transfer into their major. Applications are available in the Counseling Center.

Step III—The students must complete the transfer application with the assistance of the freshman advisor to assure proper completion.

Step IV—The completed application must then be submitted by the student to the appropriate division chair.

Advisement is critical to each student's academic survival. Advisement is all of the information needed to successfully assist the first time college student in meeting all of the requirements for becoming a successful student, academically and socially. Advisement is an ongoing process for all students. The information that a student receives from his/her advisor can determine academic success. Therefore, all students are encouraged to maintain contact with their assigned advisor throughout their stay at Miles. The advisor will be able to inform students concerning all aspects of the academic curriculum, policies and procedures of the college. Lastly, the advisor will be able to advise the student with regard to social concerns and will be able to make referrals to the appropriate resources.

■ The Importance of Critical Thinking

by Edgar Lamar

Critical thinking is a very important academic survival skill at Miles College, and we hope that each freshman student will strive to acquire this skill as a vehicle to academic and personal success.

There are four essential elements of this basic survival skill. These elements include effective (1) writing (2) speaking and (3) listening skills. These elements are explained in other sections of this text, and are addressed through the general education courses of study.

We define a critical thinker as one who is self confident—willing to trust one's skills, and yet keep an open mind. We believe that critical thinkers are honest with themselves and others about their abilities, goals, and reasons for seeking a college education. These kind of thinkers respect the opinions of others and consider a variety of ideas and opinions on a wide range of subjects and topics. A general spirit of curiosity is a characteristic of a critical thinker. This kind of thinker enjoys exploring ideas and concepts, yet demonstrates the ability to draw analytical conclusions from the information obtained through research and exploration, and stay focused and organized. Critical thinkers demonstrate maturity with regard to their choice of life style and peers. They establish priorities with regard to work and school. They understand that they must manage their time wisely to accomplish their goals.

Critical thinkers use good problem solving methods, as evidenced through their ability to correctly define a problem; brainstorm possible solutions, establish a plan of action, implement the plan, and evaluate the effectiveness of the plan.

Finally, critical thinkers are willing to take risks. This kind of thinker welcomes the challenge of difficult situations and is not afraid to ask questions and make changes as needed.

Time Management

Most people have a pretty good idea of what time management is, as well as some of the ways to use it. No matter what techniques you try to use, successful time management can only be achieved through consistency, commitment, and self discipline. Different things work for different people; the trick is to find the most comfortable technique or combination of techniques for your own needs. Time management is different for everyone, and there is no "right" way to do it. Try various things, and be consistent about using whatever feels suitable to you.

When time seems unmanageable, you may feel like you are losing control of your entire life. This can lead to frustration, stress, procrastination, and other anxiety problems which could further interfere with your daily life. Successful time management allows you to feel like you are in control of your life, rather than vice versa. In this chapter, we hope to provide you with insights which will help you learn the power of identifying your values and setting goals to realize those values. Furthermore, we hope to show you how to balance the demands of school, work, and a social life so you can find the time for the people and things that matter most to you, and still allow you to feel in control.

When you are having problems managing your time, take a moment to consider some of the techniques you have used in the past when your time seemed more manageable. Then, see if you can adapt these things to your lifestyle. For example, in high school, you may have had somebody reminding you to do things every morning before you left for school. Obviously, most people cannot have someone reminding them to do things everyday here; but you can remind yourself by making a list every night before you go to bed. Put this list somewhere you are sure to see it in the morning. Then, you will have your own daily reminder of what you have to do today.

If your problems with time management stem from a feeling of lack of control, consider your priorities. Sit down and make a list of every activity which takes up some time. Then, consider your list and decide what is most important to you. By ranking your commitments in order of priority, you can better decide how you want to divide your time. Remember to include social activities as well as academic commitments. Furthermore, remember to include such time consuming tasks as eating or walking to class. Being honest with yourself when budgeting your time is the key to sticking to your prioritized goals. If, for example, academics are your number one priority, you should block out time needed to fulfill academic obligations first, then you can block out time for your second, third, fourth priority, etc.

A good way of figuring out your priorities is to keep track of every single minute of your day for 3 or 4 days. This means writing down the exact minute you wake up in the morning, brush your teeth, get dressed, lock your front door, etc. By keeping a specific record of your time, you can pinpoint specific areas of your life which seem to take too much time. This will probably be very surprising, as few of us really realize how long we spend petting the dog, walking to class, talking on the phone, or just staring out the window. Once you begin to get a better idea of how you spend your days, prioritizing in terms of actual time available becomes easier. Use the weekly time grid at the end of this chapter to help keep track of your days. If possible, make entries as soon as events occur, rather than at the end of the day, to insure the most accurate assessment of your time.

However, sometimes tasks occur which do not fit your ordered weekly time plan. These large, time consuming tasks can dramatically impact your daily time management routine. So, how do you deal with a 20-page term paper?

You can get through any large task by doing things one step at a time. Even if we wait until the night before that 20-page term paper is due, we still have to do research, an introduction, a conclusion etc. So, if you do your research one day, your introduction another, etc., until you have finished, the entire task will not seem quite as enormous. It is much easier to write four-five page papers than it is to write one 20-pager the night before it is due. This technique can also be applied to reading. It is extremely hard to stay focused when reading 10 chapters the night before an exam. But, if you read two chapters each night of the week before the exam, you would probably retain a lot more information.

Now you have to decide how you should break down your task and the goals you want to set for yourself regarding its completion. Before you decide on your goals, consider this question: Do high achievers set high, intermediate, or low goals for themselves? Before you answer, refer to the exercise at the end of the chapter titled "Goal Setting." For this exercise, you will need a pen, a stopwatch, and the worksheet. On the top bar, you will see the numbers one through six, with characters corresponding to each number.

1. Set the watch for 30 seconds. During this 30 seconds, memorize the six characters as well as you can.

2. Then, set the watch for another 30 seconds. Pick a starting point. During this time, fill in as many characters as you can on the rest of the sheet. Go on to the subsequent lines if necessary.

3. Now add up the number of correct characters you filled in. How many?

Now, you are going to go through the process again, but before you do, estimate how many you think you will get correct the second time around. Say, for example, you got 16 right the first time, you may estimate that you would get 20 right the second time. Then, decide, on a scale of 1–100% how sure you are of your ability to improve your score. So, if I estimated I would get 20 right the second time, I might feel 90% sure that I would be successful. So, go through the process of memorizing, and filling in characters again.

Having completed the exercise for the second time, how many characters did you get correct this time? Did you meet your goal? If not, how do you feel about that? Did your estimation of your ability match your second score? (For example, if you were 95% sure you would reach 20, and you got 19, you did a pretty good job of estimating.)

You may not see it now, but this exercise can provide you with a great deal of insight into how you set goals, how you accomplish those goals, and how you react to achievement. Being able to foresee what you can achieve before you set a goal is a difficult task. If you can foresee what you can achieve, then you are a person who knows how to set realistic goals for him/herself. This is a characteristic of a high achiever. High achievers have the tendency to know themselves, know their capabilities, and they are realistic with themselves when it comes to knowing their limits.

Referring to the earlier question of whether high achievers set high, intermediate, or low goals for themselves, the answer should now be more clear. People who are always setting high goals for themselves, but do not quite reach the mark can often become disappointed, as they never really meet all of their expectations. People who set goals which are too low may feel as though they never get anywhere, and this can prove to be just as problematic as setting goals that are too high. The correct answer is to set realistic goals. In setting realistic goals, a person is likely to achieve his or her task and feel good about the process. That person then can move forward to another task that may be incrementally more difficult, but still feel confident about achieving it.

When you set goals for yourself, it is crucial to consider possible distractions, other commitments, and actual time necessary to complete a task. If you eat dinner at 6:30, don't plan to get two chapters read between 6:00 and 7:00. That is not a realistic goal and chances are high that you will not be able to accomplish it. If you know you might go out on Friday night, don't plan to write your paper that night. Even though it may be hard to realize that some aspects of your life may take priority over others, once you do, your time will seem more manageable. Plan ahead of time to go out Friday night, and instead of having it interrupt your other plans you will feel more in control of your time.

So how do you keep track of your priorities, commitments, goals, assignments, etc.? The most common way to keep track of things is a day planner. Write everything down in your planner. When you first begin using one, refer back to the lists you made with your commitments ranked according to priority. Go through your class syllabi at the beginning of the quarter and write all the reading assignments, exams, papers, etc. into your planner. This way, you get an accurate idea of how to budget your time for the rest of the quarter and minimize the need for cramming. One key to help minimize surprises is to allow more time for a task than you think you will need. By allowing yourself that extra hour, you won't be as disrupted by a phone call, or your roommate's crisis, etc. If your day planner becomes so full it becomes confusing, consider color coding your entries. Use red for academics, blue for social events, green for work, etc. This should help to minimize the confusion.

So now, you have a day planner, you are breaking down your tasks, and you are setting intermediate goals for yourself. What is next? COMMITMENT, CONSISTENCY, SELF-DISCIPLINE. It is easy to have a day planner, but it takes more effort to actually refer to it on a daily basis, or stick to your goals. An easy way to make yourself use your day planner is to find some small amount of time every day. For many, the best time is right after dinner. You have just eaten, are feeling tired and lazy. So, before you turn on the TV, glance through your day planner. If you find that there are things you need to do in the next couple of days, scribble them down on a note and put this on your backpack, mirror, alarm clock, etc. (someplace where you will be sure not to miss it).

Finally, remember to take time out for yourself. Reward yourself for meeting a goal or deadline. Successful time management is extremely difficult. Always remember that you can't plan for everything, and when the unexpected happens, try to make the most of it.

GOOD LUCK!!!

Name: _____ Date: _____

■ Week Time Grid

	Sunday	Monday	Tuesday	Wednesday	Thursday	Friday	Saturday
7–8 AM							
8–9 AM							
9–10 AM							
10–11 AM							
11–12 AM							
12–1 PM							
1–2 PM							
2–3 PM							
3–4 PM							
4–5 PM							
5–6 PM							
6–7 PM							
7–8 PM							
8–9 PM							
9–10 PM							
10–11 PM							
11–12 PM							
12–1 AM							

■ Goal Setting

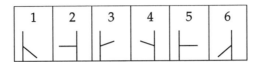

4	1	3	1	2	5	6	6	5	2	3	1	4	2	5	4
2	5	6	4	2	1	3	4	4	1	5	3	2	5	6	4
3	1	4	2	6	5	3	1	5	6	4	3	2	1	5	6
1	3	5	4	2	6	1	2	1	3	6	4	6	2	5	1
5	3	1	6	2	1	5	4	6	2	3	1	4	2	1	3
4	2	3	5	2	6	2	6	1	3	5	2	1	1	2	5
1	6	2	5	4	3	1	6	2	4	3	1	2	6	4	2
5	1	6	4	3	2	4	6	2	1	5	3	4	3	2	5
2	3	2	1	5	6	4	1	5	4	3	2	4	6	4	5
1	5	3	6	2	6	4	1	3	5	2	6	4	1	6	4
6	4	2	1	3	5	3	2	6	4	6	1	2	5	3	2
4	2	3	5	6	1	2	5	4	6	1	2	5	4	1	3

Name: _____ Date: _____

■ Time and Academic Demands Schedule

☐ **Available Time**—per week
  ☐ In a seven-day period you have   168   hours
  ☐ Subtracting 7 hours/day for sleeping, 2 hours/day for eating, and
     1 hour/day personal grooming and maintenance (10/day × 7 days)   —70   hours
                                 TOTAL AVAILABLE TIME: 98   hours

☐ **Necessities**—per week
  ☐ Working _____ _____ hours
  ☐ Travel to and from work _____ _____ hours
  ☐ Travel to and from school _____ _____ hours
  ☐ Housekeeping chores _____ _____ hours
  ☐ Family Obligations _____ _____ hours
  ☐ Other Demands and Obligations _____ _____ hours
  ☐ _____ _____ hours
  ☐ _____ _____ hours
  ☐ _____ _____ hours
                TOTAL TIME FOR NECESSITIES =   _____ hours*

☐ Available time before necessities   98   hours
☐ Subtracting time for necessities   −   _____ hours*
  ☐ TOTAL AVAILABLE TIME FOR ACADEMIC DEMANDS
     AND EXTRACURRICULAR ACTIVITIES   =   [   ] 1

☐ **ACADEMIC DEMANDS**

Time per week for	Courses		
	1	2	3
1. Attending class (lecture & discussions)			
2. Reading Assignments			
3. Written Assignments			
4. Problems			
5. Laboratory work			
6. Meeting with Professors or Teaching Assistants			
7. Library Research			
8. Review Lecture Notes			
9. Test Preparation			
10. General Study and Reflection			
11. Study with Other Students			
12. Use of Support Services			
13.			
TOTAL TIME PER CLASS			

TOTAL TIME NEEDED TO MEET ACADEMIC DEMANDS   [   ] 2
Determining Available Time for Extracurricular Activities   [   ] 1
Enter time available after necessities (above)   [   ]
Subtract time for academic demands   −   [   ] 2

Remaining time for Extracurricular Activities   [   ]

Name: _____ Date: _____

■ Self Assessment Inventory for Time Management

Do these items reflect you as a student?   No   Yes

1. I keep a careful record of the dates of upcoming major events   1 2 3 4 5
   such as tests and assignments.

2. I often feel really panicky about being behind with my work.   1 2 3 4 5

3. During a study session, I set small goals and work to achieve them   1 2 3 4 5
   (e.g., read 5 pages of text and do 3 math problems.)

4. I tend to miss classes.   1 2 3 4 5

5. If I need to solve a problem quickly, I get help from another   1 2 3 4 5
   student, the teacher, or other help resources.

6. I often miscalculate how much time homework tasks will take.   1 2 3 4 5

7. I have set up a regular plan for my study activities.   1 2 3 4 5

8. I find my current course load too heavy.   1 2 3 4 5

9. I begin assignments early so that I will have time to do a good job.   1 2 3 4 5

10. I have difficulty concentrating while doing homework.   1 2 3 4 5

11. I plan ahead so I can be flexible about putting in extra hours if I   1 2 3 4 5
    have a lot of school work to do.

12. I always seem to be behind with my work.   1 2 3 4 5

13. I regularly use a day planner to plan my activities.   1 2 3 4 5

14. My marks tend to suffer because of last minute cramming for tests.   1 2 3 4 5

15. Each day I have clear goals of what I wish to accomplish.   1 2 3 4 5

16. I am easily distracted from school work by my friends, TV, etc.   1 2 3 4 5

17. I really enjoy working on the courses I am taking.   1 2 3 4 5

18. I can only work if I feel like working.   1 2 3 4 5

19. I prioritise tasks effectively.   1 2 3 4 5

20. I have a hard time deciding just what school work I should be   1 2 3 4 5
    doing outside class.

▶ **Scoring the inventory**

Total up your scores for all of the odd-numbered items. Odd-numbered items in the inventory reflect positive components of time management that can contribute to effective use of time. Then do the same for the even-numbered items. Even-numbered items reflect negative components that can take away from effective time management. Subtract the total for the even from the odd-numbered items. If you have a positive total score, this indicates a proactive-approach to managing time. If your score is negative, your time management strategies can be improved. However, remember that there is not one right way to manage time. You need to find the right approach for you that will allow for tasks to be completed on time, without necessitating super-human effort. It will also ensure that your stress level is reasonable.

From *Power over Time: Student Success with Time Management.*

How to Deal with
Your Procrastination Habit

Procrastination is a bad habit we must deal with in every area of our lives. In school or in the workplace, procrastination often impedes on the completion of necessary responsibilities. As students, we know that there is often an extreme tendency to put work off until another day; doing so however, only reduces productivity, efficiency, and often, quality. In an effort to combat the propensity to procrastinate, you must first understand a few things about yourself and how you procrastinate?

Take a few moments to think about the top three ways in which you procrastinate. Fill out your answers below:

1. _____

2. _____

3. _____

It is important to write down and recognize what it is exactly that impedes your ability to complete a task. This is the first step in dealing with your tendency to procrastinate. The second step is to realize that you are not alone. Thousands of students at every college campus struggle with procrastination, and many of them may procrastinate in the very same way as you! Just for fun, let's play a little game. We surveyed 100 students and asked them the same question we asked you to fill out above, "In what ways do you procrastinate?" Their responses have been narrowed down to the top five answers. Try to guess what they were by filling out numbers 1–5 below:

In what ways do students procrastinate? (Answers listed at bottom of the following page.)

1. _____   4. _____

2. _____   5. _____

3. _____

There are different levels of procrastinating, ranging from beginning a research project the day before it is due, to not completing any required assignments at all. In addition, there are many ways to procrastinate, as you may already know, or that you found out in the above survey. Some people procrastinate by going out, while others stay in and clean. Others may eat, sleep, play their computer, or talk on the phone. Everybody is different. It is important to understand that regardless of the manner in which you procrastinate, procrastination has a negative impact on you and your work. We have identified that procrastination has a negative impact on you academically, physically, and socially. In the space below, jot down a few of your thoughts on how procrastination affects you negatively in each of three categories mentioned above. (It's OK if you don't get three examples for each).

Academics	Physical	Social
1. _____	1. _____	1. _____
2. _____	2. _____	2. _____
3. _____	3. _____	3. _____

Some of the common responses are: **Academic:** bad grades, no time for other work, not totally satisfied with achievement; **Physical:** tired, unhealthy, sick, nauseated, and stressed out; **Social:** look bad, smell bad (no shower), and no time for fun.

Just as it is true that people procrastinate in different ways, it is also true that different people procrastinate for a variety of different reasons. Before we explore **WHY** others procrastinate, why don't you take a few minutes to think of the reasons why you procrastinate.

As before, please fill out the spaces below by answering this question: Why do you procrastinate?

1. _____

2. _____

3. _____

Some of the most common reasons students present to justify their procrastination are (just to name a few): boredom with the material, feeling overwhelmed by the material, lack of interest, fear of failure or commitment, not enough time to complete assignment so why start, do not understand assignment, and laziness. Obviously, this is just a small list of countless justifications often referred to as *crooked thinking*. *Crooked thinking* is the delaying techniques we employ to justify our bad behavior or bad habits.

There are three general delaying tactics:

1. **Perfectionism:** I don't have time/resources to do the task perfectly, so why do it at all.

2. **Inadequacy:** I am not capable of doing well, so why start, I'll just do poorly anyway.

3. **Discomfort:** I don't like the work in the first place, I do not want to do it.

Once we can adequately recognize and break down these justifications, we can address the real problem, the bad behavior itself. Getting started on a task is often the most difficult aspect of task completion and often seems impossible. Nobody is going to get your work done for you and the work is not going to be completed on its own, so it is imperative to address the concept of inertia and how it relates to procrastination. **Reverting back to old science classes, fill out the blanks in the sentence below:**

A mass at rest tends to stay at _____.

A mass in _____ *tends to stay in motion.*

Hopefully this task was not too challenging. The correct answers are: A mass at rest tends to stay at rest. And, a mass in motion tends to stay in motion. **Now, I want you to go back to the two sentences above you just filled out and replace the word "mass" with the word "task."**

The sentence should now read as follows:

A task at rest tends to stay at rest.

A task in motion tends to stay in motion.

Understand that greater forces are required to facilitate change than to sustain change. Consider for instance, this visual example: Procrastination is a huge boulder. Cluttered in front of it are many smaller rocks (excuses), keeping us from pushing the boulder. Once we get the rocks out of the way, and push hard, the boulder starts moving. Once it is moving, it is easier to keep it going. The boulder is now the task we need to get going. In the sections below, we will provide some useful tips on how to get started on difficult or cumbersome assignments.

So what can we do to stop procrastinating? Well, we have narrowed this troubleshooting section down to four major problem areas which we will go over below. Keep in mind that not all solutions will work for you, and many of the solutions are interrelated. We do ask that you be honest with yourself and give merit to each technique, as sometimes we do not know which technique works best until we try.

Often, students feel **overwhelmed by a task** or they **dislike the task** at hand. By overwhelmed, we mean the assignment is too large to even begin to tackle, or so confusing that we don't know where to start. The most effective way to approach such a problem is to set **SHORT-TERM GOALS**. These are goals that you wish to complete anywhere from one day to about a week. How do you set short-term goals? Take for example the following humorous, if not grotesque scenario. Let's say that there is a gigantic, dead, smelly elephant in your dorm room. You don't know how he got in, but you sure as heck know you can't get him out. How would you get this elephant out of the room? **Fill in your answer below:**

_____

_____

Although you may have come up with a creative response, probably the simplest way would be to chop the elephant up into small pieces. The same is true for overwhelming tasks. Break down the task into small, reasonable parts. After you complete each manageable section of a project or task: **REWARD YOURSELF!** A fitting reward may be a snack, exercise, some TV time, playing a video game, or whatever it is that you like to do in your spare time. Be sure to limit your reward time by watching the clock or setting an alarm. Also, **SET REASONABLE AND MANAGEABLE LIMITS**. It is not effective to set goals that are unattainable (e.g., I am going to finish this 12 page paper in three hours and then reward myself by watching "X-Files"). This only leads to frustration, anger, and feelings of low achievement. Lastly, **KNOW YOURSELF**. What do we mean by this? Well, know where and when you study best. Do you study best in a group or alone? Do you work better before sleeping or when you first get up? Ask yourself these questions and provide yourself with ample study time in the conditions you find most constructive to your academic achievement.

Study Skills

■ Introduction

In this chapter you will learn about several strategies to make your study time more efficient and productive. First, we'll look at ways to use your textbooks more effectively: how to read for better understanding, how to mark your textbooks to aid in later study, and the technique of surveying the textbook. We'll introduce you to some formal study systems, including the SQ3R system, as well as special systems for handling classes like math, science, and foreign language where practice exercises and memorization tactics will be useful. Next, we'll look at your study habits: the study environment itself, tricks for planning and use of time, and methods of motivating yourself to study productively. We'll also touch on ways to develop concise study guides, and we'll discuss the pros and cons of study groups. Finally the chapter delves a bit into "intellectual inquiry": how to use the library and other research tools, and how to understand research studies and statistics. With the appropriate systems and tools, your study time can be utilized to its fullest, and your comprehension—and grades—are sure to improve!

■ Pretest

PURPOSE: to help you focus in on areas of study techniques where there's room for improvement.

		Yes	No
1.	When I get a new textbook for a class, I always look it over in detail to find out what the course will cover.	_____	_____
2.	I know how to find the topic sentence in a paragraph.	_____	_____
3.	I always look up words that are unfamiliar while I'm reading.	_____	_____
4.	I mark my textbooks with highlighting and margin notes.	_____	_____
5.	I use the highlighted material and margin notes when I review for a test.	_____	_____
6.	Before I read a chapter for the first time, I survey its headings, graphics, examples, and review questions to get a grasp of what material will be covered.	_____	_____
7.	I plan my time to study when I will be at my physical peak of energy and concentration.	_____	_____

From *The Community College: A New Beginning*, Second Edition by Aguilar et al. © 1998 by Kendall/Hunt Publishing Company.

8. I keep my study materials organized and in one place. _____ _____

9. I have given some thought to my study environment: lighting, temperature, furniture, potential distractions. _____ _____

10. I plan rewards for myself when I meet my study goals. _____ _____

11. When I begin studying a subject, I review materials from the previous study session before tackling new material. _____ _____

12. Whenever possible, I study new material right after the class or lecture. _____ _____

13. I develop written study guides before each major test. _____ _____

14. I have been or am a member of a study group, or I have found a study partner for appropriate classes. _____ _____

15. I have taken a tour of my college library, and know how to access periodicals, use the computer lab, and borrow materials from other libraries. _____ _____

■ Using Your Textbooks

Reading for Understanding: What's in a Paragraph?

The basic building block of all reading material is the simple paragraph. Most paragraphs contain three major parts. The **topic sentence** states the main idea or point the author is trying to get across. The **body** of the paragraph contains one or more supporting sentences which develop or prove the point being made. The **conclusicn** will either re-state the main idea or topic, or will provide a transition to the next paragraph. Let's look at the three main parts of this sample paragraph:

It is time that America elected a woman President.

} **TOPIC SENTENCE:** States the main idea, the author's point of view.

Many women have a great deal of experience in the political arena; from being Senators or Representatives, to state Governors, to powerful executives in large companies. Some women have learned about the role of the President from close observation, such as being members of the Cabinet, or even relatives of the President himself. Many times it has been obvious that inherent feminine personality traits could be very useful in the role of Chief Executive. For example, women may use compassion for the feelings of others to come to fair judgements on sensitive issues. Furthermore, there are many issues of great importance to women that male-dominated government has not yet addressed; such as affordable child care.

} **SUPPORTING SENTENCES:** Gives facts or opinions to support the main point.

These are some of the many excellent reasons why the idea of a female President should be taken seriously by Americans today.

} **CONCLUSION:** Re-states the main point, sometimes summarizes the supporting statements.

Variations of the Standard Paragraph

Sometimes a paragraph will contain no topic sentence, but a series of supporting sentences (facts or opinions) leading to a conclusion. The preceding example, minus its topic sentence, would work this way. Another stylistic variation might be a paragraph which has no formal conclusion, but invites the reader to come to his or her own conclusion from the evidence provided. Here's an example of this variation:

What will you find at Founders' University? At Founders' you'll find a beautiful, wooded campus with a lovely blend of old and new architectural styles. At Founders' you'll find the latest scientific and technical equipment, always available for your use. At Founders' you'll find an enthusiastic and friendly student body. And at Founders' you'll find the finest instructors ready and willing to give you plenty of time and individual attention.

The paragraph might have concluded with a sentence like, "Everything you're looking for, you'll find at Founders'." Instead, the author chose to leave the paragraph open-ended, inviting the reader to draw the obvious conclusion about the merits of Founders' University.

In summary, to understand a paragraph, find the topic sentence and grasp what the author is trying to tell you. Read the support sentences and glean the new information. Feel free to form opinions about the support sentences: are they facts or opinions? Do they really support or prove the main point? Then read the conclusion, if there is one, and re-state the main point of the paragraph in your own words. Complete Activity 1 for more helpful practice in understanding paragraphs.

■ Marking the Textbook and Study Materials

Why Mark the Textbook?

"Why would I want to mark up my textbook?" you ask, "I can sell it to the bookstore at the end of the term and get some of my money back!" Think of the cost of your textbooks as an investment in your education. If you want to save money, buy used textbooks to begin with!

There are three good reasons to mark your textbooks for your own study. First, the marking process itself forces you to concentrate as you read—you can't be physically marking the book while falling asleep at the same time! Marking also helps you understand the material as you go along—it helps you organize the reading in your mind. Finally, you'll have ready-made focal points for later review and for making study guides.

How to Mark the Textbook

First you'll want to mark certain items with highlighting or underlining:

1. The topic sentence (main idea) of the paragraph

2. Main (key) words of the supporting sentences

3. Names and dates if studying history, psychology, etc.

4. Definitions

Here is an example of a highlighted paragraph:

> *Language* *is a* *system* *we* *infer* *from the* *sounds* *that come out of the mouths of* *speakers* *and the marks that come from the hands of* *writers.* *Variation within a language is of* *two main kinds.* *From* *one kind,* *we* *identify those who use the language:* *we infer* *where* *they come from,* *what* *groups they belong* *to,* *when they learned the language,* *and* *what* *they are like* *as individuals—their age, sex, education, and personality.* *Such variation* *is called* *dialect.* *From the* *other* *kind, we* *identify the uses* *to which language is put:* *the* *subjects* *it treats, the* *circumstances* *in which it is used, the* *medium* *of its expression (for example, speech versus writing), the* *social relationships* *among its users, and* *the* *purpose* *of its use.* *Such variation is called* *register.*

Next, use the margins of the page to make notations to yourself:

1. Definition (def.), comparison (comp.), similarity (sim.), differences (diff.)

2. Memory cues—dates, names, key words

3. One or two word description of the paragraph's main point (assuming it's not in the heading)

4. Summaries, contents of the material in your own words.

Here's the same paragraph, with margin notes added:

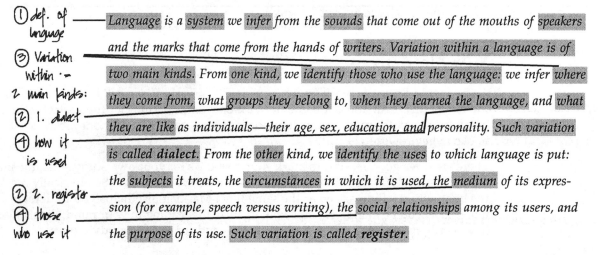

Turn to Activity 2 and highlight/mark the sample paragraphs.

■ Surveying

Surveying a Textbook

Using the technique of surveying a textbook can be helpful in two situations. First, suppose you're thinking of taking Underwater Basket Weaving 101 next semester. Go to the bookstore, find the textbook for that class, and use the surveying technique we're about to show you. You'll learn if the book covers material you'll find interesting, whether it might be too difficult, or if topics are covered that you've studied before. Second, if you survey the textbook before you show up for the first class meeting, you can confidently take your seat, knowing you've got the advantage of already knowing how the textbook is organized and what material it covers.

Here are the eight steps in surveying a textbook:

1. Examine the **title page**. It contains not only the title of the book, but also the author's name and credentials such as degrees and university or college affiliation. You will also find the name of the publisher. Pay special attention to words like "Second Edition"—this tells you the book has been revised or rewritten.

2. The **copyright page** is usually the "flip" side of the title page. It will tell you the year the book was published. Obviously, the more recent the book, the more up-to-date the material it covers.

3. Read the **introduction** or **preface**. It is directed to you, the reader or user of the book. It will explain how the author came to write the book, about his or her point of view, and some of the topics the book will cover.

4. The **table of contents** is the place to spend the most time while surveying the book. It lists the organization of the material of the book, by sections, chapters, and headings. Remember, these are the topics that will be covered in the course.

5. Many textbooks will have a **glossary**, where you can look up the definitions of unfamiliar terms. This is a very helpful feature, as you can look up terms without having to go to the trouble of finding a dictionary.

6. Some books have an **appendix**, which contains supplemental materials like charts, statistical materials, maps, articles, or answers to exercises or problems.

7. Most books contain a **bibliography**, which refers you to all the books and articles the author used in researching the textbook. If you have an interest in further information about a topic, you can check the bibliography for a book or article to read.

8. Finally, take a look at the **index**. Here you'll find an alphabetical listing of all the topics in the book, including names and places that are mentioned in the text. The index contains the page number where you'll find that topic.

Activity 3 guides you in surveying a textbook.

Surveying a Chapter

Now that you've got the basic idea of surveying, we'll check out the concept of surveying a chapter.

Why survey a chapter? Before you read the chapter for the first time, surveying helps you find out exactly what material is covered. You'll get an idea if the chapter will be time-consuming, contain a lot of unfamiliar material, or have many exercises to complete. Before taking the test, you'll want to survey the chapter again, to focus on areas which might need more study.

Here are the six steps in surveying a chapter:

1. Read the chapter title—it will, of course, tell you what the chapter is about.

2. Read the chapter introduction (or first paragraph) to find the thesis statement, or the main idea of the chapter. Ask yourself, "What am I supposed to learn from this chapter?"

3. Read the major headings within the chapter. Again, ask yourself, "What am I supposed to learn in this section?"

4. Check out all the visual aids—photos, charts, cartoons, graphs. Usually visual aids relate to topics the author thinks are important.

5. Read the summary. This is a review of the chapter, usually containing major points and new vocabulary.

6. Look over the questions or exercises within the chapter or at the end of the chapter. Again, you can see what you're expected to learn.

■ Study Systems

SQ3R "An Oldie but a Goodie"

The SQ3R study system was developed in 1941 by Francis P. Robinson. It's such an easy and comprehensive system, it's hard to find anything better even after more than fifty years. The system consists of five steps:

S = Survey. Using the surveying techniques we've already studied, survey your textbooks and chapters to get a head start on understanding their content and organization.

Q = Question. Re-word the chapter headings as questions, which you will then answer as you read the material. Later on, we'll show you how to use this step to make study guides.

1R = Read. We've already talked a lot about how to read your textbooks. Be sure to make notes in your book, and underline or highlight. Answer the questions, aloud if you like, while you read. Writing down the questions and answers will help with later study.

2R = Recite. Especially if you're an auditory learner, reciting material out loud can be very helpful. It helps "burn it into your brain." Read aloud your margin notes, your questions and answers, lists, definitions, names and dates. Reciting also helps you to memorize material.

3R = Review. Review, review, review. Review right after reading, and the next day. Review at least every other day to retain the information in your memory. Review just before the test.

Special Situations

Math involves problems (i.e., demonstrations and practicing of material covered). Remember, math material is usually cumulative, meaning it builds on material previously learned. Usually it helps to do a couple of problems from the previous chapter before tackling the new material. If you are studying a new math topic before it is covered in class, try studying the sample problems, copying the original problem, closing the book and re-working the sample problem.

Foreign language uses memorization skills. Recite new vocabulary out loud. Use a study partner to drill you on new material. With your study partner, converse in the language, trying to use new vocabulary. Write a page in the language, using as much of the new material as possible.

Chemistry, Biology, and Other Sciences include both problems and memorization! Use the tactics from math and foreign language, and add diagrams or charts, especially if you are a visual learner. You can use charts for almost all subjects. For more information see the section on written study guides later in this chapter.

In all cases, studying as soon as possible after a class is most beneficial, as it reinforces new concepts. This is especially important for math, science and foreign languages, where memorization is an integral component of the course.

■ Study Habits

Planning for Effective Use of Study Time

Your best bet is to design a schedule for each study session. Here's the schedule Margie May made up for a particularly heavy pre-midterm study session:

Margie May's Study Session Schedule:

To-Do List for this Session:

TUES, MARCH 11:

Math—Read Chapter 11 and do problems 1–15.

Review Chapters 1–11 for midterm THURS.

Psychology—Read Chapter 6.

Prepare topic paragraph for midterm paper, due WED.

History—Study for midterm WED.

French—Study for midterm FRI.

Schedule:

7:00–7:30—Read pages 1–5 of psychology chapter, mark & recite.

7:30–8:00—Read pages 6–10 of psychology chapter, mark & recite.

8:00–8:15—Break

8:15–9:00—Read math chapter and do problems.

9:00–9:30—Do 2 or 3 problems from math Chapters 1–4.

9:30–9:45—Break

9:45–10:00—Review French vocabulary lists

10:00–10:30—Prepare topic paragraph for Psychology, and type.

10:30–11:00—Extra time for delays or interruptions.

You'll notice Margie May used the two major rules of thumb regarding study schedules:

Rule of Thumb #1

Always build in extra time—it always takes longer than you think it will.

Rule of Thumb #2

Study no more than one hour to one-hour-fifteen-minutes without a break (even a quick break like going to the bathroom or getting a soft drink).

Also remember that when reading is part of the study session, break it into manageable chunks (how long is your attention span?), mark the text as you go, and follow with reciting out loud to help focus your attention.

Here are some quick tips to maintain concentration and stick to your study schedule:

1. Break large assignments into smaller, manageable "chunks," and schedule them separately.

2. Study the most difficult subject first, while your mind is still fresh.

3. Don't study two similar assignments right after each other—separate them with something different (don't do two reading assignments in a row, for example).

4. Plan for breaks, and plan for rewards.

5. Study from your own familiar, well-marked textbooks.

■ Your Study Environment and Materials

Planning Your Environment

Have you ever noticed that it's much easier to study and concentrate in some environments than in others? A study location and environment is a personal thing. Some people love to study outdoors, while others need a less "natural" locale. Many students swear by studying with loud music playing, while others require absolute quiet to concentrate.

Here are some things to think about and plan for as you design your prime study area:

1. Location—for most people, having one definite area designated for study works best. Use that place only for studying; it helps put you "in the mood." Usually it should be in a relatively quiet room, away from the hustle and bustle of families or roommates, and away from distractions like the TV.

2. Comfort—to avoid eyestrain and fatigue, try to make sure you have overhead light, or a lamp that does not cast a glare on your work area. Make sure your work area is not too hot or too cold. If you are too hot, you will begin to feel sleepy. Too cold, and you'll be unable to concentrate. Finally, take inventory of the furniture you use in your study area. A sturdy table or desk with plenty of space for books and computer, a writing area, and supply storage is ideal. A supportive chair which can be adjusted to the right height for you is also important.

3. Supplies and Organizational Tools—keep all your supplies nearby and ready for use. There's nothing more annoying than sitting down to work, only to have to jump up and search out a pencil. If your desk doesn't have storage, put everything into a file box or plastic storage container, so it can move from place to place with you, if need be. Use a filing system (folders, a cardboard file box, a stacking tray system) to organize returned papers and tests, study guides, rough drafts, and other papers you need for your work. It's a good idea to have a bulletin board or cork board near your study area—preferably one you can see each time you look up. Here's where you post your semester calendar, weekly schedule, study schedules, etc. Keep your study area as organized as possible, and it will become an inviting and efficient aid to your study system.

Other Study Locations

Sometimes you'll have to do some studying in locations or environments over which you have little or no control. Some examples include the library, science labs, foreign language or music listening labs. Try to at least find a comfortable chair, good lighting, and enough room to spread out your materials. Limit your time in these areas to just what you must do there, and schedule the lab or library session just like you would any study session. Allow for breaks and extra time for interruptions.

Another potentially difficult situation can be meeting someone else for a study session. You may need to work with a partner, for example, or a friend or boyfriend/girlfriend may suggest studying together. In this second situation, you are not study partners, working on the same material; rather, you are studying in the same place so you can spend time together. It's difficult in college to maintain a relationship when so much time needs to be devoted to study; sometimes "studying together" seems like the perfect solution. Usually the drawbacks are significant and the benefits minimal, but if you must do it, try these rules:

1. If the environment is less than ideal (i.e., someone gets the desk and someone has to sprawl across the bed), try to match the activity to the locale. It's easier to read on the bed than to write a term paper there. Also switch off whenever possible.

2. Design a study schedule for each of you that synchronizes breaks. This minimizes tempting distractions and provides opportunities for socializing with time limits!

3. Make sure the study session requirements are compatible—it's almost impossible to read sociology when your friend is listening to opera!

4. End the evening at a pre-arranged time and leave at least half an hour to enjoy each other's company (take a walk, watch the news on TV).

5. In every relationship, there is one person who is better able to enforce the rules than the other. Make an agreement at the start—who is the "timekeeper?" Then, the other person must agree to abide cheerfully by the schedule.

■ Study Partner and Study Groups

Finding a Study Partner

For each class for which you'd need a study partner, ask yourself if it would be more beneficial to have a partner with the same or different learning style. For example, a visual learner will be happy to make the charts and graphs, while an auditory learner will be willing to read lists of vocabulary out loud for memorizing. And, do yourself a favor—DON'T select a study partner because she/he is someone whom you find attractive. Studying and dating are usually like oil and water—they don't mix.

Rules for Study Partners and Groups

1. Designate a regular time and place to meet that incorporates each member's peak energy times and study needs (quiet, comfortable locations, materials, etc.).

2. Divide the work early on: "You survey Chapters 1 and 2, I will make study guides, you draw the diagrams of the cat's stomach and label the parts . . ." Remember to fully utilize the strengths and weaknesses of each person's learning style.

What's in It for Me?

It's a standard phrase in motivational jargon—"reward yourself!" But how? We've already talked about planning break times—those are small rewards for working steadily and sticking to your schedule. But what about the concept of really rewarding yourself for accomplishing a big task, or a "job well done"?

Here's a list of some suggested rewards . . . and add your own—things you know will motivate you!

1. A walk to the ice cream store

2. A ride in the car in the country

3. A movie or renting a video

4. A sporting event—college or professional

5. A new outfit, or sports equipment, or video game

6. A "mental health" day (like a Saturday)— schedule everything for another day and just "veg out."

7. A long phone conversation with a friend you haven't seen for a while.

8. Work out, get a massage, or schedule a tanning session

9. Prepare a favorite meal or go out to dinner

List Your Own:

10. _____

11. _____

12. _____

---

3. Set a realistic goal, i.e., preparation for a particular test or completion of a project. Don't just say, "We'll study together."

4. Deal with problems immediately; be kind but direct. "When you don't complete your part of the assignment, it makes more work for the rest of us and sets us back."

■ Developing Study Guides

Using the "Q"

A written study guide is a valuable tool for organizing your readings, lecture notes, and other materials into a coherent unit. The study guide not only helps you prepare for short exams, quizzes, papers, or midterms, it can also be a ready reference when reviewing for the usually cumulative final exam.

Cherney, et al. in their book *Achieving Academic Success: A Learning Skills Handbook* have noted that although we are often taught facts and figures and vocabulary (the "learned material"), we are often tested on the application of that material. We must solve problems by drawing inferences from the learned material and applying them to the problem.

Remember in the SQ3R system, we mentioned the "Q" stands for "Question"? You can use the "Q" to help you design a study guide that will clarify and organize all that "stuff" from each unit or topic. For each heading or major topic covered, write down a question or two starting with: Who? What? Where? When? Why? Then answer your question, in *outline form*, using your textbook margin notes and your classroom lecture notes.

I.   Definition of language: system inferred from
   A.   Sounds from speakers
   B.   Marks from writers
II.   Two kinds of variation within language
   A.   Dialect
      1.   Identifies those who use the language
         a.   Where they come from
         b.   What groups they belong to
         c.   When they learned the language
         d.   What they are like as individuals
   B.   Register
      1.   Identifies how language is used
         a.   Subjects it treats
         b.   Circumstances of use
         c.   Social relationships among users
         d.   Purpose of use

Hints for Outline Form

1. *Organize your outline with Roman numerals, capital letters, numbers, lower case letters.*

   I.   Main Idea
      A.   Divisions within main idea
         1.   Supporting statements
            a.   Details

2. *Try not to copy phrases from the book. Translate them into your own words so you're sure you understand them.*

Organizational Patterns

The next step is to notate and organize the material you've outlined in terms of patterns you'll commonly find over and over again when studying certain subjects. For example, in a behavioral science class, you will learn a lot of definitions; thus your study guide should be organized like a glossary. In a history class, you will do well to organize material in chronological order. Other examples of patterns and hints for organizing your study guides follow.

Intellectual Inquiry

Familiarize Yourself with the LRC/Library

By now you're surely aware that your college Learning Resource Center (LRC) has a lot more to offer than just books. Magazines and professional journals, published research studies, encyclopedias, newspapers, articles on microfiche, multi-media materials, cassettes, videos . . . the list goes on and on. Now add to that the products of contempo-

Patterns

1. *Writing Class: Example, proof, details*
   Remember the good old topic sentence, supporting sentences, and conclusion? Study written materials for these standard items, then fashion your own writing the same way.

2. *Behavioral Sciences: Definitions*
   Make glossary-style lists of vocabulary and definitions for use in study/memorization.

3. *Natural Sciences: Concept and illustration*
   For every scientific theory or concept, your book or instructor will give you an example or illustration. Write them down together, draw pictures if necessary.

4. *Courses Containing Research Data: Cause and effect*
   All sciences from psychology to sociology to biology to chemistry will include results of research studies. A large proportion of research is done to prove that one thing causes another—cause and effect. Make two columns: in one write out the causative factor (i.e.,"neglect during childhood") and in the other note the effect ("antisocial adult behavior").

5. *Literature and Humanities: Compare or contrast*
   To compare means to find similarities, to contrast, find differences. You can compare and contrast characters in a novel, time periods of history, pieces of music. Again, use the column system: "Similarities" and "Differences."

6. *Mathematics and Sciences: Simple to complex*
   You must understand the basics (like addition and subtraction) before you can get to the harder concepts. Review previous material whenever necessary.

7. *History and other Social Sciences: Cause and Effect and Chronological order*
   Cause and effect . . . see point 4. Names and dates . . . that's what you'll need to remember. List things in chronological order in your study guide. It will help you get a mental picture of what happened first.

8. *Sciences: Problem-Solution or Question-Answer*
   Just like the SQ3R system, write out the question first and then the answer. Put both into your own words for best results.

rary technology: fiber optic information transmissions, FAX copies, CD-ROMs, articles and research through the Internet . . . this list is growing faster than any author or publisher can keep up!

So where do you find out what library material you need, which source it comes from, and how to get your hands on it? It's the same age-old answer: your friendly librarian.

Just as the contents of libraries have changed, librarians have too. No longer will you find Marian, granny glasses on her nose, finger pressed to her lips, hissing "Shhhh . . ." Today your librarian is probably an experienced researcher, fully conversant with the computer, unafraid to venture into cyberspace to help you get your paper done. So feel free to put yourself into his or her capable hands!

Step one: Take a tour of your college LRC, taking notes as you go along about what resources it offers, where they're located, and how to access them. Some colleges have a class you are encouraged (sometimes required) to take your first semester, which familiarizes you with your library and with research techniques. Other schools offer regularly scheduled group or individual tours; at other schools you must make a request of the library staff. Librarians are usually more than happy to show off their facility; it's fulfilling to them when students take full advantage of the materials and sources they've worked so hard to provide.

Step two: Familiarize yourself with the card catalog or computer search database, and with the indices and abstracts which organize the information available in periodicals. Ask for help if anything is confusing. Do a few trial runs to obtain a book or periodical with ease.

Step three: Visit the library soon after you get your first research assignment. Use your tour notes to help you get started, then again check in with a librarian. She/he can help you determine if there is material available from another library source that can be ordered to help you. In some cases, ordering material takes a little time, so the earlier you get started, the better.

Dig in to the Technology

Well, it's almost the 21st century, and computers are here to stay—whether you like it or not. Most students who have come up through junior high and high school in the current generation are not afraid of computers—they've grown up with them, so to speak. But for those who remember what a keypunch card was, things are a bit different. Computers were huge, awesome things which you could not dream of even turning ON, much less actually operating, without knowing some indecipherable mathematical formulas which only engineers were privy to. The computers themselves took up rooms the size of gymnasiums, and you needed 17,000 keypunch cards to program one to print, "Now is the time for all good men to come to the aid of their party."

Now people are talking about bits and bytes, RAM and ROM. And, heaven forbid—the Internet! How can I make sense of any of this if I'm afraid I'll push the wrong button and the whole thing will blow up?

Fear not, flower child. Using a computer is like plugging in an electrical appliance. You don't have to know how the electricity gets into the outlet, and you don't have to know how it gets to the appliance. You don't have to know how the appliance sucks dirt or plays music. You just have to know how to use the appliance—how to push the steam button or adjust for the carpet height, or find the oldies station. Just remember the battle cry of computer use: Save! Save! Save! Not to scare you again, but computers are not perfect; just like vacuum cleaners, they can break down and when they do, they can erase any unsaved data you've been working with. If you master the habit of saving your work both to the hard drive and to disks on a regular basis, you shouldn't have any trouble.

Your college library will have access to the Internet, which is a system linking computers (via a telephone line) throughout the world. You will need detailed instructions to get started, and usually it helps if you know exactly what information you're searching for before you start. You can try out the Internet by searching one of the on-line services such as America Online, Prodigy, or Compuserve. Through the "web page" or "home page" you can get massive printouts of all kinds of information, services, and merchandise. Learning techniques for downloading or ordering information from these sources will be an important step in your "surfing" expedition. Two words of warning: 1) don't download anything until you've established if it has a cost and 2) don't send out any messages of your own until you're fully familiar with the Internet and the person or address to whom you're sending "E-mail."

■ Summary

In this chapter, we studied first the techniques of reading for understanding, and hints for marking your textbook for later study. We covered the topic of surveying the textbook and chapter to get a head start on understanding their organization and content.

Next, we took a look at an old "classic" study system, the SQ3R, and some ideas for customizing study systems for particular subjects. We learned about how to develop good study habits, how to schedule a study session, and how to design an efficient study environment. We found out how to make written study guides. Finally, we took a look at some of the components of research tools: the library, the personal computer, and scientific research studies.

■ Journal Assignment

Analyze your current study habits. Describe what you are doing right and list some potential ways to improve. Survey your study area(s) and provide examples of how your study needs are being met and/or what improvements you need to make.

■ Activity 1.

A. Find and underline the topic sentences in the following paragraphs:

1. Because there is so much more to a college than can be stated in catalogs and brochures, we encourage students to visit our campus. While on campus, prospective students may attend classes, explore Diploma Mill College's facilities, meet with faculty and students, speak with personnel from the Offices of Admissions and Financial Aid, and learn more about the Diploma Mill difference. The campus visit is the best way to experience Diploma Mill life.

2. The quiet town of Shipshewana is the home of the renowned auction and flea market, and it bustles with treasure-seekers on market days. Over 900 outdoor vendors display their wares, and the gigantic indoor antique auction is a sight to behold. Situated in northern Indiana in the heart of Amish country, the flea market and auction hold something for everyone. You will need a whole day to explore the market, which is located in the center of town. You'll also want to take time to stroll along the main street of this tiny town, where you'll find friendly shopkeepers and wonderful quilt, craft and other country stores. Your day at Shipshewana will be a memory you'll talk about for years to come.

B. Summarize the main point of these paragraphs:

1. The Americans with Disabilities Act (ADA) took effect in January, 1992. The Middleville Park District complies with the legislation, which prohibits discrimination on the basis of a disability. The Middleville Park District makes reasonable accommodations in its recreation programs to enable participation by people with disabilities who meet essential eligibility requirements for the specific programs and facilities. The ADA requires that recreation programs offered by the Middleville Park District be available in the most integrated setting appropriate for each individual. If you believe you have been discriminated against, a procedure is available to help address and resolve your complaint.

   _____

   _____

   _____

   _____

   _____

   _____

2. Exploration in the art department at Academia Junior College is possible both for the art major and for students simply interested in pursuing their creativity. Basic courses in studio work such as drawing, painting, figure drawing, and composition are structured to encourage students to explore their own creativity. Studio courses in ceramics, printmaking and sculpture serve as a foundation for those students pursuing further advanced study in a variety of media—oil, acrylic, charcoal, watercolor, clay, metals, and stained glass. Art history is divided into four sections: origins of art, the Renaissance, modern art, and American art. Because of flexible prerequisites in the art program, it is possible to pursue a program leading to education certification as well.

   _____

   _____

   _____

   _____

   _____

   _____

◼ Activity 2.

Mark these paragraphs with highlighting and margin notes:

1. Engineering opportunities are exceptionally good, and continue to open in energy-related areas, environmental projects, defense and health care fields. Medical electronics engineers are in demand to assist in the development of new techniques in health care. These engineers tend to work in research, design and development, or as clinical engineers, which is the fastest growing of these areas. Another field of engineering which is growing is environmental engineering. These engineers work with air and water pollution, sewage treatment, surveying and mapping, and industrial hygiene.

2. Understanding the difference between memory and disk storage can help you use your personal computer more productively. Memory is your computer's temporary storage area; it is where data resides when you work with it. Every time you enter or change data, you use more available memory. If you continue to add data, you will eventually run out of memory. The data in memory is lost when you end an application or turn off your computer. To store this data for future use, you must save it on a physical disk such as a hard disk or a diskette. Disk storage is permanent storage; it is not the same as memory. You may have a large-capacity hard disk (such as 110 megabytes), but have only 640 kilobytes of memory in your computer. The large amount of disk storage you have does not mean you necessarily have enough memory for the kinds of programs you want to run. The size of the memory is unrelated to the size of the disk storage.

■ Activity 3.

Get a textbook from one of your other classes. Survey the textbook and answer the following questions:

1. What is the title of the book?

   _____

2. Has the book been revised?

   _____

3. What is the author's name?

   _____

4. When was the book published?

   _____

5. What is the author's stated purpose for writing the book?

   _____

6. How many chapters are in the book?

   _____

7. Find a term with which you are unfamiliar, and look it up in the glossary.

   _____

8. Does this book have an appendix? What does it contain?

   _____

9. List one book or article used as a source for this book.

   _____

10. Look up any topic in the index, and write down the page number on which it is covered in the text.

    _____

Name: _____ Date: _____

■ Activity 4.

Make your own study schedule. Start by listing this week's assignments for each course you are taking:

Class	Assignment

Now, schedule one or more study sessions to complete your assignments.

To-Do List (for this study session)	(time)	Schedule (activity)

Remembering to Concentrate

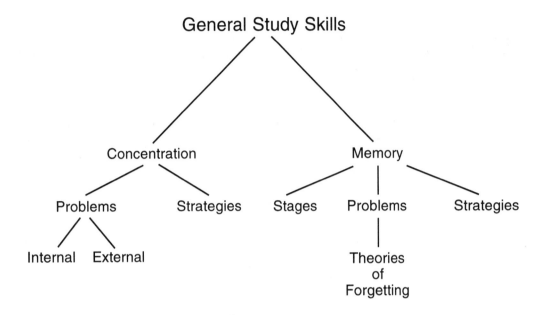

Concentration and memory are both important factors in your learning process. The ability to concentrate affects how much you can accomplish while you are studying. The ability to remember information is going to determine how well you will be able to apply this information in your life and how well you will score on tests.

Concentration is a by-product. It only happens when we don't think about it. If you are engrossed in a Civil War battle in your history book and suddenly realize that you were concentrating, then at that moment you would have broken your concentration on the battle.

Concentration is the process that permits you to focus your attention on a particular task. This process requires continual monitoring of distractors. You will have a better chance of improving your concentration if you know what causes you to lose it.

■ Why Is Concentration Difficult?

Concentrating on a subject is not something that just "happens." Albert Einstein was the typical "absent-minded professor." His enormous intellectual powers were so concentrated on the problem at hand that he lost all connection with routine activities. A good example today would be the teenager engrossed in playing a video game. He loses all touch with routine activities. "I can't concentrate" is a common student complaint. The habit of concentration can be developed by self-discipline and practice in "becoming involved."

■ What Are Some Problems in Concentrating and Their Solutions?

1. *Problem:* Mental and/or Physical Fatigue—It is difficult to concentrate when you are tired. Studying late at night can be a problem because of this. Mental fatigue can be caused by too many things to do, depression, fear of failure, lack of interest, and many more factors. When you are physically tired, it is hard to care about anything, not to mention trying to concentrate on it. Sometimes boredom can be the cause of the fatigue feeling.

   Solution: Determine the time of day you are most alert. Use this time of day for your most difficult assignments. A proper diet, rest, and exercise will also help you be more alert. If boredom is the culprit, find something in the class that will help you build an interest. Look until you find it! Be alert to ways in which your class relates to your life. Read actively and converse mentally with the author. It also helps to study in a well-ventilated room. Take short breaks and do something active.

2. *Problem:* Too Much To Do—Procrastination is usually the cause here. Often we are more overwhelmed by the idea of all that we need to do than the actual work that needs to be accomplished. When we try to think of several things at once, it is impossible to concentrate.

   Solution: Keep a calendar of test and assignment deadlines. The deadline for one class will probably coincide with the deadline of another class. Make a schedule with definite times for studying and completing specific assignments. Stick to this schedule! One way to do this is to set goals for each study session. Plan ahead exactly what you expect to accomplish in that session. It is important to set realistic goals. Divide long assignments into short sessions. Reward yourself after your objective is completed. Your objective should not be to just cover the pages, but to understand the assignment.

3. *Problem:* A Poor Attitude—If you do not care about what you are studying, you obviously will not be able to concentrate!

   Solution: Accept the fact you need to learn the material. Many people have spent long hours in deciding what courses were necessary to fit a particular program. Decisions are not always based on simply turning out good teachers or lawyers. These people were also concerned with producing good, well-rounded individuals.

   Before you allow your attitude to ruin any hope of good concentration and retention, give the subject a chance. Be an active reader. Dig in and question, agree, or disagree with the author. Talk to students who are majoring in this field and see what interests them. Could it be possible that your lack of background is causing the dislike? Explore this field in an encyclopedia. Look in bookstores for review and workbooks. If you can build a background, maybe you can help your attitude!

4. *Problem:* No Concentration Habit—If you have been out of school for a period of time, did not apply yourself previously, or have not been involved in an activity that required concentration, maybe you have "lost" the habit of concentration.

Solution: You had it at one time. You have concentrated when you were learning to ride a bicycle, when you learned to read and write, drive a car, and many other basic skills you possess. You can re-develop this skill by being aware of how important it is. This could take some practice!

5. *Problem:* Noisy Study Environment—Are you trying to study with your favorite television program? How about your favorite music? Do you take your textbook to a ball game?

   Solution: Two or three hours of study in quiet surroundings does more good than ten hours of study in a noisy place. It is important to have a designated study place that is used only for studying. Concentrating will be aided by associating studying with a particular locale.

6. *Problem:* Poor Reading and Study Skills—It is difficult to concentrate if you are having problems understanding what you are trying to learn.

   Solution: If your vocabulary is limited, you need to work on this! Practice vocabulary exercises, word games, and read as much varied material as you can. You improve reading by reading. Learn basic effective approaches to textbook study.

7. *Problem:* Deciding Who Is in Control—It is difficult to concentrate if you're not aware of who controls your concentration efforts.

   Solution: You should be cognizant of what contributes to your concentration. If you are in control, then you are the one who can make the decisions necessary to increase your concentration. If the control is something else, is there anything you can do?

■ What Are External and Internal Distractors?

A learner must be able to cope with internal and external distractors before starting to concentrate and learn.

Internal Distractors

Any form of negative self-talk is an internal distractor. In order to concentrate, your mind must be quiet and controlled. Sometimes a small voice inside that should be full of confidence blurts out, "You are probably going to say something stupid," and, sure enough, this proves to be true. But luckily, there is also another voice hiding in there. You feel confident and knowledgeable about what you are about to say, and it comes out right! These inside voices determine to a great extent the "tone" of your world—whether it is good, bad, or indifferent. We can change how we feel by what we say to ourselves.

Negative self-talk can be produced by insecurity, fear, anxiety, frustration, defeatist attitudes, indecision, anger, daydreams, and personal problems. This self-talk is obviously influenced by your feelings. If your self-talk seems to lean more on the negative side, you are not alone! Richard Fenker says 80–90% of students with learning problems have self-talk that is predominantly negative. Fenker believes you can control these negative voices using your right brain and substituting more positive self-talk. If you are afraid of speaking in public, imagine yourself giving a report in front of a class. If you have test anxiety, imagine or picture yourself being relaxed and calm in that testing situation. Spend a few days listening to yourself. When a negative opinion surfaces, try to replace it with a neutral or a positive thought!

What Internal Distractors Affect You?

Take a look at the following list of internal distractors. Do any of these distractors seem to be a problem for you? If so, note the possible answer for this distractor.

Hunger	Eat before you study.
Fatigue	Plan study time when you are most alert and get at least 7 to 8 hours of sleep. Don't forget some exercise!
Illness	Postpone until you feel better.
Worrying about grades or work	Try to focus on the task and better grades will be the result. Focus on work while you are at work.
Stress	Attempt to focus on what you are trying to accomplish.
Physical discomfort	Study in a comfortable place.
Not understanding assignment	Always clarify assignments before you start.
Personal problems	Make a note of the problem and tell yourself you will cope after you study.
Lack of interest	Try studying with someone else, find something that you can relate to, or look at related material.
Negative attitude	Remember negative thoughts take away from getting a job done! Convince yourself there is something positive in the class.

Please note that some of these distractors can be eliminated if you anticipate your needs!

External Distractors

External distractors originate outside of you. They are those things that draw your attention away from a learning task.

Take a look at the following list of external distractors. Do some of them seem familiar? Many of these problems can also be eliminated if you anticipate your needs.

Lack of proper materials	Before you start your study session, have paper, pencil, etc. in place.
Music, television, noise, lighting too bright or too dim, temperature too high or too low, people talking, telephone	Choose your study location carefully. These should be eliminated by just choosing a proper spot.
Party or activity that you want to attend, family or friends wanting you to do something	If possible, plan your study session ahead of activity and use it as a reward.

Do the Concentration Worksheet to determine your specific problems.

■ Why Is a "Place of Study" So Important?

By looking at internal and external distractors, you can see how many can be controlled by the place you choose to study. It is important to have a definite and permanent place to study. Psychologists believe a conditioning effect is created between your desk and you. Do not do any other activities at your study desk. You should associate your study place with studying alone. Don't write letters, daydream, plan activities, or visit with friends in your study place. You need a study place where you feel comfortable and where you are likely to have few distractions.

A Program to Increase Concentration While Studying

Purpose

This program is designed to help you learn deep and effective concentration while studying.

How Does It Work?

Primarily by capitalizing on the concentration powers you already possess. This is done by developing an extremely strong association between one particular physical location (such as the desk in your room) and deep concentration on your studies.

What Must You Do?

To set up a strong association such as this, you must: Remove old associations that your "study spot" might have for you. This means removing pictures, telephones, souvenirs, etc., from your study area. When seated in your "study chair" only materials being studied at that moment should be seen. This sounds simple and in fact it is not extremely difficult, but it does require some self-discipline—especially at the beginning. You learn this new association by merely making sure that the only time you are in your study spot is when you are concentrating on your studies. Get up and move to another chair, or at least turn around in your chair so that you are looking at an entirely different set of visual stimuli every time your mind wanders, a friend comes in to talk, your roommate asks you a question, etc. Don't be discouraged if you have to change locations or turn around every few minutes for the first several days. It takes this long to develop this new association for most people. It's vital that you do absolutely nothing except concentrate while in your study spot. If you feel like letting your mind wander, go ahead . . . but make sure you move out of your study spot or turn around in your chair. Also, don't force concentration, or you'll end up associating your study spot with discomfort rather than concentration. Concentration is also helped if you switch study subjects every half hour or forty-five minutes, rather than working so long on one particular subject that you tire of studying for that course.

What Can You Expect?

Between 75% and 90% of the students who try this program find they can dramatically increase their periods of deep concentration within a period of a week or so, if they have been faithful to the system. Going from periods of concentration as short as two minutes to more than 45 minutes within several weeks is not at all unusual. But remember, the first three or four days will be the hardest, because it is during that time you will not notice much change. After the third or fourth day (assuming you have studied several hours each day), you will begin to notice a difference. Some students find the number of times they have to turn around in their chairs the first few days to be discouraging, and feel that the system results in their wasting time. However what is probably the case is that they have finally become painfully aware of just how much time they have actually been wasting in the past!

■ How Do You Improve Concentration while Reading?

Dr. Walter Pauk, noted study skills expert, believes the best way to gain and maintain concentration while you read is by having a lively conversation with the author. (No one will have to know!) Agree or disagree with the author. Interject your thoughts and ideas. This will also lead to more comprehension.

One reason your mind may wander during reading is because material is unfamiliar or too difficult. You cannot concentrate on what you can't comprehend. Formulate a purpose for reading! It also never hurts to look up words when you do not know the meanings!

■ What Are Some Strategies to Strengthen Concentration?

1. Learn to beat boredom—If boredom is causing a problem with concentration, study in small groups occasionally, buy review manuals and workbooks and look at the material from a different angle. Perhaps a tutor could provide new insights.

2. Become more active in studying—Highlight, underline, make questions out of the material, paraphrase, construct mnemonics, and/or form imagery associations. Think about your learning style and put it to work.

3. Ignore external distractions—Λ vibrating tuning fork held close to a spider's web sets up vibrations in the web. After the spider makes a few investigations and doesn't find dinner, it learns to ignore the vibrations. If a spider can control external distractors, a student should be able to eventually ignore external distractions.

■ Memory

Your brain is constantly being attacked with all kinds of information. You need to learn to process all of this by selective attention. Unimportant information signals are discarded immediately, such as a dog barking, a bird chirping, or the wind blowing. Other signals are only recalled for a moment. These signals will either be stored or dropped. As you are reading, you may recall the sentence you just finished. But, it may be difficult to recall that sentence when you finish a paragraph. The exact wording of that sentence has probably been dropped. If you can remember the concept of the sentence, you have probably stored that information in your memory.

It is important to note that without memory, there would be no learning.

Before you start reading this portion of the chapter, complete the Memory Worksheets.

What Are the Three Stages in the Memory Process?

1. Respond—If you don't understand material you are trying to remember, you don't have a chance to respond. One method we have of understanding new information is to relate it to what we already know. It will be helpful when starting a new chapter in a text to stop and think about what you already know about the material. What does this information mean to you before you learn anything new about it? To help you respond to information it is advantageous to use all of your senses: Listen to the lecture, take notes on it, and read about it.

2. Reserve—The key to reserving or retaining information is to make a conscious effort to remember. You need to find a reason to remember! One of the best ways to reserve information is to use or practice this information.

3. Remember—Our mind enables us to remember or recall information we have retained. Organization is an important factor in recall. Using your preferred learning style is also an asset. Review is vital for recalling information.

The immediate memory is called your short-term memory. This information is either discarded and forgotten or it is transferred into your permanent memory. This permanent memory is your long-term memory. Not all information stored in your long-term memory is in a form that can be retrieved. Short-term memory plays an important role in our everyday life. It is also vital in reading and study situations. The transfer of memory from short-term to long-term is enhanced by organization, repetition, and association with what we already know.

A study conducted at Southwest Missouri State University by Dr. Charles Tegeler revealed information on the value of review to help you remember. Students were given information and they studied it until they had 100% mastery. The group was divided into two groups. One group did not review the material and at the end of 63 days when they were retested, they averaged 17% comprehension. The other group reviewed once a week. At the end of the 63 day period, they averaged 92% comprehension! (See Figure 1.)

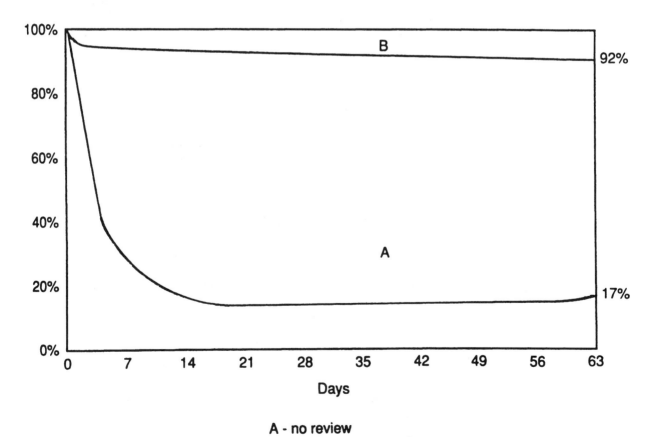

A - no review
B - review once a week

Figure 1 ■

Why Do You Forget?

Forgetting can be defined as a failure or loss of memory. Your mind remembers only what you need and discards the rest. Do you remember grades you made in your classes in the eighth grade? Do you even remember what classes you had? You probably don't remember. Information that is not used is forgotten.

Research has proven over and over that the greatest amount of forgetting occurs during the first day. Remembering what you have heard is even more difficult to remember than what you have read. When you read, you have control over the material. You can slow down, regress, or speed-up your reading.

People often say they forgot something when they actually never knew it. If you just met someone and didn't really catch their name, you didn't forget it—you probably never knew it.

There are a variety of theories about forgetting. Think about these as you read them and see if you can understand how the theory relates to your own "forgetful" experiences.

1. It's There Somewhere!—Some psychologists believe once we have thoroughly learned something, it remains in our memory our entire life. This theory suggests that the concept is there, but we are just having trouble finding it in order to be able to retrieve it.

2. Interference Theory—Old facts and ideas cause us to forget new facts and ideas. The reverse is also true. New ideas and facts can cause confusion with old ones. We are continually adding ideas to our memory bank. If you learn three similar facts at three separate times, the middle one will have the most difficult time surviving. This is also true of lists you need to remember. The first and last items are easier to remember than the middle ones.

3. Use It or Lose It—If you don't use a fact you have learned, it gets more difficult to remember it. This is why review is so important!

4. Motivation and Attitude Theory—Here are our two favorite words again! Sometimes we choose to forget. Things we associate with unpleasant memories or mistakes we have made we would like to forget. A poor attitude in class can definitely affect memory ability. You have the power to influence both remembering and forgetting.

How Can You Enhance Your Memory?

Our most powerful attack against forgetting is cognitive processing. This simply means deep thinking. It is deep thinking that makes a long-lasting memory trace. According to Walter Pauk, there are three steps in cognitive processing or deep thinking:

1. Understand the fact thoroughly; be able to explain it in your own words.

2. Analyze the fact by viewing it from all sides.

3. Relate the fact to information you already have.

Using memory effectively is being able to recall information at the right time. Our memory system needs to be flexible.

The following ideas should help improve your memory:

1. *Organization*—The first step in organizing is to get a broad overview. Learn general concepts before you learn specifics. If you have a "feel" for the general idea, the details will have a place to fit.

   Research has shown that our short-term memory has a limited capacity. Seven unrelated items are about maximum for most people to remember. In various college classes, you will need to remember more than seven unrelated items. The way to handle this is through meaningful organization.

   Chunking or Clustering—This is a method whereby you categorize similar items you need to know. For example:

   As you walked to the grocery store, you realized you didn't have your list with you. You did remember there were twelve items. The items you had on your list were:

   onions, lettuce, ice cream, bananas, green beans, eggs, cheese, peas, apples, grapefruit, milk, and oranges.

   Look at these items for 15 seconds. Close the book and see how many you can recall. You are doing well if you remember 6 or 7.

   By clustering or chunking these items, we can make them manageable. We can have three major items instead of twelve.

Vegetables	Dairy	Fruits
onions	ice cream	bananas
lettuce	milk	apples
green beans	eggs	grapefruit
peas	cheese	oranges

   When we think of the major headings, the individual details fall in place. The thought of dairy products automatically reduces our thoughts to dairy products. This procedure will work well in your textbooks. Learn to associate details with the major headings.

   John Morris suggests a similar organizational technique. A good way to consolidate and summarize information you need to remember is to use the "poker-chip" strategy. In the game of poker, the blue chips are worth the most, followed by red chips and then the white chips. By analogy, the most important ideas in any message are the blue chips. Next to the blue chip ideas are the red chip, and subordinate to the red chip are the white chip ideas, which may be considered details.

   Around a poker table, you'll usually find a player has many more white chips than red or blue. Usually he will also have a few more red chips than blue. A writer has few blue chip ideas, a few more red chip, and many more white chip ideas. When you are summarizing, mark white chip ideas with a W, the red chip ideas with an R, and the blue chip ideas with a B. This technique makes main ideas easy to remember. The main ideas act as magnets holding together the subordinate ideas and the supporting details.

2. *Visualize Relationships and Associations*—Knowing individual facts does not help you understand a topic. Relating details provides a basis for the main idea. Also, it is important to relate new ideas to what you already know. Visualizing uses a different part of your brain than when you just read. This will also aid in reten-

tion. Often students will remember a picture, table, or graph that explains a theory easier than they will remember the words that described it. The better our background, the easier this will be.

3. *Make It Meaningful*—We remember things better when we can apply them to ourselves. If we can match the information we need to remember to a goal we have set, it will be easier to recall.

4. *Intend to Remember*—Your mental attitude plays an important role in your memory. Intending to learn can create a positive attitude that will include other important characteristics, such as active learning, paying attention, and writing to understand.

5. *Motivated Interest*—Research has shown that interest is important to learning, but remembering is almost impossible without interest. If you are not interested in a class you are taking, find some way to create an interest. We tend to forget information that contradicts our opinions. If you feel bored, consider the possibility that you are creating your boredom. Take responsibility for your attitudes.

6. *Recitation*—This technique is probably the most powerful one that will allow transfer from short-term to long-term memory. When you want to remember something, repeat it aloud. Recitation works best when you put concepts you want to remember into your own words.

   Arthur Gates did a series of recitation experiments in 1917. His experiments suggest that when you are reading a general text (psychology, sociology, history), 80% of your time should be spent in reciting and 20% in reading. It is also more effective to start recitation early in the reading process. Do not wait until you have read everything before you start to recite.

7. *Spaced Study*—Marathon study sessions are not effective. It is much better to have intermittent spaced review sessions. A practical application of this would be using the small blocks of time you are now wasting during the day. It is also important to take breaks while you are studying. After 45–50 minutes, reward yourself with a short break. When you come back, you will be more alert and more efficient. If significant learning is taking place and you are really engrossed, go for it! You don't have to stop, but memory is more productive when you space your studying instead of trying to accomplish everything in one long session.

8. *Brainstorming*—If you are having a problem recalling an answer on a test, try brainstorming. Think of everything you can that is related to what you are trying to remember. For example, if you are trying to remember your fifth grade teacher's name, think of other elementary teachers you had. By association the name you are trying to remember should pop up during this brainstorming.

9. *Reflecting*—It is important to give information time to go from short-term memory to long-term memory. This is considered consolidation time. Researchers vary on their opinions, but a safe rule is to leave information in your short-term memory 4–15 seconds. This gives information time to consolidate and transfer to your long-term memory. This is important to remember when you are reading quickly and not stopping to think what you have read. The information will be discarded quickly if you do not allow time for transfer. Stop and think about what you have just read, recite it, paraphrase it, and relate it to what you already know.

10. *Use All Your Senses*—The more senses you involve in studying, the better your memory process will work. Read and visualize, recite key concepts, devise questions, and write answers.

11. *Combine Memory Techniques*—You can combine organizing, reciting, and reflecting in one task. Different techniques can reinforce each other.

12. *Repetition*—Simply repeating things will aid memory. Advertisements hook us in this way. We learn a jingle by hearing it repeated again and again. For example:

   "You Deserve A Break Today" . . . McDonalds

   "It's The Real Thing" . . . Coke

   "Ring Around The Collar" . . . Wisk Detergent

   "You've Got The Right One, Baby" . . . Diet Pepsi

13. *Mnemonics*—Mnemonics are easily remembered words, rhymes, phrases, sentences, or games that help you remember difficult lists, principles, or facts.

   An example of a rhyming association could be:

   "In fourteen hundred and ninety-two Columbus sailed the ocean blue."

If you have a group to remember or a list of items, you can make-a-word mnemonic. An easy way to remember the Great Lakes is by the word HOMES—Huron, Ontario, Michigan, Erie, and Superior.

Similar to this is an acronym. An acronym is formed by the first letters of the words you want to remember. A good example of this would be the note taking system introduced in this text.

   TRQ: T ake notes
   R evise notes
   Q uestion main points

Another mnemonic device is to make a sentence you can remember. You make the sentence using words you devised from the first letter of the words you need to remember. For example:

You need to remember the factors that are involved in the quality of your sleep. These factors are the habit of your sleep, the environment where you sleep, the duration, your general health, and the use of drugs.

Your mnemonic sentence could be: "Hey everyone, don't have drugs."

You made these words using key words in the list you needed to remember:

   Hey—habit

   everyone—environment

   don't—duration

   have—health

   drugs—drugs

It is important to note that mnemonics do not help you understand the material. They assist in rote memorization.

■ General Study Skills

The next section is to make you think of different areas in general study skills. Answer the questions honestly and, after each major section, write a brief paragraph describing your habits in these areas and whether they are potential problems. Awareness of the problems in these different areas is the beginning of more efficient study.

■ Summary

The best way to improve your concentration is by identifying and eliminating internal and external distractors. You are in control of internal distractors. External distractors may be beyond your control, but you can learn to control your reactions to them. A proper place to study and how you study also affect concentration. Take frequent breaks and reward yourself!

Recall ability is controlled by your memory processes. Forgetting occurs very rapidly unless you take certain steps to prevent this. Realizing the importance of organization, visualization, intention to remember, interest, recitation, combining memory techniques, spaced study, brainstorming, reflecting, using your senses, and mnemonics will help you in strengthening your recall ability.

■ Concentration Worksheet

During your next study session, keep a record of internal and external distractors. On the chart below, write what the distractor was. After your study session determine whether the distractor was internal or external. Write in a brief solution.

Distraction	External/Internal	Solution
1.		
2.		
3.		
4.		
5.		
6.		
7.		
8.		
9.		
10.		

When considering the solutions—how many do you feel you can control? Write a brief paragraph explaining how you can possibly prevent these distractions.

_____

_____

_____

_____

_____

_____

_____

_____

_____

_____

_____

_____

_____

_____

_____

_____

_____

_____

_____

_____

_____

■ Memory Worksheet

List five things easy to remember.

1. _____

2. _____

3. _____

4. _____

5. _____

List five things difficult to remember.

1. _____

2. _____

3. _____

4. _____

5. _____

List three reasons why there is a difference between these two lists.

1. _____

_____

2. _____

_____

3. _____

_____

Name: _____ Date: _____

▮ Your Memory Habits

Answer *yes* or *no* to the following questions.

	YES	NO
1. Do you intend to remember your course work?	_____	_____
2. Do you try to get interested in your classes?	_____	_____
3. Do you honestly focus your full attention while studying?	_____	_____
4. Do you review lecture and textbook notes once a week or more?	_____	_____
5. Do you use organization in your study sessions?	_____	_____
6. Do you study in short spaced (45–50 minutes) sessions with breaks?	_____	_____
7. Do you keep an open mind when being introduced to new material?	_____	_____
8. Do you recite material you are trying to remember?	_____	_____
9. Do you make an effort to understand the material, not just read it?	_____	_____
10. Do you use several methods to reinforce memory, i.e., reciting, discussing with friends, and effective note taking?	_____	_____

If you answer *yes* to seven or more of these, you are on the right track! If you have three or more *no* answers, you need to evaluate your study habits.

Write a brief paragraph explaining what you intend to start doing to develop your memory.

_____ _____

_____

_____

_____

_____

_____

_____

_____

Name: _____ Date: _____

◼ Work and Study Habits

	YES	NO
1. Do I study alone?	_____	_____
2. Do I listen to the radio or TV while I study?	_____	_____
3. Do I plan my study time so that I can finish what I start?	_____	_____
4. Do I prepare for exams?	_____	_____
5. Am I flustered by exams?	_____	_____
6. Are my study periods interrupted by family or friends?	_____	_____
7. Does illness interfere with my studying?	_____	_____
8. Do I smoke while I study?	_____	_____
9. Is my work of an inferior quality?	_____	_____
10. Do I feel that I am accomplishing anything when I study?	_____	_____

Evaluate your work and study habits:

_____

_____

_____

_____

_____

_____

_____

_____

_____

Note Taking Habits

	YES	NO
1. Do I try to write down everything the instructor says in class?		
2. Do I take more notes only on those things which interest me?	——	——
3. Are my notes meaningless after I leave the class?	——	——
4. Do I put my notes in good order soon after writing them in class?	——	——
5. Do I feel too much pressure in class to take notes effectively?	——	——
6. Do I have difficulty taking notes and keeping up with the lecture?	——	——
7. Has note taking been very helpful in the past?	——	——
8. Am I able to pick out the important points in lectures?	——	——
9. Is my background so weak I cannot make sense from the lecture to write effective notes?	——	——
10. Do my feelings about some of the instructors make it difficult to take notes?	——	——
	——	——

My Problems:

_____

_____

_____

_____

_____

_____

_____

_____

_____

Name: _____   Date: _____

▉ Reading and Thinking Habits

	YES	NO
1. Do I like to read fiction?	_____	_____
2. Do I read books not related to classwork?	_____	_____
3. Do I formulate questions during reading?	_____	_____
4. Do I read newspapers and magazines?	_____	_____
5. Do I read too slowly?	_____	_____
6. Does my mind wander when I read?	_____	_____
7. Do I daydream in class?	_____	_____
8. When I read something long, do I finish?	_____	_____
9. Is my best reading done at a certain time of day or night?	_____	_____
10. Do I read word-for-word?	_____	_____
11. Do I preview the material before reading?	_____	_____
12. Does the mood I'm in play an important role in my reading?	_____	_____
13. Does my weak vocabulary cause me to read slowly?	_____	_____
14. Do I read for leisure?	_____	_____

Evaluate your reading and thinking skills:

_____

_____

_____

_____

_____

_____

_____

■ Leisure-Time Habits

	YES	NO
1. Do I participate in physical activities (in school or out)?	_____	_____
2. Do I like to work with a hobby?	_____	_____
3. Do I loaf with my friends when I should be studying?	_____	_____
4. Do I "try to get away" occasionally in order to think?	_____	_____
5. Am I bored when I am at home?	_____	_____
6. Am I fatigued long before bedtime?	_____	_____
7. Do I work for pay when I am not in school?	_____	_____
8. Do my family obligations take the place of studying?	_____	_____
9. Am I unable to schedule time for family and friends?	_____	_____
10. When I do get leisure time, I am not able to enjoy it because of stress of guilt feelings about not spending enough time with my family.	_____	_____

My Problems:

_____

_____

_____

_____

_____

_____

_____

_____

Taking Notes of Lectures

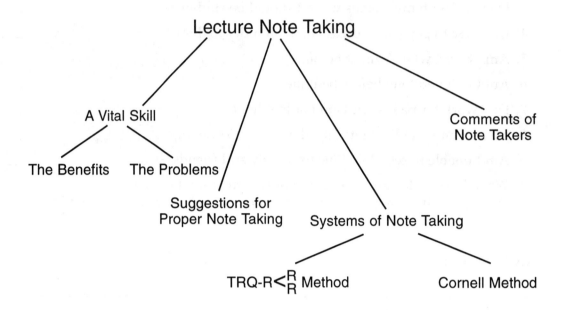

In the previous chapter, we discussed the important skill of listening. You spend about half of your college time doing this vital task, and yet it has been called the most used and least taught of communication skills. It has even been noted that, in respect to amount of words, we listen a book a day, speak a book a week, read a book a month, and write a book a year. Yet have you ever heard of a class called Listening 101? Somehow it is assumed that we need classes to improve our speaking, reading, and writing skills, but we all know how to listen and do not need improvement in this area.

We hope you realize by now that the skill of listening can be improved, but only by practice and hard work! You can't really listen half way—it's either on or off. Unless you mentally rehearse material you are trying to listen to, you can't retain the information in short-term memory for more than twenty seconds! Yet listening comprehension affects your college grades more than reading comprehension does! Evidentally, something must be done to give us a back-up system, since we cannot count on our memories.

Some of you may not be convinced of this fact. You may feel that if you really set your mind to it, you WILL remember that lecture. An interesting study was done several years ago to see how well we really can remember when we are interested and pay attention. The members of the Cambridge Psychological Society (obviously, intelligent people!) had

From *Practical Approaches for Building Study Skills and Vocabulary*, Second Edition by Funk et al. © 1996 by Kendall/Hunt Publishing Company.

an enjoyable discussion one day that was secretly taped by the experimenters, and two weeks later they were asked to write down all the specific points of the discussion they could remember. These learned members—who spend their lives learning and remembering—could only remember 8% of the major points, and what is even more startling was that 42% of those points were wrong![1] Do you really think you could do much better? The simple truth is this: if you want to remember, you must write it down so that you can review it. In short, you've got to take notes!

■ Why is Note Taking So Vital in College?

It's really not vital to take notes, unless you want to remember what you are learning! It has been said that "we learn to listen in order to listen to learn." It is a proven fact that the normal student will forget 50% of what they have just heard within twenty minutes after a lecture. Unless you are terribly abnormal (and we doubt that!), you do not stand a chance of doing well on a test three weeks after a lecture unless you have some way to review that lecture—and there is no way to do that without notes. Material taken from lectures is usually a major portion of the material you will be tested over, and without notes you are almost guaranteed to go into the test situation only remembering a very small percentage of the material! You can always go back and review your textbook material, but your lecture notes are your ONLY lecture reference. They are vital to your college success! Add to these facts the sad but true thought that you will forget MORE and FASTER in lectures than in text reading or in writing, and you should begin to see the importance of note taking.

Another value of note taking is that it keeps you alert and listening during lectures. Note taking almost forces you to listen so that you can get the ideas to write down. Plus, the physical act of writing activates another one of your senses, thus helping you to retain a greater amount of what you are hearing. You will also tend to focus more on main ideas and begin to realize the relationship of sub-points to those main ideas as you try to take good notes. Even as you evaluate what is important to write, you are increasing your learning potential! Do we have you convinced yet? Well, let us give you one more huge benefit of lecture note taking. A proper note taking system will set up a way to review and make that review manageable, and that is at least half the test-battle won!

Don't plan on getting someone else's notes instead of taking your own. We can see those mind-wheels turning and planning to ask a very good note taker to let you borrow his notes. You are thinking, "A lot less trouble for me, and just as efficient in the long run!" Sorry, but that's not the way it works. As we have already mentioned, the act of writing and evaluating is important for the individual note taker, plus it is really difficult to make sense of most people's notes. They have a different style and use different symbols or abbreviations, and therefore, for the most part, someone else's notes—no matter how good they are for THEM—are not as effective for you. You must share the responsibility for communication, or it will not be as beneficial or effective for you. Sharing the responsibility for communication during lectures means taking a good set of your *own* notes.

If you leave a lecture totally unchanged, you have wasted your time and money. In order to get the most value out of any lecture, consider these three questions:

  a. How important is the lecture *to you?* Does it directly influence your major, your career, or even your life in general? The more pertinent you can make the lecture to you, the more apt you are to listen attentively and retain the information.

---

[1] Hunter, Ian M.L. "Memory Facts and Falacies," (Baltimore, Penguin, 1957) p. 83

b. How important is the lecture *to the lecturer?* Whether you think it's important to you or not, if it appears to be important to your professor you are apt to see that information again—probably on a test! How do you know if it is important to your professor? These are a few signs which may clue you in: time spent on topic, repetition of topic, change in tone, pause in speech, change in posture (as in moving closer to the audience), writing on the board, or signal words, such as "Remember this," or "This is important to note." Mark these clues in your notes and make sure you MAKE these points important to you!

c. Does the lecture *duplicate* the textbook or *go beyond* it? If it's a duplication, a little of the pressure is off you because you have a second source with which to check information. But if the lecture goes beyond the textbook, it is doubly important that you conquer that information.

■ What Are Some Common Mistakes in Note Taking?

It has been said that most of us do one of two things when it comes to taking notes: we suddenly become a stenographer who feels that we must get everything down word-for-word, or we do the other thing—absolutely nothing! Both of these practices are incorrect and will lead to problems in learning. Another common problem involves worrying too much about grammar or spelling, and thus not getting enough information down on paper. A possible solution to this problem is to spell phonetically (or the way the word sounds) and correct it later that day. If you have no idea how to spell the word, leave a blank and write the first consonant. Then rely on the rest of the phrase or sentence to clue you in later that day as you look the word up and find out how to spell it. We have also seen problems with students who take notes, but do not take **enough** notes. They wait for the professor to write on the board before they write any information down, or they keep waiting to write the BIG idea only. Try to get as much information down as possible while still keeping up with the lecturer. You can always delete, but it is much more difficult to add on later.

Two final note taking mistakes are the failure to review notes and relying on tape-recorders. It defeats the purpose of note taking if you do not review the notes. Although it is beneficial just to write the information down, don't leave out the review step! As to whether to tape record lectures, our advice is that it is usually not a good idea. For one thing, if you rely on a machine you will probably not listen as actively. Secondly, if you find it difficult to listen to a live lecturer, how are you going to make yourself listen to an inanimate object? That is even more boring than the most boring of lectures! Finally, when will you find the time to listen to (and hopefully take notes from) the tape? You may soon find that you have a whole set of tapes to listen to and that is just one more thing to get you behind! If the lecturer speaks very quickly, you write very slowly, or the lecturer is difficult to understand due to an accent or other condition, it might be beneficial to tape record, as long as you follow these guidelines:

1. Take notes as if you did not have the tape recorder so you will promote active listening on your part.

2. Revise your notes with the tape THAT SAME DAY.

3. Only use 1 tape per subject so that you will be forced to stay caught up with your notes.

Take a minute to NOTE YOUR NOTE TAKING SKILLS by completing the checklist. How do you measure up in this important skill? Your college grades—and more importantly, how much you learn from your college years—may depend on it!

■ What's the Best Way to Take Lecture Notes?

The first item that is needed in order to take good notes is a well-organized notebook. It is best to have a separate notebook for each subject, preferably one with pockets or a three-ring binder so that you can add handouts to the proper place in your notes. At the very minimum, you need a separate section in the notebook for each subject. It has been stated that you can tell how a woman keeps house by the way that she keeps her purse organized. We're not sure how accurate that is, but it is fairly safe to say that a well-organized notebook helps to promote well-organized thinking, and should also promote the possibility for a higher GPA! If your notebook is similar to the organization of a flea market, perhaps there is a reason for that confusion in your brain!

Now that you are armed with the proper notebook, consider the following suggestions as you begin to take notes and fill up that notebook:

1. ASSUME A POSITION OF ALERTNESS. This statement involves two suggestions: watch WHERE you sit, and watch HOW you sit. If you want to give yourself every advantage, SIT FRONT AND CENTER. Students who sit closer to the lecturer get higher grades—it's just that simple. No one seems to know for sure why this is true. Could it be because there are less distractions, or could it be that better students naturally navigate closer to the front? For whatever reason, it will be to your advantage to DO IT! Besides watching where you sit, make sure you also watch your posture. For the most part, an alert body helps to promote an alert mind, and outward manifestations of interest may even create genuine internal interest, so watch how you sit. Slump in your seat, and your mind may slump with you! As you sit alertly, INTEND TO REMEMBER what you will be hearing. Pretend you are going to have a pop quiz after the lecture. It **will** make a difference in how carefully you listen!

2. BE PREPARED! Have all your SUPPLIES together. You will need your trusty notebook, of course, and a pen with which to take notes. But you also need to prepare by making sure you have kept up with your TEXTBOOK READING, and also by REVIEWING YOUR PAST LECTURE NOTES before class. These two suggestions will make a large difference on how easily you can follow the lecturer. Keep your class SYLLABUS handy and refer to it often. It is a contract between the professor and yourself, and you are both obligated by what it says. Make sure *you* know what it says! Part of class preparation starts before the beginning of the semester by trying to SCHEDULE your classes in an organized fashion. Consider your own biological clock as you decide when the best time would be to take each class. If it is at 12:00 P.M., you may have difficulty concentrating due to hunger. So, as much as you can, prepare adequately before you start the class by considering all possibilities. Finally, prepare by ASSUMING YOUR RESPONSIBILITY. You will decide how much you get out of the lecture largely by this one act. If you are a responsible, self-motivated student, you will FIND reasons to listen and take notes. If you do not assume this responsibility, you will be a more passive listener who expects the instructor to GIVE you reasons to listen by motivating you and capturing your interest. Don't count on this happening. It's nice when it does, but the responsibility has to be yours—as is the education you gain or lose.

3. ATTEND CLASS AND BE PUNCTUAL. You can skip class physically (as many do), or you can realize from the very start how much you are paying for each class period, and that it's your loss if you skip. Unfortunately, the habit of skipping is an easy one to get into and a hard one to stop. Don't start it. Be there, and be there on time! You need to also be aware of the fact that you can skip mentally even if you do not skip physically. If you do not listen actively or if you do not take notes, you might as well have skipped the class.

4. KEEP YOUR EYES ON THE INSTRUCTOR. It does take PRACTICE to listen, watch, and write, but your skill will improve with practice. It is important to WATCH THE PROFESSOR FOR THOSE VISUAL CLUES mentioned earlier, and to NOTE THOSE as you take notes. Mark things with which you tend to disagree. For some reason we tend to remember best the things we agree with and ignore the rest. Try to listen with your mind, not your feelings. Is the lecture boring? You have some control over that, believe it or not, by your attitude and by your facial expressions. You can ENCOURAGE THE LECTURER by nodding your head, smiling, and looking alive and interested, and the lecture may improve. If you want it to get even more boring, try looking bored or even putting your head down on your desk. You can spice up the lecture by making your face look interested! Try it! VISUALIZE AND CATEGORIZE as you listen. See it as well as hear it and write it, and you will be planting it more firmly in your mind. Since the mind can only retain about seven "chunks" of information at a time, try to think in main ideas. These main topics will be easier to organize in your notes AND in your mind. Lastly, NEVER HESITATE TO ASK a professor to explain a point if you've read your assignment and been listening to the lectures. You're probably not the only one who has that question!

5. TAKE NOTES AGGRESSIVELY! Do not wait for something important to be said. It will be too late to get it down if you put your pen down and wait. You never know the importance of the statement until it is past, so keep your pen in hand, and use it! Perhaps the most crucial component of this suggestion is your attitude. The proper attitude has been called the most important requirement for good note taking. Realize that the lecture is supposed to save you time and effort, and that the teacher is a partner in your future success for your chosen career. This will make it a little easier to share the responsibility of the communication and cooperate in active listening. Take advantage of your professor's knowledge and time. It will add to yours—and we're speaking both of knowledge and time! Don't just write down what you think will be on the test. You are trying to learn all you can learn, remember?

6. WRITE IN TELEGRAPHIC STYLE. Even though it is important to get down all the information you can in the time you have, it is beneficial to leave out words that are not crucial to the meaning of the message—like you would if you were paying for each word in a telegram. Invent your own symbols and abbreviations to make your notes more meaningful. For example, put a star by material that the lecturer mentioned might be test material, or put a box around material that was written on the board. Abbreviate words such as without (w/o), because (b/c), or a name that is used repeatedly can just be the first initial with a blank after you have used it several times. Make sure you USE YOUR OWN WORDS. If you try to copy the professor's words down word-for-word, you may bypass your brain! Rephrase the main idea into your own words, and you will increase your learning power. All of the above take practice, but you will improve with each good set of notes that you take.

7. NEATNESS COUNTS! Don't waste valuable study time trying to decipher notes that can only be read by a mind-reader. BLOCK PRINTING is often more easily read than cursive, and can also be much faster to write, so consider printing your notes in manuscript. Be sure to LEAVE PLENTY OF WHITE SPACE. Use blanks for words or ideas missed and fill them in after class by asking your professor or a friend for clarification, or by looking it up in your text. Review your notes as soon as possible after class so you can do some fix-ups. Add to or correct whatever is needed. "White space" aids in this revision process. KEEP YOUR NOTES DATED AND NUMBERED to avoid confusion at a later time and to be able to tell where test coverage will start. Remember, if the problem of spelling slows you

down, use the first letter plus a blank space, or use phonetic spelling. Also, USE INK as you take your notes. It is less likely to smudge or fade, and you will not have as much difficulty reviewing your notes several weeks later—or even years later, as the case may be!

8. DON'T DOODLE! If you do doodle—or write letters, or sleep, or knit, or whatever—you are making a judgment call that what you are doing is more important than the lecture, and you may be right! But remember, you must also be willing to accept the consequences of your actions, and usually that's a high price to pay. If you get bored, try reviewing your notes, questioning them, or predicting what's going to be said next. All of these strategies are important comprehension tools, and may help to revive your interest. Even if that doesn't happen, you are not wasting your time as you are with the doodling syndrome!

9. GO FOR MAIN IDEAS, NOT DETAILS. Note taking is a process of selection, condensation, and compression, and this very process is a wonderful learning experience. If you do it correctly, the act of note taking is a valuable study tool. Try to think in terms of headings and sub-headings, and USE SOME TYPE OF AN OUTLINE SYSTEM to show the overall organization of the lecture. Headings or labels are extremely important! If you are not sure what the topic is, leave a blank, get down the information, and come back to create a heading later. You need to see some visual organization in order to think in an organized fashion. The outline form itself is not important—that there is some organization for main points and sub-points is vital!

10. ALWAYS COPY EXAMPLES AND BOARD WORK. These will tend to be the items that make the most sense to you and will be more easily remembered. They may help to clarify the rest of the material.

11. LISTEN CAREFULLY TO THE VERY END of the lecture! Professors typically get behind in a lecture, and they may be cramming in two last pages of notes while you are busy gathering up all your junk! Or they may be reviewing some important test questions right at the last minute, so you must listen until the "bitter end." Some of the most important information may be squeezed into the last few seconds. Take a few minutes to get the full benefits, or you may live to regret it!

■ Is There a System to Make Note Taking Easier?

There are many good systems to help you organize your notes, and we will present two excellent ones here.

The TRQ-R$<^R_R$ System

This system was created by Dr. Charles Tegeler of Southwest Missouri State University, and is an acronym standing for Take notes, Revise, Question, and Review. It is probably not that much different from the system you are using now, but it could make an enormous difference in your grades. Why? Because of the difference in the two words RECALL and RECOGNITION. Most of us have learned to study lecture notes by simply reading over them several times (if we're lucky), and hoping that we will recognize the correct answer on the test. We never reach the point where we can pull up (recall) the information without the clues. TRQ-R$<^R_R$ builds in a set of questions so you are forced to recall, not just recognize, and that difference will change those C's and B's to A's!

Reprinted with permission of Dr. Charles Tegeler, SMSU Reading and Special Education, Springfield, MO.

So here is what you should do:

Step 1: *Take Notes*

After you have dated your notes and made a title for what the lecture is about, write down the information as clearly and quickly as you can. But one very important aspect of this system is that you only write on the right page of your notebook—leave the left page blank for Steps 2 and 3. Make sure you keep up with the professor. Don't get behind. Go on when he/she goes on, and fill in missed information after class. Try to keep eye contact with the lecturer, and get as much down in your own words as possible. As soon as the class is over, take a minute or two to summarize what the lecture was about at the bottom of the last LEFT page. This summarizing will aid in your comprehension and retention.

Step 2: *Revise Notes*

Some time after the lecture—and it must be the day of the lecture or this step will not work properly—take a few minutes to fix your notes. Although many students try to recopy or type their notes, we feel that this is not an efficient use of your time or an effective way to study. You could better be using this time by studying your notes, and recopying or typing does not necessarily mean you are learning the information. Instead of recopying, use the left page you have left blank to REVISE your notes. If some sections of your notes are fine and need no revision, then make a checkmark on the left page directly across from the notes and leave them alone. The checkmark will remind you that those original notes needed no revision. But for that section for which you now remember more information or need to clarify a point, add that information directly across from the old information. This section can also be used to REDUCE or condense information, or make up mnemonic memory strategies to aid with retention. When you study, you can then study back and forth as you follow your numbering or outline system.

Step 3: *Question main ideas*

Now, in the margin of your left pages, come up with a good summarizing question for EACH main idea and sub-point of your notes. If you have used an outline form, this step will not be difficult. Good questions usually involve words such as describe, explain, how, or the 5 W's—who, what, when, where, why. Write the question directly across from the information that answers it, and as you study you can flip the right page over to cover the notes and revisions and see only the questions to make sure you are studying for recall, not recognition. If you do not know the answer, all you have to do is look directly across from your question to review the information in your notes. Make sure your question is a "reciting question," such as "What are the seven suggestions to improve listening skills?" or "Discuss the six major causes of the Civil War." It is helpful to clue yourself into how many answers you are trying to remember—if you remember six, was that good or were there twelve more you should have known? This question step is the most vital part of the system and is why this system will almost guarantee raising your grades, if you use it properly. The only way you will know if it works is to try it!

Step 4: *Review your notes* < Review what you know / Relearn what you have forgotten

Your first review should happen as soon as you revise and question your notes—on the same day as the lecture. But since you have set up your notes for review, this is not a difficult process. Simply read your questions aloud (to involve more of your senses), and try to recall and recite the information. This review step consists of two parts—REVIEWING WHAT YOU REMEMBER, and RELEARNING WHAT YOU HAVE FORGOTTEN. The first time you review your notes, unfortunately most of the review is in the second category—the relearning portion. But each time you review, and we would suggest you review each set of lecture notes once a week, more of the material should fall in the RE-MEMBERED category. You're not ready for a test until it is ALL in that category! Although it seems it would be impossible to review each set of notes weekly, each time you review you will remember more information for a longer period of time, so very soon you will be able to breeze through this set of notes. What a difference you will feel the night before the test if you have practiced weekly review!

The Cornell System of Note Taking

This system, devised by Dr. Walter Pauk of Cornell University, is another excellent way to organize your notes. You will need to make two-column note sheets for this system by drawing a vertical line 2½ inches from the left edge of your paper. End this line two inches above the bottom of the paper and draw a horizontal line across the paper there. In the narrow left column you will write questions about the notes which have been written in the wide column on the right. In the bottom two inch space you will summarize your notes. Now that your paper is set up, these are the steps you should follow in more detail:

1. Record

In the wide column, get down as many of the facts of the lecture as you can. Remember to use the suggestions that were given earlier in the chapter, such as printing if it is more legible for you, using pen, and using telegraphic sentences. As soon as possible after class, "fix" any major errors in your notes, or add clarifications.

2. Question

You now need to take a few minutes to reread your notes and make up questions based on the main ideas. Put these questions across from the main ideas in the narrow column on the left. Make sure they are broad, "reciting" questions.

3. Recite

To recite means that you say the information in your own words AND aloud, without looking at your notes. It is such a valuable learning strategy! Not only are you using several of your senses, but you are working for recall again—not recognition. Studies have shown that students who recite remember 80% of the material. Those who only reread remember only 20% when tested two weeks later. You choose which will be the case for you. If you choose to remember 80% (or hopefully even more), cover up your notes, read the question, and recite your answer. Then take a minute to check your notes again, and recite any information that was left out or incorrect. Continue in this manner through the rest of your notes.

4. Reflect

With "real" learning, you want to be able to do more than give back information verbatim, so this reflection stage is crucial. You now need to try to apply what you have learned to your own life. Make it pertinent and significant to you. Ask yourself how this new information "fits in" with what you already know. This added step will make you more enthusiastic and curious

Critical Thinking

Two skills that are crucial to good note taking are summarizing—being aware of the main ideas, and paraphrasing—being able to state those ideas in your own words. Take a minute to look back over a set of past lecture notes. Try your skill at summarizing each page, and then go one step further and summarize the whole lecture at the end of the last page. Look back over the lecture notes. Did you record the information in your own words, or in the words of your professor? Paraphrasing the information will require understanding of it, and summarizing will then be an easy step with which to follow-up.

about what you learn, and will mean that you will retain the knowledge longer than you possibly could if you omit this important reflection step.

5. Review

Of course, no system could work without the necessary step of reviewing. We suggest you review your lecture notes before class, and also plan a time during the week to review all past lecture notes for each subject. Thanks to the organization of the system, the review step is set up for you. Now you just need to read the questions—aloud, recite the information, double-check the answer, and continue through your questions. Each review will prove you are remembering more information for a longer period of time.

6. Recapitulate

This term simply means that you summarize each page of notes at the end of the lecture. This summarizing step requires a higher level of thinking, and will help you to gain a deeper understanding of the material. Dr. Pauk also suggests that you go one step further for optimum learning and summarize the entire lecture on the last note page for that lecture. To be able to summarize will mean that you really got the "meat" of the lecture. It is also a fast and easy way to review just before a test is handed to you.

■ Does a Note Taking System Really Make a Difference?

We feel that you will be pleasantly surprised at what a difference a system WILL make! But don't take our word for it. Prove it to yourself! You may choose to adapt one of the systems in a few ways that would better suit it to your own needs. But in the meantime, read these comments of students who—just like yourself—had to try it before they would believe it.

- I've only had one test using TRQ-R and got a B+ up to an A. It worked well!
- With TRQ-R I got a 10% raise (in my grade).
- TRQ-R helped me raise my grades. I went from a D in Econ to an A!
- In religion—F on first test
    —C on second
    —B on third
- In Communications I went from a D to a C. My overall grades have gone from D's and F's to B's and C's. My study skills have improved tremendously using time and study habits with TRQ-R.
- My fourth Soc test was returned to me during class today. Unlike my first three test scores which averaged 79%, the grade I received on this test was 91%.
- I've not been able to tell a difference in my tests because I made high percentages before, but I have noticed an advantage in a reduction of needed study time.
- Using TRQ-R raised my test grades. On the first test, I made a high F (58%); on the second test I made a 74%.
- My letter grades in my classes have gone from C− to B+.

And finally, just one more comment:

- I didn't use (TRQ-R) but I wish I had—I definitely will next semester!

So, try a system to organize and revitalize your notes. You'll be glad you did! All you have to lose is lower grades and frustration. But think what you have to gain!

■ It's Worth It!

Since most of our learning will take place by the work of our ears and mind combined, the adding of our hands with the skill of note taking will help to ensure that the knowledge stands a better chance of sticking in our brain. Yes, it does take more time and effort to write it down, but the improved results show that it's worth that time and effort! Have you ever stopped to consider how much you are paying for each lecture? You have to take into consideration not only what you are spending for classes, books, gas, and rent, but also what you could be making if you were working full time instead of investing in college. If you find out—as most of our students did—that you are spending at least FIFTY DOLLARS per lecture, you may decide that note taking is the least you can do to get the most for your money. Spend your time, your energy, your study efforts, AND your money in the best way possible. Find an effective system of note taking that works for you, and use it!

■ Summary

This chapter has stressed the necessity of taking lecture notes. Too much will be forgotten, or not even heard correctly in the first place, if a student does not write it down. The benefits are numerous and worthwhile. They include keeping you alert during lectures and involving added senses to your sense of hearing. Often students get bogged down in note taking because they focus on the wrong things—like details, grammar, spelling, or the exact words. The best way to take notes includes using your own words, getting as much of the information on paper as possible, using ink, headings, and an outline form, and also using a note taking system. This chapter has presented the reader with two excellent ones—the TRQ-R System and the Cornell System. Either of these systems will help to organize your notes and set them up for efficient review—and that is what mastering lectures is all about!

◼ Note Your Note Taking Skills!

Put a check by each necessary skill of note taking that you currently practice. How do you rate?

Before the Lecture, I

1. Read all textbook assignments.

2. Review yesterday's lecture notes.

3. Make sure I have all necessary supplies, including:
   a. an ink pen.
   b. my notebook for that class.
   c. the syllabus for that class.
   d. any special notebook set-up markings for my note taking system.
   e. any other special supplies needed for that particular class.

4. Arrive on time and attend each class, except in emergency situations.

During the Lecture, I

5. Label my notes with the date.

6. Use some type of outline form to see the visual organization of main and sub-points.

7. Make sure I have a heading for each topic as well as a heading for the entire lecture.

8. Try hard to get interested in the subject and stay mentally alert.

9. Ignore distractions.

10. Listen for clues that indicate important points and mark these in my notes.

11. Write legibly.

12. Get down as much information as possible, using my own words.

13. Use my own style of abbreviations and telegraphic writing.

14. Copy all information written on the board.

15. Ask questions if I do not understand.

After the Lecture, I

16. Take a minute to write down a summary of the lecture.

17. Revise my notes that same day, adding, deleting, or clarifying information.

18. Review my notes by:
    a. making up questions over the notes.
    b. reciting the answers aloud.

19. Continue to review my notes weekly.

Listening and Note Taking

Name: _____ Date: _____

■ Exercise 1. Listening and Note Taking Awareness Check

DIRECTIONS: Please put an "X" in the appropriate box.

	Yes	No
1. The keys to learning from lectures include active listening and good note taking.	☐	☐
2. When I hear material, I am listening.	☐	☐
3. I am addicted to the fatal belief that I can listen to two things at once.	☐	☐
4. My notes are easy to read and understand.	☐	☐
5. I copy information the instructor writes on the board.	☐	☐
6. I try to write statements summarizing what the instructor is saying.	☐	☐
7. I revise and review my notes within 24 hours.	☐	☐
8. If I do not understand my notes or they seem incomplete, I ask another student for help or see my instructor.	☐	☐
9. I use abbreviations to accelerate my note taking.	☐	☐
10. I always believe I can gain new knowledge from a lecture.	☐	☐
11. I am able to follow the instructor's line of reasoning in presenting ideas.	☐	☐
12. I can narrow my focus when I listen to a lecture, so that other student activities, both in and out of the classroom, do not serve as distractions.	☐	☐
13. I consider students' comments and questions to be an important part of the lecture, and I listen to them, preparing an answer to their questions.	☐	☐
14. Even when I don't agree with the instructor, or I don't understand some part of the lecture, I remain an active listener.	☐	☐
15. I make up test questions from my notes.	☐	☐
16. An important function of notes is their availability for use for later review or study.	☐	☐
17. Organization is important in note taking.	☐	☐

Positive answers to the questions in the Awareness Check (except items 2 and 3) suggest that your note taking skills resemble those of other successful students. Few people, however, are this efficient with their note taking skills.

As you read this chapter, begin to incorporate some of the listening and note taking techniques that are new to you in your classes and when you do your assignments.

■ Introduction

Learning to listen and take useful notes requires practice. As these skills are developed for use in the academic setting, notes become valuable in helping the student to understand the nature and purpose of academic lectures and other resources. Notes are used to help the student establish an active learning attitude. They direct the student's attention to getting meaning out of lecture material, accompany the studying process, and provide a record of material for further study and review. As the student listens, abstracts, organizes and condenses material, he/she is working to integrate and assimilate new information.

■ Listening

Active listening is effective listening

In the academic environment, you are continually exposed to lectures. If you wish to learn the information that is being taught, you must know how to listen. Listening is a very neglected communication skill. It is an active process in which you transform the material that you hear into meaning for you. Allowing words to pour into your ear is not listening. You must organize material, relate it to your experiences, and make it part of yourself.

You can learn to listen more effectively.

Research indicates that the following statements are true (Carmen and Adams, 1972).

1. **We listen in spurts.** Your attention wanders so that you listen intently for 30 seconds or so, tune out for a short time, and then return. You are usually not aware this is happening.

2. **We hear what we expect to hear.** Your prejudices, past experiences, expectations, and beliefs determine what you hear. You tune out what you do not want to hear.

3. **We do not listen well when we are doing other things.**

4. **We listen better when we are actively involved in the process.** When we listen to satisfy a purpose, we hear more and better.

Identify purpose of listening

You may first need to identify the instructor's purpose in lecturing. Is it to show you how the course material relates to your own life, to help you solve a particular problem, to discuss and raise questions, to demonstrate certain trends, to encourage you to think critically and analytically? The instructor often states the purpose of the lecture on the syllabus as well as at the beginning of the lecture.

When you go job hunting, you need to hear what the employer is going to require of an employee. Employment expectations and knowledge generated while listening and communicating in an interview is very valuable. Hours to be worked need to be understood, responsibilities must be clarified and clearly defined, and work hours, environment, benefits and advancement opportunities all need to be discussed.

Active listening is a critical skill involving much more than just passively hearing the words someone else has spoken.

Restate

There are several active listening techniques. One is to restate or paraphrase in your own words what you have just understood the other person to say. In the classroom, this tech-

Paraphrase

nique is used to check your understanding of what is being said by the instructor or other class members. In the employment situation, restating is a powerful skill to ensure accuracy and precision. Paraphrasing also helps to demonstrate your interest in what the instructor is saying, and encourages the speaker to explain more fully.

Watch for non-verbal clues

The second active listening technique is to respond to non-verbal clues. Observe and understand the impact of words, watch for non-verbal clues when messages are delivered and received. Responding to non-verbal clues helps to get more information.

Summarize key points

A third active listening technique is to summarize the key points that have been made during the course of the lecture. Summarizing includes all key points that have been made and helps to keep you aware of what is important as well as to illustrate what has already been covered.

Ask questions

A fourth active listening technique is to ask questions that will help generate responses you can listen to. Use open-ended questions which will help when you need further information or explanation. Open questions begin with "what, how, who, when, and where."

Listen carefully for key points. Like important announcements, these are often given in the first few minutes and the last few minutes of class and meetings.

■ Note Taking

Any effective study system must include skills for note taking. An organized, planned approach to the lecture helps to increase on-the-spot learning, maintain a longer attention span during the lecture, boost retention of the material, and have valuable notes for later study as students review and at exam time.

Note taking is a very real, immediate and practical college success skill. As a beginning college student, you will discover that there is an enormous amount of exposure to the lecture method of instruction.

Look, listen, and write

Taking notes helps the student remember what the instructor said during the lecture, and utilizes many of the sensory skills. You use your auditory skills as your ears take in information through careful listening; your visual skills as your hands and brain transform the words and ideas into a visual form that can be read, reread and reviewed. You might be aided by diagramming the information presented, highlighting, starring, and/or drawing circles around important/key points. Writing information down forces students to encode it, creating a deeper impression on their brains.

Concentrate

Another important reason for note taking during lectures is to help you concentrate in the classroom, to focus and to be an active listener.

Prepare

Good note taking skills are essential in helping you to prepare for tests. Frequently, "studying for a test" consists of reviewing and memorizing information from lecture notes. It

Readable, accurate, well-organized

becomes even more important that these notes be complete, readable, accurate, and well-organized. In addition, notes are often a source of valuable clues to what information the instructor thinks is most important, and therefore what may be included on exams.

Notes often consist of information that is not found elsewhere.

> **T**he student needs to prepare for each class session. Stay up-to-date with the readings. Review your notes from the last time. What questions were left unanswered from the last lecture?

Instructors frequently use lecture time to explain concepts introduced in the text, and to add professional examples the student can use in understanding this information.

Your ability to listen and take notes is closely linked to how well you will do in class.

Taking the Right Kind of Notes: Developing Your Listening and Note Taking Skills

Over the years, a special system of note taking, known as the Cornell system, has been developed (Pauk, 1984). It can be applied to almost all lecture situations. Its goal is simple efficiency. Every step is designed to save time and effort. There is no rewriting in this system. Each step prepares the way for taking the next natural and logical step in the learning process.

Phase I: Before the Lecture (adapted from Long, 1992)

1. Take a few minutes to review your notes on the previous lecture, to provide continuity with the lecture you are about to hear.

2. Divide paper in half, preparing to take notes on one side.

Phase II: During the Lecture

1. Record your notes on one side of the paper, completely and clearly enough so they will still have meaning for you long after you have taken them. Strive to capture the main points of the lecture, the general ideas rather than illustrative details. Do not be concerned with developing an elaborate formal outline using Roman numerals, capital letters, numbers, etc. Subtopics under main points can be indicated with numbers or simply with a dash placed in front of each subtopic.

2. Write so that you will be able to read the material. This may mean practicing a form of printing or developing a system of abbreviations. Be careful to use only those abbreviations you are familiar with.

Phase III: After the Lecture

1. Consolidate your notes as soon as possible after the lecture by reading through them to clarify handwriting and meaning. Underline or box in the words containing the main ideas. Restructure the notes by reading them and then jotting down key words and key phrases from the lecture on the left side of the paper. This procedure helps you to recall the lecture. The process of writing summarizing words and phrases helps to fix the information in your mind.

2. Cover your notebook page so that you are looking only at the key words and phrases. Use the jottings as cues to help you recall and recite aloud the facts and ideas of the lecture as fully as you can in your own words.

   Uncover the notes, then verify the accuracy of your work. This is known as using your skills of recall. Recall is a skill you will need to demonstrate on your examinations.

3. Review your notes. Work on recalling the contents of the lecture. Meeting with other students in the course is another profitable way to review your notes. Not only

Reduce ideas to concise summaries as cues for *Reciting, Reviewing, and Reflecting.*　　*Record* the lecture as fully and meaningfully as possible.

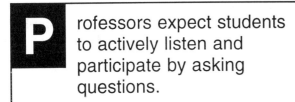

Professors expect students to actively listen and participate by asking questions.

can you review the main points of the lecture with each other, you may also discover that other students have heard points that you haven't. Perhaps they saw the relationship of points to each other differently than you did. Input from other students can be one more source of information for you as you try to give meaning to what you are studying.

In summary:

1. **Record.** During the lecture, record in the main column as many meaningful facts and ideas as you can. Write so that you can read your handwriting.

2. **Reduce.** As soon after the lecture as possible, summarize (reduce) these ideas and facts concisely in the recall column. Summarizing clarifies meanings and relationships, reinforces continuity, and strengthens memory. It is a way of preparing for examinations gradually and well ahead of time.

3. **Recite.** Now cover the main column. Using only your jottings in the recall column as clues, state the facts and ideas of the lecture as fully as you can, not mechanically, but in your own words, and with as much appreciation of the meaning as you can. Then, uncovering the notes, verify what you have said. This procedure helps transfer the facts and ideas to your long-term memory.

4. **Review.** If you will spend thirty minutes every week or so in a quick review of your notes, you will retain most of what you have learned, and you will be able to use your knowledge more and more effectively.

Good note taking is a powerful skill. You will be motivated to enhance this skill when you find your notes are useful in preparing for exams. Good notes may save you hours of study time.

When you take notes on a lecture, you must be well-prepared to focus on the information being presented, and to use a technique that will allow you to receive large amounts of academic material efficiently.

Poor note taking wastes a lot of time and is essentially useless. A student must be able to read his/her notes, to develop study questions from his/her notes, to use key words from the notes to prepare essay and multiple-choice practice questions, and to feel that he/she can achieve mastery of the material presented in the classroom from a review of his/her notes.

■ Tips for Strengthening Your Note Taking Skills

Tip 1

Organize and plan your approach to note taking. What will you write with?

Come to class prepared. Have a pen or pencil to write with. Black ink is usually best because it is a dark color which is easy to see and does not fade into the page. Ink lasts longer than pencil markings. A student is more receptive to studying when the ink is readable, not very light and fading.

What will you write on? Where will you keep your notes?

Have a separate spiral notebook for each subject area. Leave the front pages clean so that you may develop a table of contents for your notes as the semester develops. Number all other pages in the notebook so that you will have an orderly progression to your notes. If it is more comfortable, use a sectioned ring binder to which you can add loose-leaf pages for each subject. Again, keep a separate loose-leaf for each subject.

Leave space in your notes to add information and explanatory details.

Tip 2

Take an active role in note taking. Be an ACTIVE LISTENER.

Use questions

Set up questions to keep yourself in the lead. Turn your reading and your instructor's lecture titles or opening sentences into questions. These are not questions that you ask your instructor, but ones around which you plan your listening. Make up your own questions, then listen for the answers.

Jot down basic ideas

Pay attention to the instructor's organization, and his or her major points. Then jot down the basic ideas as you grasp them. Get in the habit of listening for major points and conclusions. Identify main ideas and the connections among them. Identify those general assertions that must be supported by specific comments. Identify the specific information (supporting details). Information presented to you in a series or a sequence is frequently worthy of note, (e.g., "There are four reasons this occurs . . ."). Active listeners pay attention to what they hear and try to make sense of it.

Ignore distractions that compete for your attention. Keep your focus on the material the lecturer is presenting.

Tip 3

Develop your own abbv. for commonly used wds.

Your own shorthand style will save time and make sense later when you are reviewing your notes. For example, psychology may be abbreviated as psy. You are already familiar with many abbreviations: days of the week, months of the year, states, college courses, etc. You also have many abbreviations you can use from your math studies, = (equal to); > (greater than); < (less than).

There are times when you shouldn't use shorthand. When you are given a precise definition, you will want to make sure you record exactly what is presented. This is also true when you are given a formula or an example of an application of the formula.

Tip 4

Identify the main ideas.

Lecturers sometimes announce the purpose of a class lecture or offer an outline, thereby providing you with the skeleton of main ideas and details. Use this information to structure your notes, identifying the major points and the details that support them.

During the lecture, there are many clues which indicate that some of what is said is more important than other information. Some lecturers change their tone of voice, stamp the podium, or repeat themselves at each key idea. If your instructor emphasizes the same information repeatedly, it should become obvious to you that the instructor feels this information is important. Chances are good that you will see these topics again on the exam.

Some lecturers ask questions to promote classroom discussion. This is a clue to what the lecturer believes is important. Identify the theme of the question.

Tip 5

Bring your textbooks to class as supportive material.

Many instructors refer in their lectures to information in the textbook. Sometimes they will ask you to do an exercise from the text, or review the interpretation of a graph or visuals accompanying data presentation. Some instructors lecture on material contained in the book and supplement this material. If you have your text in class, you will be able to follow along and note important material.

Tip 6

Make a personal commitment to learn and use good note taking skills. Assume personal responsibility.

A positive frame of mind will strengthen your motivation to be an active listener. Assume that you will learn something useful, that you will expand your knowledge, and that your understanding of the course will increase.

Tip 7

Write down what the instructor puts on the board.

If a professor takes the time to write points on the board, you need to give that information special consideration.

Tip 8

Write down and use the dictionary to learn unfamiliar words.

Ask the instructors in class what unfamiliar words mean. Use these new words in your vocabulary.

Tip 9

Be an active participant.

Summarize statements of information presented in the lecture in your notes or to the class-at-large. **Take notes with a purpose.**

Don't be afraid to ask questions. If you don't understand some of the material, it's very likely that your classmates have similar concerns.

Ask questions

When you realize that you have missed an important point, ask the instructor to repeat it. If you don't understand what is being said and need time to dwell on it, leave a space in your notes and put a question mark (?) in this place. Fill this void in your notes by asking a classmate or the professor prior to the next class session.

You may find graphs, charts, and drawings to be helpful. When these are used to illustrate a point, make your own sketch of what the instructor has presented.

Tip 10

Do not rely on a tape recorder for note taking.

If you use a tape recorder, do not allow this crutch to encourage you to become a passive learner. You still need to write the main points the instructor is lecturing on.

Tip 11

Recall

Create a recall column in your notes. This remains blank while you take notes during class. It is, however, used within 24 hours of the note taking to review and integrate (synthesize) your learning of the material. Write the main ideas and key information covered in the notes in the recall column.

Tip 12

Recite

Use key words or phrases highlighted in the recall column to recall and recite out loud what you understand from the class notes. This summarization of your notes can then be used to prepare for test-taking.

Tip 13

Review

Before lectures begin, review notes from the previous day. This is a "warm-up" to help your mind focus on the material to be covered and to prepare you to think critically during the lecture.

Notes are to be used frequently. Within 24 hours after the lecture, go through your notes and complete any information which might have been recorded hastily or with the intention that you would provide more detail after class. During this quick trip through your notes, make sure concepts are clear and understandable. If not, read your book; check your notes against the text, especially if you missed some main points while writing them down; speak with other students; or check with your instructor. You may also bring these questions up with the professor at the beginning of the next class.

Compare notes with other students and discuss for better retention and understanding.

Work on condensing many thoughts, ideas or facts into a few words or phrases which will be meaningful to you at a later date.

Tip 14

Find out who's the best note taker in your class.

Compare notes, borrow notes, restructure notes. Should you miss a class, make copies of these notes.

Tip 15

Build test questions from your notes.

Once you have identified the key points in a lecture, you can identify exam answers by making up your own set of exam questions. This is exactly what the instructor does in making up an exam, giving most of the same questions—and the answers, too. In a study conducted at one eastern college, a group of students was asked to use this study method. It was found that up to 80% of the actual exam questions were among the key point questions the students had made up ahead of time. The grades of these students were 10 points higher than students not using this method of study (Olney, 1991).

After you have developed all of your questions, use your notes to highlight the answers for each question. If you find an answer is incomplete in your notes, fill in the necessary detail. You may want to transfer questions and their answers to note cards for easy and "portable" review.

Tip 16

Apply your note taking skills as you study and mark your books.

Use your pencil as you read.

Underline important points.
Write notes in the margins.
Draw arrows connecting important material.
Circle material you want to focus on.
Find a system of marking your textbook that is right for you.

These activities help you to be actively involved in note taking. Activity such as this forces you to focus on the material and to concentrate.

Active reading and note taking helps you consciously to search for what is important. Your markings serve a similar purpose to the recall column while the underlined text provides supporting detail.

The benefits of good note taking are many. Increased immediate learning, longer attention span, more interest in the material, an enhanced ability to apply the material in many situations, better retention, and improved notes for later study.

It does take time and self-discipline to use a note taking study system. As you progress in college, you will be forming new habits with regard to your listening skills, improve and monitor your attitude when attending a lecture, adjust where you write information on a sheet of paper; and cultivate a new standard of note taking that ensures you have studied and used your notes well.

■ Summary

Notes provide a useful and convenient record for study and review. Properly used, they are an important reference component and study supplement. With clear and complete notes, a student may identify key lecture points and integrate academic information as well as develop and practice exam questions which focus on the mastery of academic material. In the career review situation, you will use your notes to learn about the nature of careers, compare and contrast occupations, analyze correlations with your personal strengths and weaknesses. In the interview situation, your notes remind you to ask the questions most meaningful to you. Taking notes also helps you determine if the answers you've received are satisfactory or if you need to gather further information.

■ Journal Questions

1. What did you expect to learn from this chapter?

2. (a) What problems do you have when you take notes?

   (b) How can you eliminate those problems?

3. How can you be a better student in class?

4. Identify at least two things you learned about yourself from this chapter.

5. Did this chapter teach you what you expected? If not, what would you have liked to learn?

■ References

Carman, R. & Adams, W., Jr. (1972). Study Skills: A Student's Guide for Survival. New York: John Wiley and Sons.

Lawson, H. H. (1989). College Bound Blacks. Dubuque, Iowa: Kendall/Hunt Publishing Company.

Long, Kenneth F. (1992-a). "Listening and Learning in the Classroom," Chapter 8 in Cooper, C. (Ed.), Keys to Excellence (first edition), Dubuque, Iowa: Kendall/Hunt Publishing Company.

Long, Kenneth F. (1991-b). "Listening and Learning in the Classroom," Chapter 4 in Gardner, J. & Jewler, A. J. Your College Experience: Strategies for Success. Belmont, California: Wadsworth Publishing Company.

Maring, G., Burns, J. & Lee, N. (1991). Mastering Study Skills. Dubuque, Iowa: Kendall/Hunt Publishing Company.

Miami-Dade North Campus SLS Orientation Files (1992).

Olney, C. W. (1991). Where There's a Will, There's an A. Paoli, PA: Chesterbrook Educational Publishers, Inc.

Pauk, W. (1984). How to Study in College. Boston: Houghton Mifflin.

■ Exercise 2.

Choose two pages of notes from one of your academic subjects. Read your notes and fill in the recall clues or formulate questions that would help you study and learn the notes for a test.

Recall Clues and/or Questions

_____

_____

_____

_____

_____

_____

_____

_____

_____

_____

_____

_____

_____

_____

_____

_____

_____

_____

_____

Exercise 3. Comparing Notes

Pair up with another student and compare class notes from your core courses such as humanities, social environment, psychology, natural sciences, and this class. Are your notes clear? Can the other student identify important points from your notes? Do you agree on what is important? Take a few minutes to give feedback and explain to each other your note taking system.

_____

_____

_____

_____

_____

_____

_____

_____

_____

■ Exercise 4.

Note taking is a critical skill you continue to develop throughout your academic career. It is essential to survival in college. Compare your present style of note taking with the approach suggested in this chapter. Where are you having the most success in taking satisfactory notes which are a good resource when you are studying for exams. Why? Discuss at least two of the note taking suggestions you will implement immediately to improve your note taking skills.

_____

_____

_____

_____

_____

_____

_____

_____

_____

■ Exercise 5. Summary

1. Why is it a good practice to make a habit of reviewing all of your notes within a 24 hour period?

   _____

   _____

   _____

2. What is the purpose of a recall column?

   _____

   _____

   _____

3. List several verbal and visual cues the instructor may use to indicate certain information is important and belongs in your notes.

   _____

   _____

   _____

4. How do you want to improve your note taking skills?

   _____

   _____

   _____

5. What factors would you consider important to take notes on when researching careers?

   _____

   _____

   _____

6. Describe the importance of the skill of writing and listening when succeeding in a career.

   _____

   _____

   _____

Test Taking I

■ Introduction

Ask students what they hate most about school, and I'll bet taking tests is probably somewhere near the top of the list. Think back to the beginning of the semester when you were asked to write in your journal what you thought would be the hardest part of being in college, or what you were dreading the most. If you're anything like the students in my classes, you probably at least mentioned midterms and final exams. If everyone hates them so much, why do we even need to bother with tests?

Tests are given for several reasons. The first is to motivate you to learn. What is the basic question on everyone's mind when the teacher is presenting new material? "Is this going to be on the test?" If the answer is yes, the class gets busy taking notes. If the answer is no, everyone sits back and relaxes; not a pencil or pen is raised to a notebook anywhere in the room. Your instructors have noticed this trend! What insures that students will pay attention in class and study later? Let it be known that this is going to be on the test.

Another reason, perhaps even the best reason, for taking tests is to give you (and your instructor) some feedback on how much you really have learned. Why, then, does everyone fear them? The problem is we have our thinking all wrong about tests. Tests are a time for you to strut your stuff and show off. Tests give you an opportunity to assess how well you learned the material and to prove to your instructor that you really were paying attention and really did read the textbook. Teachers know that not everyone feels comfortable talking out in class or participating in discussions. Written and other out-of-class assignments are a great way to evaluate, but the instructor has no proof that it was you who actually did the work. So, somewhere in the history of education the concept of giving tests was invented. The same teacher probably came up with the idea of giving final grades.

At this point I can almost hear you thinking, "That's great, but what if I don't have that much stuff to strut? There's a lot to learn in college, and I never was that good in school." I'm so glad you're reading this chapter! Isn't that why you're taking this class? You can learn the strategies and skills that will help you be one of those confident, assured students who take good notes, have a great study system, and don't fear tests.

There are two factors that contribute to good test scores. You need to prepare for them properly, and you need to know how to take tests. Both are important, so let's analyze them one at a time.

■ Strategies for Test Preparation

Thorough preparation throughout the semester is the only avenue to success. Start by attending class on a regular basis, even if attendance is not required. Whether the instructor actually takes attendance or not, he or she expects you to know all of the material covered in class. It is rare that a student who doesn't come to class will make a passing grade. OK, we all know some of those super bright people who never read their textbooks, never take notes, skip class all the time and still make good grades. The problem is, we aren't one of those people. We have to get our grades the old fashioned way: we have to earn them!

I can't emphasize the importance of class attendance enough. If you aren't there you don't have an opportunity to ask questions when you don't understand something. This is especially true if your instructor is an adjunct faculty member. (That's a fancy college term for part time instructor.) They are not required to have office hours to meet with students, nor do they have to give out their home phone numbers so you can call them at your convenience. Even if your instructor has an office on campus, how likely is it that s/he will want to repeat the whole lecture/discussion/directions/etc. to you during office hours? If you want to know what's going on, be in class. Being in class regularly also shows the instructor how serious you are about passing the course or getting a good grade.

Another thing you must do throughout the entire semester is study. You cannot wait until the night before the exam to start reading the textbook and your notes. Cramming is not a productive way to study, and the night before the test is not the time to learn new material. Begin with the very first class meeting and develop your study habits so they become a continuous process throughout the semester.

I know we've already covered time management, note taking and study systems, but let's review quickly how to incorporate these skills into your test preparation. Using the great notes you now take in class and when you read, look at them for potential test questions. Summarize all your notes so you have a manageable system that can be reviewed often, and especially before a test. Make up a study guide and study small sections of the material at a time. Plan and write out a workable schedule for studying that includes daily and weekly reviews. Begin at least a week before the test to get all of your materials together. Then, divide them into parts and study some each day. This will help you avoid procrastination. At each study session quickly review all the material from prior study sessions, then add a new section. Start with the most difficult parts or sections. That way you will review the hardest stuff every day.

You may want to form a study group or join one that is already in existence. Working with other students to share ideas, questions, information, notes and other materials is usually helpful. Students tend to learn well from one another. Besides, being able to explain the concepts to someone else means you've learned them yourself.

When you study, it's not enough just to memorize things in your notes and textbooks. A good test taker will know the vocabulary in every subject. Make a list of words with their definitions and practice using them. Or better yet, put them on flash cards for quick review. Ask someone to help you by quizzing you on the meaning of key terms. Your study should also help you understand the major concepts and see relationships between the important points. Often tests will ask you to apply what you have learned to new situations. Be prepared for those kinds of questions.

Performers and athletes will tell you that in order to be good at what they do, they must practice. In order for you to be a good test taker you have to practice. How? Make up your own tests. Look at your lecture notes. Is there anything the teacher said would be on the test? Use your homework, notes from class and reading assignments, quizzes, study guides and textbook aids to help you develop test questions. Pay attention to the objectives for each unit. They tell you what the teacher (or textbook author) thinks you should know by the end of the unit—i.e., *it will be on the test*. Look at the introductions, summaries, glossaries, examples, chapter review questions, etc., etc. Turn all this material into questions. Write out the answers; test yourself periodically. Should I say it again? Put those questions on note cards so you can recite and review! In math, make sure you work additional problems. Practice every kind of problem that's likely to be on the test.

■ More About Test Preparation

Have you ever followed all of the advice given in this chapter so far, studied for hours and hours, and still done lousy on the test? I often hear the lament, "I studied, but everything I studied wasn't on the test, and the stuff I didn't study very much was all that the teacher asked!" What else can you do? What do those people who always get A's do differently than you do? How do they seem to know what to study?

Let me share a couple more secrets to good test preparation. They're not really secrets at all, but you'd think they were considering all the students who were never taught these skills.

Attending the class before the exam is critical. Not too profound, huh? But you'd be surprised how many students skip the review session. I hear comments like, "I'm not really going to miss much, Dr. _____ is only going to go over the stuff we've already learned." What a mistake! That's one of those self defeating behaviors you need to change if you're in the habit of thinking you can use that class time more productively on your own. Why do I say that? Usually during the session before the exam, the instructor will give you all kinds of information you need to know to properly prepare for the test. If she/he doesn't tell you, ask! Be assured your classmates want to know as badly as you do what the test will be like, and they will be so glad you had the courage to ask.

What Exactly Should You Know About the Test?

- ■ What type of test is it going to be?
- ■ How many questions of each type will there be?
- ■ What topics will the test cover?
- ■ Will any material that was covered in class be omitted?
- ■ What percentage of the questions will come from each unit or chapter?
- ■ How much weight should you give to studying materials such as textbooks, lecture notes, handouts, lab work, outside readings, etc.?
- ■ Are the questions from the textbook's test bank or did the instructor make them all up?
- ■ Will there be essay questions? If so, will you have to answer all of the questions or will you be able to choose your questions?
- ■ How long is the test? If it is longer than two hours, will you get a break?

What Exactly Should I Do with All of This Information? Or How Will This Information Help Me Prepare for My Exam?

Knowing what kinds of questions will be on the test will determine what kinds of sample questions you should make up and practice. If there will be essay questions on the test you should practice answering some essay questions. Yes, that means writing out the answers, not just thinking them in your head. Your written expression often differs from your mental thoughts. You don't have to use proper grammar and punctuation in your head, and you always know what you mean when you're thinking. But you don't always say what you mean when you're writing, especially when pressured for time.

If you know the test will not cover everything, that should help you focus your study to what **will** be on it. Also, knowing whether the questions come mainly from the textbook or if they will be from videos shown in class, labs, extra readings, etc., will help you determine what to spend the most time studying. Usually instructors will give you clues or even tell you outright what to study the most, especially if you ask them directly. Don't be afraid to use the best resource for knowing what's on the test—the person who made it up.

If you somehow managed to get into a class with the one teacher on campus that never reveals what the test will be like, there are still ways to get that information. Ask students who were in his/her class last semester what kinds of tests are given. Although instructors may vary the questions they ask from semester to semester, very few vary their style. What I mean is, the tests themselves may be different, but the format is likely to be the same. An instructor who prefers multiple choice or objective type questions usually will use them consistently. Instructors who think essay or short answer questions are best will probably have those on every test. Talk to friends who have previously taken the course about how to study and what to expect on the test. They may even have copies of some of their tests that you can use in your study. And don't forget that the other tests and quizzes you've already taken in the course should give you ideas about future exams.

■ The Day of the Test

Actually, let's back up to the day before the test. Complete your study, and if possible, review your notes just before going to bed. Make your class material the last thing on your mind before falling asleep. Your subconscious will continue to work on it through the night, and your memory won't have the interference or distraction of new information crowding out what you've so carefully put in. I know this will sound like something your mother would say, but I'll say it anyway: get to bed at a reasonable hour and get a good night's sleep. Staying up late to cram is a self defeating behavior. Too much cramming tires both mind and body, produces anxiety, and brings about mental blocks.

On the day of the test get up on time so you don't have to rush to school. Your mind needs time to focus and become alert. Plan to get up more than 20 minutes before the test, even if you do live in the subdivision across the street from the college. Remember your nutritionist's instructions to eat a light, healthy breakfast. Heavy meals tend to make you sleepy, and you will also want to avoid fried, greasy foods, those that are high in acid, or any other kinds of food that might upset your stomach. Too much sugar, caffeine, or other stimulants will make your energy level peak and fall like a roller coaster.

Even the clothes you wear can affect your test performance. Does that sound absurd? It's not! Wear something comfortable that you like; something that makes you look and feel good. Consider wearing layers. That way you can adjust if the room is too cold or too hot. Nothing can destroy your concentration like being physically uncomfortable.

If your test is later in the day you may have time to review between classes, but don't plan on cramming until the last minute. Take some time to relax, and follow the above mentioned guidelines for a healthy lunch. Remember, now is not the time to worry about family, work situations, or other personal problems. Put that stuff out of your mind. Trust me, it will still be there waiting for you after the test. The difference is by then you can focus some solution generating energy to those problems instead of distracted, fruitless worry, and you won't have a bad test grade to add to your troubles.

One more thing about test preparation: bring the proper supplies with you. If you will be using computer scored answer sheets, make sure you have several No. 2 pencils with erasers. The student, not the instructor, is responsible for making sure s/he has pencils, pens, erasers, paper, exam booklets, calculator, ruler, dictionary, or whatever is required for the test.

And now, drum roll, please . . .

- *Make sure you arrive on time*
- *Read and follow all directions carefully*
- *Jot down memory cues*
- *Survey the entire test before you start*
- *Plan and use your time wisely*
- *Answer the easiest questions first*
- *Make sure you have answered essay questions completely*

- *Work math problems out to the last step*
- *Check your answer sheet as you go along to make sure the numbers match the questions as you fill in the circles*
- *Don't be distracted (or pressured) because others are finished*
- *Go over your test one last time before you turn it in*

■ The Test!

Ok, you're here. It's the day; it's the time; you've studied; you have everything together; and you are still nervous! Here are a few more tips to consider:

Get yourself off to the best possible start by being on time for the test. You will have the maximum amount of time to take it (especially important on long essays or timed tests), and you will not miss any important instructions or questions that were asked before the exam.

Be sure to write your name on your paper and/or fill in the name part of a machine scored answer sheet. (Yes, you do need to fill in the circles for the letters of your name!) It is very frustrating for the instructor to have exam papers without names. If there is more than one anonymous paper in the class, it may be impossible to tell whose black circles are whose!

Read the directions and ask any questions you may have about the format of the test. Are you allowed to write on the exam itself? May you use scratch paper? What is the point value for each question and what are the time limits? Are you penalized for guessing? Listen for verbal instructions given by the instructor in addition to the written ones.

Jot down your memory cues before you start reading the test. On the reverse side of the test, in the margins, in scratch paper, or wherever possible, write down formulas, mnemonics, and any other memory aids you can. Dump as much information from your mind as possible so you can concentrate and won't "go blank" on later questions.

Survey the test before you actually start writing. This will help you figure out exactly what you have to do. Plan your time according to the point values of the questions. Spend more time on the ones that earn more points. If you are slow to organize your thoughts or are a slow writer, you will need to allow more time for essay questions. If you are a slow reader, you will need to spend more time on the objective questions. Be sure to leave five minutes at the end to check your answers.

Don't think that you have to answer the questions in the order they are asked. Always get the easy ones out of the way first. This builds confidence, and confidence reduces test anxiety. Skip questions you do not know, but make sure you mark them so you can return to them later. You might want to develop a system such as circling the numbers of the questions about which you are unsure and placing a check next to the ones you don't know at all. The correct answer may occur to you later. In going back, first deal with the circled questions, secondly with those checked. Sometimes you might find the answers to those difficult ones in another part of the test. Be sure not to spend too much time on any one problem or question. This is a classic test taking error. If you sense yourself going over your time limit, move on to the next question. You can always return to it later.

Write clearly so your answers will be easy to read. Make sure your "T" (true) doesn't look like an "F" (false). Even though you will be writing quickly, make sure your handwriting is legible. Please take time to proofread what you have written. It is easy to leave out words and proper punctuation when you're in a hurry. Make sure your sentences make sense. On a math test it is really important that the instructor be able to identify your answers (from among that mess of chicken scratch) and be able to read your numbers. Also, check to see that you have carried the problem out to the last step. Reread the original question. Does your solution answer it? Often, to do the problem you use an equation that solves for "X," but the question asks the value of "Y."

Don't become distracted or anxious because other students are done with the test and you're still working. The person who finishes first may not necessarily know all the answers. Instead that student may have failed to study, not known much of anything, and given up in frustration!

That age-old advice about not changing your answers arbitrarily is still true. Assuming that you studied and paid attention in class, your first impression is often the correct one. Change your answer only if you know for certain that your first answer is wrong (you found a clue somewhere else in the test, you had a sudden memory surge, etc.).

Always, always go over your paper one final time before turning it in to check for careless mistakes, to add more information to your essays, to guess on those questions you left blank, etc. Reread each question with the answer you chose to make sure it is correct. On foreign language or English tests, proofread for grammar, spelling, placement of accent marks, and such. On math tests be sure you have the numbers labeled properly, check the signs, exponents, decimal placement, number of zeros, etc.

Relax, keep a positive attitude. You're doing just fine.

■ Test Taking Strategies

I'm ready to reveal the last few tricks up my test taking sleeve. Being properly prepared is the best strategy for getting a good grade, but there may come a time when despite your best efforts, you just don't remember everything. This is the time to pull out your aces: some good guessing skills. "Guessing skills?!" you say. Yes, there are some skills that you can learn to make you a better guesser. They're often called good test taking skills or being test-wise. Remember those smart students? The ones who get A's without really trying? Somewhere they learned and practiced these skills. Why didn't your grade school and high school teachers tell you this stuff years ago and save you a lot of bad test grades? I don't know. Maybe they thought you already knew. Maybe they did tell you, but you were on a mental vacation at the time. Anyway, you're serious about school now, and serious about improving your GPA, so now it's time to pay attention and add these skills to your personal repertoire.

Exams basically test your memory in two ways: they find out what you **recall** and what you **recognize**. To answer recall questions you have to come up with the information yourself. Essays, short answer, and fill in the blank are the most common recall type questions. It's much easier to respond to recognition type questions where the choices are given to you. Multiple choice, true/false, and matching are favorites in this category. Since there are specific strategies to use for each type of test question, let's look at them one at a time.

True/False Questions

You already know these are about the easiest kind of test questions. You start with a 50/50 chance of guessing right no matter what. Let's increase those odds even more.

1. Read true/false questions carefully. They are easily made into trick questions by the way they're worded.

2. To be marked true, a statement must be true without exception. If **any** part of a true/false statement is false, the whole thing is false. Consider this example:

    For a goal to be attainable it must be realistic,
    measurable, and rigid.

    This is a false statement. Goals need to be measurable and realistic, but they also need to be flexible. To be true the statement should read:

    For a goal to be attainable it must be realistic,
    measurable, and flexible.

3. Watch out for statements with absolute words or extreme modifiers like all, never, none, always, no one. They are almost always false because they do not allow for exceptions. Few things in life are 100% true or false.

    It never rains in the desert.

4. Be careful, though, because there are times when absolute statements can be true.

    When calculating your GPA on a four point scale an A is always worth 4 quality points.

5. Statements that contain qualifiers allow for exceptions or leave open the possibility that there is more than one right answer. These items are likely to be true. Qualifiers are words such as sometimes, seldom, usually, often, occasionally, almost, most.

    An instructor's teaching style determines
    to some extent the instructional
    methods used in the class.

6. Statements that have reasons in them tend to be false. Because, therefore, consequently, the cause of, as a result of, etc., are all words used to indicate reasons. True/false items like these do not always give all the reasons or they might give the wrong reasons. Would you answer the following true or false?

Cancer results from environmental pollution.

This statement is false. Cancer has many causes and does not only result from pollution. And all pollution does not cause cancer. If, however, the statement read as follows, the answer would be true.

Cancer can result from some forms of environmental pollution.

Absolute Words

all
everyone
none
always
only
no
invariably
never
no one
every

Common Qualifiers

many
seldom
almost
sometimes
frequently
can
most
usually
rarely
ordinarily
occasionally
few
some
likely
often
possibly
generally
might

7. Be especially careful about negative statements. Your mind is more likely to "read over" negative words, causing you to miss them. If you are allowed to write on your test paper, underline negative words as you read to draw attention to them. Also, remember that in the English language a double negative makes the statement positive. This is one of those grammar rules that you may ignore in conversations with your friends, but ignore it on a test and it will cost you valuable points. Example:

Different cultures must not be studied in an unbiased fashion.

This statement is false. An easy way to avoid the double negative trap is to cross out both of the negatives and read the sentence without them. The above example would then read:

Different cultures must be studied in a biased fashion.

8. Long statements are somewhat more likely to be true than short ones. For example, A is true and B is false.

   A. *A psychologist is a person with a master's or a doctorate degree in psychology.*
   B. *Psychologists are medical doctors.*

9. Assume that the instructor is asking straightforward questions. In other words, do not turn an obviously true statement into a false one by creating wild exceptions in your mind.

10. If you've followed strategies 1–9 and you still don't know which to guess, mark the answer true. Even though there are hundreds of things that could make a statement false and only one way for it to be true, it is easier for instructors to write true statements when making up a test. They usually want to accentuate the positive. Therefore, unless you have a teacher known for writing trick questions, assume the answer is true unless you can determine that it is false.

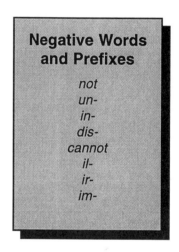

**Negative Words
and Prefixes**

*not
un-
in-
dis-
cannot
il-
ir-
im-*

Matching

You have two lists that require you to match items from the first column with items from the second, or perhaps a diagram with arrows pointing to certain parts and a list of words to identify these parts. What can you do to make this easier?

1. First, look at the two columns and figure out the pattern. Is one a list of names and the other accomplishments? It might be easier to look at the accomplishments and figure out who did what than the other way around. If it's a diagram, it might be easier to start with the list of words and find the correct location for each. Whichever way seems easier, stick to one list as a starting point and keep going down that list to avoid getting mixed up by jumping back and forth.

2. Check to see if there are enough options in each column for an even match. Will you have to use some names/words twice? Or, are there too many names/words, which means some will be left over? If there's an even match or extra names/words always mark off your choices as you use them. The process of elimination will help narrow the field for later guessing.

3. Start with the ones you know for sure. Don't guess right away because one wrong answer can increase your chances of further errors as you start a whole string of incorrect matches.

4. Use logical clues and information from other parts of the test to help you as you guess the ones you don't know.

Multiple Choice

Most typical multiple choice questions have two parts: the stem, which can be an incomplete statement or a question, followed by several options for completing the statement or answering the question. Many students prefer this type of test, as do many instructors. It is easier to grade and, like true/false or matching, it is objective. On an objective test there's a specific right answer for every question, and no matter whose paper it is or who grades the test, the score would be the same. People like to refer to these kinds of tests as multiple guess, because if you don't know the answer, you usually have a one out of four (or one out of five) chance of guessing correctly. Still, those odds are stacked against you. Let's look at some ways to improve your score.

1. As with other kinds of questions, read the item carefully. Underline key words, especially negative words that can give the question an entirely different meaning. Watch out for those double negatives!

   In some states it is not illegal to
   a. *pass a school bus stopped to pick up children*
   b. *drive faster than the posted speed limit*
   c. *ignore a school zone warning sign*
   d. *turn right on a red light after stopping and yielding the right of way*

   In case you're not up on the rules of the road, the correct answer is "d." All the others are illegal in every state.

2. Of course, you are already on the look-out for absolute words for all the same reasons we mentioned in our discussion of true/false questions. You also need to read carefully statements with phrases like "all but one" or "all of these are true except." These are just like negatives. Consider:

   All but one of the following cities in the United States boast a population exceeding one million people.
   a. *Washington, D.C.*
   b. *Los Angeles, California*
   c. *Hartford, Connecticut*
   d. *Atlanta, Georgia*

   The question is asking you to identify the one city from the list of alternatives that has less than one million people in its population.

3. Avoid choosing the first option that seems plausible without reading all of the possibilities. When you read the question, try to figure out the answer first. Read all of the options and match each of them with the stem to see if they make a true statement. Discard the obvious distractors. At least you will improve your odds of guessing the right answer.

4. Choose the best or most complete alternative. Don't be fooled into selecting a response that is true but only partially answers the question. In the following example, the correct choice should be "e."

An aria is an operatic solo sung by a
a. *tenor and bass*
b. *contralto*
c. *harpsichord*
d. *soprano*
e. *tenor, contralto, soprano or bass*

When alternatives seem equally good, select the one which is longest and seems to hold the most information. For example:

In the United States inferior intellectual development is most often caused by
a. *poor nutrition*
b. *divorce*
c. *the combined effects of inherited ability and environmental deprivation*
d. *television*

You did choose "c," didn't you?

5. Check out responses that include combinations such as "a and b" or "all of the above." These are often the correct answer, especially if you think more than one of the options are true, or if none of them seems right. However, be aware that "all of the above" and "none of the above" can be the test writer's way of "copping out" when s/he can't think of any more plausible choices. Be cautious here.

6. When two of the options are identical, then neither of them is correct.

A kilogram is approximately equal to
a. *2.5 pounds*
b. *2.2 pounds*
c. *22 pounds*
d. *2 pounds 8 ounces*

In this example you can eliminate "a" and "d," which should make choosing between "b" and "c" a lot easier.

7. When two responses are similar, one of them is likely to be correct.

The Hawaiian Islands are located in
a. *the Atlantic Ocean*
b. *the Pacific Ocean*
c. *the Adriatic Sea*
d. *the Gulf of Mexico*

Now, all you have to do is remember which ocean is which.

8. Whenever two of the options are opposites, one of them is always wrong and the other is often, but not always, right.

A person who prefers to work in a neat, orderly fashion, doing one thing at a time, and using an outline is probably:
a. *a right brained thinker*
b. *a realistic thinker*
c. *a left brained thinker*
d. *an artistic thinker*

Which is it, "a" or "c" ?

9. When statements contain numbers, the correct answer is usually neither extreme, but rather, a middle number.

   In the labor market what percent of available jobs are ever listed in the want ads?
   a. 0 to 10%
   b. 15 to 20%
   c. 30 to 40%
   d. over 45%

   In this example "b" is correct. An exception to the rule is when the true answer is a lot higher or lower than the average person would think.

   If artistic talent, mechanical aptitude, musical aptitude and athletic potential were considered, _____ out of 20 children could be labeled as being "gifted."
   a. 10
   b. 12
   c. 17
   d. 19

   You might not have guessed that "d" is right before you read this tip. That's why some knowledge of the subject helps!

10. Remember that the correct answer will agree in number, gender, and person with the question, and will match the stem grammatically. Eliminate choices that don't match.

11. When all else fails, guess. If you studied at all, choose something that sounds familiar. Options with words that you've never heard of are probably wrong. If you're taking a random guess, choose either "b" or "c." There is a slightly better chance that answers in one of the middle positions are correct.

Essay Exams

The dreaded essay questions—usually you love them or hate them. These are the ones my students always moan and groan about. They are tougher because they're tests of recall rather than recognition. There is no faking here. You have to supply the information as well as be able to organize and present it in a logical way. That means you first have to know the material and then develop and support your ideas in writing. That's a lot more difficult than just recognizing or being able to guess right answers from a list of options. Although they are a lot harder and more time consuming to grade, essays are favored by teachers because they often give the best picture of what you do know. But there's something else you should realize about essays. They are graded subjectively. The teacher, no matter what criteria she/he establishes for evaluating the answers, will still be influenced by those "between the lines" kind of factors. Take advantage of this and you may be able to gain extra points by employing good essay writing techniques. So, even though there aren't any guessing strategies to use on an essay test, there are ways to improve your score.

1. Ask for clarification if you don't understand something. Sometimes the questions are worded in such a way that you're not sure what the instructor wants. Don't guess, ask and be sure you are on the right track. Pay attention to details such as whether or not you have to answer every question. If you are to choose a certain number of questions to answer, do you get extra credit for answering the others?

2. Learn how to manage your time so that you will be able to respond to all of the questions rather than answering one or two thoroughly and leaving the rest blank. Select the questions you are best prepared to answer and do them first. A common test taking error is to start with the most difficult question, thinking you'll have time to get the easy ones at the end. What usually happens, though, is you don't

leave enough time and end up rushing—writing too brief an answer for a question that you really did know. If a 50 minute test has 5 questions, allow 10 minutes for each question. Check your progress, but don't be a clock watcher. (It wastes time, interrupts your train of thought, and increases test anxiety.) If the time allotted for one question has passed, move on to the next one (even if you still had more to say). Do not sacrifice one question for another.

3. To make things easier for yourself, when you first get the test, jot down on scratch paper all the information that might be lost or forgotten by the time you begin to write. Use abbreviations or key words that will jog your mind later. Before you actually write out the complete answer, outline your thoughts. Don't spend too much time on this; it doesn't have to be perfect. However, it will give you a chance to organize what you want to say. As you are outlining, you may think of extra details to add to an earlier point. You can change things around in your outline and make sure your answer will flow smoothly. Answer the questions in simple, direct language. Get to the point and avoid lengthy, complicated sentences. Don't be repetitious. You will not get extra points for saying the same things over and over. When an instructor is grading your paper, s/he will be more impressed by an answer that covers each point thoroughly and then moves on to the next one. Papers that jump around from point to point, or ones with extra stuff squeezed between the lines or in the margin are harder to understand. If the teacher doesn't understand (or can't read) what you've written, you won't get full credit.

Direction Words

Argue—give reasons, pro or con

Analyze—separate into parts and show function and relationship

Comment—express your opinion

Compare—discuss similarities and differences

Contrast—stress the differences

Criticize/Critique—judge positively or negatively

Defend—state reasons

Define—give clear and concise meanings

Demonstrate—provide evidence

Describe—provide a detailed account

Diagram—make a sketch, drawing, chart, graph, or plan

Differentiate—show the difference

Discuss—examine in detail by providing facts and reasons both pro and con

Enumerate—provide a concise list or outline

Evaluate—express an opinion

Explain—give reasons, clarify, or interpret

Identify—give meanings

Illustrate—give examples or use a diagram or picture

Interpret—give the meaning in your own words

Justify—same as defend; prove a point

Label—name

List—same as enumerate

Narrate—tell a story

Outline—provide the main points in an organized manner

Paraphrase—express ideas in your own words

Prove—give evidence or reasons

Relate—show how things are connected

Review—examine critically and comment on important points

State—provide the main points omitting details

Summarize—condense the main points

Support—prove

Trace—describe a series of events or steps in narrative form

4. Know the meaning of direction words and answer the questions according to the directions. Be sure you answer all the parts of each question. Decide if the answer calls for facts, opinions, or both. Use the terminology learned from the textbook and used in class lectures. Define the terms you use if they are not self explanatory. Provide evidence to support your answers. Give specific examples and/or details.

5. In drafting your answer, use the principles of writing you learned in your English class (even if this isn't an English test). Use an introduction at the beginning and a conclusion at the end. Start the introduction by rewording the question into a statement. For example, if the question asks you to enumerate the reasons for the U.S. Civil War, you might start your paper by writing:

There were many compelling and complicated reasons for the U.S. Civil War.

Use paragraphs containing main ideas and supporting details. If possible, answer the question directly in the first sentence. Then expand on that sentence to develop your answer.

Some reasons for the U.S. Civil War were the political, economic, and lifestyle differences between the North and South, as well as the many problems of the slavery issue.

It is most important that you follow the conventions of standard English when you write. Even though your teacher may say s/he doesn't take off points for spelling or grammar, remember the subjective element in grading. If you want to sound educated (like you know what you're talking about), pay attention to details like subject/verb agreement, correct use of pronouns, run on sentences, phrases that aren't sentences at all, confusing logic, etc.

Some Final Thoughts on Writing Answers to Essay Questions

Be aware of your instructor's personal opinions, biases, feelings, likes and dislikes which might enter into the scoring of the questions. Never leave an unanswered question. If you are running out of time, outline the important points on your paper. This will show that you do know the material. If you do not know the answer, write down what you do know—anything that may apply to the question. You might receive partial credit, and some points are always better than none. If the question has multiple parts, be sure your answer includes at least a sentence addressing each part. When you are in doubt, qualify your answers. If you don't remember an exact date, give an approximate or a general time period.

Transition Words

however
finally
therefore
furthermore
similarly
besides
for example

Leave space between questions so that you can make additions, corrections, clarifications, rewrites and examples if time permits. Use transitional words to move from one idea or point to another. It will make your paper sound better. Summarize a long essay or write a conclusion at the end. Always allow time to edit your paper, and please, proofread your answers.

Fill in the Blank Exams and Sentence Completion

These are statements with a missing part (or parts) that usually require you to supply the missing information from memory. Although more difficult than recognition questions, these are not impossible. Read them carefully and decide what kind of answer you need. Is it a name, date, location, or other fact? Often the way the statement is expressed may help you decide how to complete it. Key words in the question may help you determine what topics the question covers. That is why it is important to be familiar with the vocabulary in the course.

When the blank space is preceded by "an" rather than "a" the answer should be a noun that begins with a vowel. The number of blanks or the length of the blank space may also be a clue to the correct answer. More often, however, the length of the blanks are the same and the blank space will be preceded by "a/an." Still, the statement, when complete, should make sense and be grammatically correct. The verb form may indicate whether the answer you are looking for is singular or plural.

As with any other test question, never leave a blank space. If the question is vague and you are undecided what type of answer is required, ask the instructor for clarification.

The War of the Roses was fought in _____.

You might ask the teacher if the correct answer is the place or the year the war was fought.

Math Tests

Use all of the strategies we've already discussed like writing down formulas right away, reading directions, scanning the entire test, budgeting your time, doing the easiest problems first, leaving difficult problems and returning to them later in the test. When you return to a problem, start it again without looking at your previous work. You may have made a simple mistake the first time that kept the problem from coming out right. Human error, not lack of understanding, is often responsible for wrong answers.

Draw pictures or diagrams to help you visualize the problem. Break down complex problems and do the steps one at a time. Show your work in an organized fashion. If your answer is incorrect you may receive partial credit for the steps you worked out correctly. Strive for accuracy and write neatly.

Some Tips for Avoiding Common Math Errors

■ *If multiplying by 2 digit numbers, the answer must be at least 4 digits.*

■ *Any quantity multiplied by zero is zero.*

■ *Any quantity raised to the zero power is one.*

■ *Any fraction multiplied by its reciprocal is one.*

■ *Only like algebraic terms may be combined.*

■ *Break down to simplest form in algebra.*

■ *In algebra, multiply and divide before adding and subtracting.*

■ *If an algebraic expression has more than one set of parentheses, get rid of the inner parenthesis first and work outward.*

■ *Any operation performed on one side of the equation must be performed on the other side.*

Remember to check your work. Check computations from step to step. Be sure you are using the proper equations, formulas, functions, order of operations, etc. Is your arithmetic correct? You can check your work by estimating what the answer should be. Always make sure your solution is logical and makes sense. Remember, if the problem involves subtraction, you check your work by adding; if division is involved, check your work by multiplying. Use the opposite operation to proof your work.

Open Book Tests and Take Home Tests

You might think these sound like the best kinds of tests yet. But neither exempt you from studying. In fact, you should study for an open book or take home exam exactly as you would for any exam. During open book tests students may refer to their textbooks, notes, handouts, etc., as they complete the answers to the questions. Open book tests seldom include questions where answers can be copied directly from the text. You must often know exactly where to find the material to help answer the test questions. You will only know how to do that by thoroughly covering the information prior to the test. Take home tests, too, are usually more difficult and require more lengthy answers than essay questions given in class. Once again, your best bet is to prepare properly.

Standardized Tests (ACT—SAT—COMPASS—ASSET—ASVAB)

Sometimes it is necessary to take a standardized test for college entrance, to enlist in the military, to qualify for a scholarship, or for placement in courses. Try to get a study guide for the test. Check for these in your local public or school library, the counseling office, the admissions office, or most bookstores. If it is a difficult test, you might even consider taking a preparatory course to help you do your best. Start to prepare well in advance. Use the study guide (or materials sent to you when you registered for the test) to find out what you should study. Answer the sample questions and problems. Identify the areas on the test that are weaknesses for you. By starting early, you can improve your skills through practice and study.

When you actually take the test, use the very same strategies we've already gone over in this chapter. Use any or all of these strategies every time you have to take a test. One thing to watch for, though, is that different types of tests are scored differently. Make sure you know if there is a penalty for incorrect answers. On some tests your score is the number correct minus points for every incorrect response. Blank questions are neutral. In that case you may not want to guess unless you are quite sure you are right. You can find out how a test is scored by reading the study guide, the test registration materials, the printed directions on the test itself, or by asking the proctor (person giving the test).

■ When Tests Are Returned

One of the best ways to improve your test taking skills is to review the test after it has been graded and returned to you. Note any incorrect answers and learn from your mistakes. Take time to look at your errors. Go through the exam and analyze the questions to see why you chose the incorrect answer. Is there a pattern to your errors? Did you include enough detail in your essay questions and answer what was being asked? Examine the questions on objective tests that you changed. Did you change correct answers for incorrect ones? What other test taking errors do you find?

Errors on the first third of a test are usually careless mistakes. Those on the last third of the test may result from being in too much of a hurry. It may be that the more difficult questions are left to the end, but you are not allowing enough time for them. On future tests spend extra time reviewing the portions of the test in which you typically make the most errors.

Take advantage of any class time devoted to going over the exam. Jot down your errors so you can review them later. Many teachers collect the tests after going over them in class. If they have taken the questions from the textbook's test bank, or plan to use some of the same questions on exams for other sections of the course, it would be unethical to allow students to keep copies of the exam. Pay attention to items you didn't know or with which you had difficulty when taking the test. Discuss the answers with other classmates and/or the instructor. However, don't get into lengthy arguments over correct answers. If you disagree with your grade, discuss it with the teacher during his/her office hours.

Remember to analyze the test to see where the instructor draws most of the questions. Do they come from the textbook, lecture notes, homework, etc.? Check the number of true answers and the number of false answers on the test. Are there usually more true questions than false questions? Use this information when guessing on future tests prepared by the same instructor.

Don't ever throw away returned tests before the final exam! In any course with a cumulative final exam there is a good chance that questions from the unit exams will reappear on the final. Even if that is not the case, those old tests give you lots of information about how to prepare for the next test in that class.

Decide how you can improve for the next exam. Do you need to:

- take better notes?
- review more often?
- follow directions?
- provide more details?
- develop better strategies?
- use your time better?
- spend more time studying?
- get a good night's sleep before the test?

■ Summary

We've looked at test taking more thoroughly than you've probably ever done before. In this chapter we have considered the importance of proper preparation which includes such things as good class attendance, using your notes and textbook, studying every week, making up your own sample test questions, and finding out what the test will be like. You should also have gained some insight on what to do the day of the test to enhance your preparation.

There are plenty of tips to follow when it comes to the actual test taking experience. I hope some of these ideas are helpful to you on your next test. The section on test taking strategies listed ways to be a better guesser on objective type tests like true/false, matching and multiple choice. Although there is no guess work in recall type tests (essay and short answer), there are some strategies that might help you get a better score. We looked at specific kinds of tests with which students often have difficulty. Math tests, open book, and standardized tests sometimes require extra effort.

Finally, taking tests can be a more valuable learning experience for you if you spend time reviewing your graded exam. Learn from your mistakes, figure out what you did wrong so you won't make the same errors over and over. Set goals for the next test and use the strategies you have learned in this chapter to become a proficient test taker.

■ Journal Assignment

Think about the tests you have taken during the last few weeks. Respond to the following:

What strategies did you use when you took these tests? Did the strategies work for you?

Describe the techniques you learned from this chapter and explain how you will implement them on your next exam.

■ Activity 1. How Well Do You Follow Directions?

1. Read all the directions before you do anything.

2. Put your name at the top of this page.

3. In the bottom right hand corner, write the name of this class.

4. In the bottom left hand corner put the name of your instructor.

5. Put a box around the class name.

6. Put a circle around your instructor's name.

7. Write the name of your college at the bottom of this page.

8. You have now completed this exercise, so let the class know you are finished by calling out, "Done."

9. Return to the beginning and only do number two.

◼ Activity 2. Time Management for Test Taking

You have one hour for an exam. The exam has six essay questions. You are to select four questions to answer. Allow time to preview the test, read the directions, determine the point value of the questions, and check your work. In the space below write a plan showing how you will use your time.

_____

_____

_____

_____

_____

You have a fifty minute class period for a test. Once again, allow the necessary time to preview and check your work. The test has fifty multiple choice questions and one essay question. The multiple choice questions are worth $1\frac{1}{2}$ points each and the essay question is worth twenty-five points. Plan your time.

_____

_____

_____

_____

_____

You have two hours to take a final exam. The exam has thirty multiple choice questions worth $\frac{1}{2}$ point each, twenty True/False questions worth $\frac{1}{2}$ point each, four essay questions worth fifteen points each, and fifteen matching worth one point each. Write a schedule to complete the exam. The test begins at 8:00 a.m.

_____

_____

_____

_____

_____

_____

_____

■ Activity 3. Essay Exams

Underline the key word(s) in the following essay questions. Circle the topic.

1. Describe Holland's Model of Careers.

2. Trace the development of the Industrial Revolution in the nineteenth and twentieth centuries.

3. Comment on the impact of stereotypes on the campus climate.

4. Identify the stages involved in reading a textbook.

5. Outline the advantages of career planning.

6. List the factors that influence memory and concentration, and show how these can be applied to your study habits.

7. Analyze the effect the Civil War had on the westward movement.

8. Review the procedures involved in information mapping.

9. A good listener has many qualities. Enumerate and explain them.

10. Discuss how you can overcome procrastination.

Name: _____ Date: _____

■ Activity 4. Test Taking Quotient

How well are you prepared for the tests you take? Read the following statements and rate yourself. Give yourself 4 points for Almost Always, 3 points for Usually, 2 points for Sometimes, 1 point for Seldom, and 0 points for Never.

_____ 1. I always eat healthy meals, get plenty of rest, and exercise when preparing for an exam.

_____ 2. I complete all my textbook reading prior to the week of the exam.

_____ 3. I arrive at my class a few minutes ahead of exam time to prevent having to rush into the room.

_____ 4. I avoid all last minute conversation about the test material with my fellow classmates.

_____ 5. I read all the directions carefully before answering any test questions.

_____ 6. I answer all questions on the test if I am not penalized for guessing.

_____ 7. I check the finished exam before turning it into the instructor.

_____ 8. I answer the easy questions first, then return to the more difficult ones.

_____ 9. On objectives tests, I am aware that absolutes can make a difference in how I answer the question.

_____ 10. I jot down key points that come to mind when I first receive the exam and when I first read the questions.

_____ 11. Before writing the answer to an essay question, I outline my response.

_____ 12. If I do not know the answer to a question, I mark it to return to later and move on so I do not waste time.

_____ 13. I prepare for exams by writing and answering sample test questions.

_____ 14. I prepare for exams by making and sticking to a study schedule several days before an exam.

_____ 15. I prepare for exams by reviewing my class and textbook notes throughout the semester.

_____ 16. I do not cram for an exam, and I do not try to learn any new material on the day of the test.

_____ 17. I always listen to all the instructions given by the test examiner before beginning to write the exam.

_____ 18. I check the point value for the exam questions and budget my time accordingly.

_____ 19. I preview the entire test before answering any questions so I know what I am being asked to do.

_____ 20. I am not distracted by other students during the exam.

_____ 21. I study for open book tests and take home tests in the same manner that I study for any other type of exam.

_____ 22. When using machine scored answer sheets, I always check to see that the number on the answer sheet corresponds to the number of the question.

_____ 23. I read each essay question and note the direction words in the question so I will know the kind of response the instructor requires.

_____ 24. I always review my returned tests and analyze any errors.

_____ 25. I attempt to answer multiple choice questions first in my mind before reading any of the options.

_____ 26. In studying for tests, I try to understand the material, see relationships, and make applications of the material I am learning.

_____ 27. I find out as much as possible about the test from the instructor prior to test time.

_____ 28. During the exam I never show my answers to any other student and never ask another student for answers.

_____ 29. In a matching exam, I use one list as a starting point and cross out items as I match them.

_____ 30. I always try to write neatly and legibly and show my work in an organized fashion.

_____ **TOTAL**

100–120   Test Wise: You probably do well on tests most of the time.

80–100   Test Adequate: You have mastered some test taking skills but could use improvement.

60–80   Test Deficient: You need to make some major changes in your test taking strategies.

Below 60   Clueless: Get Help Quickly!

■ Activity 5. Examining Your Test Taking Errors

Review a test you have taken recently, either from this class or another, on which you did not receive a satisfactory grade. Make a list of all of the reasons you did not do well on this test. Consider the quantity and quality of your preparation. Examine your errors. What went wrong? Write down everything you can think of.

_____

_____

_____

_____

_____

_____

_____

_____

_____

_____

_____

_____

_____

_____

_____

Review a previous test on which you got a good grade. List all of the reasons you did well on that test. What did you do right?

_____

_____

_____

_____

_____

_____

_____

_____

Now think about an upcoming test in one of your classes. What grade would you like to receive? How much studying will it take to get your desired grade? What exactly do you need to study to prepare properly for this test. List the things you will do to insure that you get a good grade. Be specific about how, when, what, and where you will study.

_____

_____

_____

_____

_____

_____

_____

_____

_____

Test Taking II

Thus far, this manual has covered goal setting, time management, note taking and reading. For many students, all that is left is rote repetition of the material. However, for effective students, testing is more than dumping material. It is more than the end point of a grading period. The actual act of taking an exam is only one step in the learning process. Advance preparation for exams is critical. Likewise, intelligent performance during an exam will often make the difference between success and failure.

■ Preparing for Exams

There are many types and purposes of college examinations. They range from the frequent short quiz through the hour exam, mid-term and final exam. The method of preparation for each exam must be adapted to the type and purpose of the exam. A wise student starts preparing for finals the first day of classes. No amount of cramming during the final week will make up for lack of study during the semester. Careful preparation of assignments removes the necessity for the frenzied type of last minute work in which many students indulge, but does not remove the necessity for intensive review before an exam.

Systematic review is effective review.

During the week or 10 days preceding final exams, a definite schedule should be set up so that all material will be covered in several sessions rather than in one long session. In reviews just as in other types of study, short sessions are much more profitable than long drawn out cramming sessions. Reviews should be directed at integrating knowledge, since isolated facts are difficult to remember, and often meaningless. Relating your collection of facts to the major points in the course will make it much easier to remember them and make them more useful. The following is a suggested procedure for test review.

■ Objective Exams

Multiple choice, matching, true-false and completion exams are considered to be objective exams. They usually have one specific answer and little variation in the answer is accepted. Some specific tips to taking objective exams are listed below. Of course none of these suggestions are more important than solid advance preparation. However, once you feel you have done all you can to prepare for an exam, a certain degree of "test-wiseness" is valuable.

From *Academic Effectiveness*, Second Edition by The United States Naval Academy. © 1994 by Eric D. Bowman.

Taking Objective Exams

1. When reporting for an examination pay very close attention the whole time you are there. Listen very closely to all directions. Ask questions if you are in doubt. Be absolutely certain of what is expected of you. Find out if there is a penalty for guessing. Are incorrect answers weighted more than correct ones?

2. Find out exactly how much time you have and try to estimate the amount of time per question or per five questions.

3. *Read closely* and pay attention. Reading directions and listening to verbal comments about the directions are vital to answering correctly.

4. While objective exams often do not allow enough time for you to read through the whole exam twice, at least glance through it to find any sections that might be more time consuming. *Plan your time accordingly.*

1. MAJOR TOPICS

Make a list of the major topics in the course. Skim assignment sheets, lecture notes, outlines of outside reading and quiz papers so you are sure that the list is complete.

2. SUMMARY

Write a summary or outline of related material for each of the major topics. Place particular emphasis on relationships among the topics.

3. SYSTEMATIC REVIEW

Go over the materials systematically. Apply more of your time to the subject in most need of work.

4. MOCK EXAM

Make out a set of probable questions. Keep in mind what you know about your professor's interests and points of importance. Using this mock exam is an excallent way to review after all the material has been covered.

5. REST

Adequate rest is essential. It is impossible to think clearly after an all night session of cramming. Many students find themselves unable to recall information which they had previously mastered. If at all possible, an early bedtime (before midnight) is critical for effective test performance.

6. RELAX!

Many students face every exam with such an emotional reaction that they find it impossible to demonstrate their knowledge. Avoiding last minute discussions is extremely important if you feel that excess anxiety interferes with your ability to perform. During exam week it is also wise to avoid post-exam discussions which may only give you a feeling of failure to take to the next exam.

5. Put off answering the more difficult or questionable items. Mark the ones you skip in the margin. Be sure and remember to return to these items before you turn in your exam.

6. Read all five choices, even when an early one seems to be the logical answer. Sometimes the fifth choice says: "All of the above," or "Two of the above," and you may only be partially correct by taking the first choice.

7. If there are five choices, read each one and cross out the choices you know to be definitely wrong. If in doubt, this narrows down the field and you stand a better chance of guessing right among two or three answers than among five.

8. Remember—almost everyone is going to miss questions. If you can avoid getting jittery over a number of missed answers and go on with a confident attitude, you will come out on top. Do not blow the exam by imagining that all is lost just because you missed what seems like a large number.

9. *Do not panic* if you see someone moving along faster than you do. If someone leaves early, he or she may have given up. Often the exams are constructed to last longer than the time given.

10. After you have left the exam room, have a debriefing with yourself. Jot down the topics covered in the exam, noting the sections of your textbooks that were covered. Note the strengths and weaknesses of your exam preparation.

11. Plan ahead to do better next time, especially in eliminating the kinds of mistakes that seem to have caused you some loss.

There are also ways to improve your performance on multiple-choice exams when your only alternative is guessing. The following suggestions are useful when all else fails.

When Studying Isn't Enough

1. You must select not only a technically correct answer, but the most *completely correct answer.* Since "all of the above" and "none of the above" are very inclusive statements, these options tend to be correct more often than would be predicted by chance alone.

2. *Be wary of options which include unqualified absolutes* such as "never," "always," "are," "guarantees," "insures." Such statements are highly restrictive and very difficult to defend. They are rarely (though they may sometimes be) correct options.

3. The less frequently stated converse of the above is that carefully qualified, conservative, or *"guarded" statements tend to be correct* more often than would be predicted by chance alone. Other things being equal, choose options containing such qualifying phrases as "may sometimes be," or "can occasionally result in."

4. Watch out for extra-long options or those with a lot of jargon. These are frequently used as decoys.

5. Use your knowledge of common prefixes, suffixes and root words to make intelligent guesses about terminology that you don't know. A knowledge of the prefix "hyper," for instance, would clue you that hypertension refers to high, not low blood pressure.

6. *Be alert to grammatical construction.* The correct answer to an item stem which ends in "an" would obviously be an option starting with a vowel. Watch also for agreement of subjects and verbs.

7. Utilize information and insights that you've acquired in working through the entire test to go back and answer earlier items of which you weren't sure.

8. If you have absolutely *NO* idea what the answer is, can't use any of the above techniques and there is no scoring penalty for guessing, choose option B or C. Studies indicate that these are correct slightly more often than would be predicted by chance alone.

■ Essay Exams

In general, essay questions are aimed at revealing your ability to make and support valid generalizations, or to apply broad principles to a series of specific instances. The question will be directed toward some major thought area. For example, in a literature course you might be asked to contrast two authors' implicit opinions about the nature of mankind. In an American History course you might be asked to discuss Madison's ideas on control of fraction, as reflected in the organization of the legislature of the United States.

Short essay questions are more apt to be aimed at your ability to produce and present accurate explanations, backed by facts. A sample short question in a literature course might be: "In a well-organized paragraph, explain Poe's theory of poetry." In a history course you might be asked to list the major provisions of a treaty, and explain briefly the significance of each provision.

Preparing for Essay Exams

1. Preparation for an essay exam, as for any exam, requires close and careful rereading and review of text and lecture notes. The emphasis in this kind of an exam is on thought areas.

2. It is often possible to find out what exam format the professor usually uses; a series of short answer types, one long essay, etc. You should ask the professor what exam format should be expected. This is not the same as asking what specific questions will be on the exam. In fact, many professors announce in advance the general areas the exam will cover—concepts, issues, controversies, theories, rival interpretations, or whatever.

3. Reviewing your lecture notes will also reveal which broad areas have been central to class discussion. Begin by asking yourself about the main concepts and relationships involved in the material you are reviewing. Review your notes with a broad view. Don't worry about detail at first. Review major headings and chapter summaries in your textbooks. Boil your material down to a tight outline form.

4. Once you have the main concepts organized in a thoughtful pattern, fill in the necessary details. On an essay exam you will be facing the task of arriving at a sound generalization and then proving it through the skillful use of detail. You must therefore have the details at your command. But remember, no detail is crucial. Select the details that best go to prove a concept.

5. Some students profit by making up sample questions and then practicing answering them. In a history course for instance you might test yourself by answering questions such as, "Explain what John C. Calhoun meant by the term 'concurrent majority' and compare his ideas to Jefferson's on majority rule."

6. Part of the groundwork for all exams is mastering the terminology used in the course. Getting this out of the way is critical.

Taking Essay Exams

1. When you first get the exam, look for the point value of each question. If the questions are not weighted equally, you need to decide how much time to spend on each question. Adjust your timing so that you allow longer time for longer answers. If necessary, borrow time from the short answers. If the point value is not listed you have a right to ask if all questions have equal value.

2. Read the directions and each question carefully. Try to understand exactly what is asked. Glance rapidly over all the questions before you start putting down your answers. An essay question always has a controlling idea expressed in one or two words. Find the key words and underline them.

3. As you skim over the test, note down key words or phrases for each question. This will serve to stimulate other ideas. Make the initial sentence of your answer the best possible one sentence answer to the entire question. Then elaborate in subsequent sentences. As ideas about other questions occur to you, immediately jot them down on scratch paper before they slip away.

4. Think through your answer before you start to write it. Use scratch paper for outlining if necessary. A little time spent on a brief outline pays big dividends for the few seconds spent. A planned answer saves you from a lot of excess words which are time consuming but worth little. If the question seems ambiguous, vague, or too broad, make clear your interpretation of the question before attempting to answer it.

5. Take care to write legibly, leave adequate margins and space your work attractively. Use good English and remember that neat papers tend to be scored higher.

6. Usually professors do not want your answer to cover everything you have learned in the course. Your essay answers should be organized, concise, to the point and with only those details needed to fill out a full picture. Do not try to reproduce the whole book. If supporting evidence is asked for, add as many details as possible.

7. Star or underline important ideas appearing late in the material. If information you have given in answer to one question ties into another, point out the interrelation. It may be worth credit.

8. Check off each question as you answer it to avoid omitting one. Reread each answer before proceeding to the next in order to correct errors or omissions.

9. Try to budget time so that you have time to proof read your answers before you turn in the exam.

10. *Use all the time allotted to you!*

CHAPTER 6

Relationships and Diversity on the College Campus

Students engage in many new relationships during college, including roommates, professors, friends and the all important significant other. As one's college career progresses, these relationships can go in many different directions. Many are healthy and will thrive and grow throughout one's college experience, while others may be unhealthy and should be examined and possibly terminated. So, what makes a relationship healthy, and what steps can be taken to help these relationships be a rewarding part of the college experience?

From *The Auburn Experience*, Fourth Edition by Deborah Shaw Conner and Wendi D. Huguley. © 1998 by Deborah Shaw Conner and Wendi D. Huguley.

Qualities of a Healthy Relationship

- Mutual respect
- Honesty
- Giving and taking
- Opportunity for support and growth
- Commitment
- Acceptance of the other person
- Recognize and adapt to relationship changes
- Effective communication
- Effective conflict resolution

You must first realize that relationships (friends, roommates, etc.) involve individuals who may view things differently, have different opinions or disagree at times. There are many qualities that help make these endeavors healthy. These qualities apply to any type of association with another person. Do your current relationships possess these qualities? If not, you may be in a situation that is unhealthy. Unhealthy associations need to be examined more closely and terminated if found detrimental to either party. One factor of relationships that is worth looking at more in depth because it is so essential to a good relationship is effective communication.

You are constantly communicating with others, whether the intention is there or not, and through communication you form, sustain and terminate relationships. Unfortunately, people are not born effective communicators. While some have natural communication skills, most have to continually work at being effective. The following table contains keys to effective communication. Each individual can find strengths as well as weaknesses. By utilizing your strengths and improving upon your weaknesses, you are well on your way to becoming an effective communicator.

Now that everyone is an expert communicator, we do not have to worry about conflict, right? Wrong! In relationships, conflict will inevitably occur. Therefore, another important quality to examine is the ability to deal with conflict effectively for the purpose of conflict resolution.

Table 1. Effective Communication Skills	
Talking	Ability to openly express information to the other person in order to send a message. Most people do not have much difficulty, but some have never learned to share.
Listening	Ability to actively listen to someone in order to receive the message being sent by that person. In a college atmosphere, this is often difficult to do. Active listening requires you to: 1. totally tune in to what the other person is saying without interrupting. 2. acknowledge you're listening by giving non-verbal cues. 3. put the speaker's ideas into your own words once they have finished. 4. question anything that may be unclear.
Understanding	Ability to comprehend the message received given the fact that actions and statements can take on different meanings for different people. This can cause misinterpretation which in turn can lead to misunderstanding. The key is to recognize and accept the differences in style, and to adjust and accommodate if needed.

Key tips to conflict resolution include:

- Introduce the problem specifically. Deal with the problem as soon as the conflict arises. If, however, the problem occurs at a stressful time in the quarter (midterms, exams, etc.), you may want to consider waiting until the stressful time passes.
- Everyone should have an understanding of the problem.
- Use "I" messages when addressing the other person. Own your feelings.
- Use effective communication skills.
- Concentrate on the present, not the past.
- Consider compromise and move toward a solution.
- Do not be a mind reader and do not assume.
- The conflict should end in a win-win situation where both parties feel good about the resolution.

Relationships play a vital as well as an essential role in every college student's life. By possessing the qualities of a healthy relationship, especially effective communication and conflict resolution, you are well on your way to gaining positive and growing relationships that will enhance your college experiences.

■ Alcohol

Alcohol is the drug of choice among today's college students, and many view college drinking as part of growing up, a rite of passage. Unfortunately, alcohol consumption has many effects not only on the person drinking, but also on those around that person. Whether an individual is or is not of legal age to drink, he or she will more than likely make decisions about alcohol consumption. Therefore, it is imperative that you as a college student be aware of alcohol, the effects it has on your body and the possible consequences that could occur as a direct result of drinking.

A Drink is a Drink is a Drink!!

Beer	Wine	Hard Liquor
12 oz.	= 5 to 6 oz.	= 1 to 1.5 oz.

Alcohol and Its Effects

The alcohol in alcoholic beverages is ethyl alcohol or ethanol. Ethanol is a depressant drug and is soluble in fat and water. It absorbs rapidly into blood and moves easily into every organ of the body. Ethanol stays in the body until it is oxidized. The slow and constant rate of oxidation places a limit on how much one can drink before becoming intoxicated. The rate is also precipitated by the following factors: weight, body size, body composition and gender.

As a depressant, alcohol is classified as a sedative drug. Circulating blood carries alcohol to the brain and disturbs the brain's work which in turn impairs other organs and body systems. Individuals may be affected in many of the following ways:

- Loss of judgment, inhibition and memory
- Loss of coordination along with speech, hearing and visual difficulties
- Impairment of breathing and heart rate
- Death due to respiratory arrest and cardiovascular failure

As stated earlier, alcohol has different effects on women as compared to men. Women can become more intoxicated than men from the same amount of alcohol, even if they weigh the same. This is due to men having more muscle on average than women. Muscle tissue contains the fluid needed to dilute alcohol. Women are also more susceptible to alcohol's influence just prior to or during menstruation.

Alcohol Abuse

For many individuals, patterns of alcohol use and abuse begin and are established in college. What starts out as drinking socially could turn into an addictive, life-threatening disease known as alcoholism. Certain signs and patterns will start emerging for those students who are having drinking problems (list not inclusive):

- Drinks to get drunk
- Drinks to handle stress or solve problems
- Drinks alone
- Drinks in anticipation of a stressful time
- Starts to see negative consequences that affect important aspects of their life as a result of drinking (i.e., school, family and friends, job, finances)
- Denies drinking
- Increased tolerance to alcohol (needs larger amounts to produce the desired effect that a lesser amount once produced)
- Dependence on alcohol (physical and psychological)
- Repeated episodes of blackouts (period during which a person is drinking and may appear normal, but later will have no memory of that period)

If you see these or other signs in yourself or a friend, you or your friend may be using alcohol in ways which are very harmful. You need to establish a healthier lifestyle or seek help if you feel that you cannot do it alone. You can get help from on-campus sources as well as local agencies.

Staying in Control

Individuals should assume responsibility to stay in control in regard to alcohol consumption. The best way to stay in control of any situation is to abstain from drinking. However, if you choose to drink:

- Know your limits and stick to them.
- Avoid punch containing alcohol—you don't know the amount of alcohol in it.
- Drink diluted alcoholic beverages.
- Drink slowly—don't binge.
- Avoid carbonation—it speeds up absorption rate.
- Eat before or while drinking.
- Avoid salty foods—makes you thirsty.

Although alcohol consumption exists on campus, the issue of drinking is your individual choice. Whatever your decision, remember the laws regarding alcohol consumption and the effects alcohol has on your body. Consider that the drinks you take can have a profound consequence on your life as well as the lives of those around you. The choice is yours!

■ Date/Acquaintance Rape

Sexual Assault—A forced sexual act against one's will. Forms include: stranger rape, gang rape, date/ acquaintance rape and incest.

"What is considered rape?" "It couldn't happen to me!" A question and statement such as these are all too common among college students. This section addresses the issue of sexual assault, specifically date/acquaintance rape.

Date/acquaintance rape occurs on virtually all campuses. Unfortunately, it cannot always be prevented. The more you know, however, the more likely you can avoid a high-risk situation. Forced sexual intercourse can occur to anyone regardless of gender or sexual orientation. Rape occurs on college campuses in part because most rapists and victims fall between the ages of 15 and 24 years. Ninety percent of campus rapes involve alcohol. Individuals need to look at things for which they each can take responsibility to avoid or minimize the risk of rape:

Date/ Acquaintance Rape—Forced intercourse by someone with whom one if familiar or has held an ongoing social relationship.

Table 2. Prevention Strategies	
Self-Assessment	Know wants, needs, desires and expectations for relationship before becoming intimate ■ Trust your instincts ■ Know your rights ■ Go to parties with friends and leave with friends ■ Study in coed groups, not alone with someone ■ Treat other person with respect
Communication	Clearly communicate your limits and wants verbally and nonverbally ■ Make sure that you receive verbal consent before progressing intimately ■ Listen to other's limits, wants and desires and respect them
Alcohol/Drugs	Know your limits and how alcohol affects your system ■ Do not exceed your limits and avoid drug use

We can all take the responsibility in trying to prevent date/acquaintance rape. Despite our best efforts, however, rape can still occur. As a friend or victim, there are certain steps to take if raped:

Physical Health

1. Get to a safe place if still in the situation—call someone you trust (friend, RA, etc.).

2. Call the Department of Public Safety or city police to report the incident, not necessarily to press charges.

3. Do not shower—go to a medical center—take a change of clothes and someone for support.

4. Have a rape kit done—other testing is optional (HIV, other STDs and pregnancy).

Mental Health

1. Because rape is a very traumatic experience, victims may think that the situation is their fault. Victims should be assured that they are not to blame and did not deserve to be violated.

2. Support the victim without questions and judgment throughout the entire process.

3. Counseling should be sought as soon as possible to counteract associated feelings of guilt and shame.

The last issue to address is the option of taking legal action against the accused. This is an individual choice, and there are different options to consider:

- Go through the school sexual harassment procedure—contact school officials for specific details of the procedures and consequences.
- Go through the judicial system—officially press criminal charges against the accused. In some states, first degree rape is considered a Class A felony and carries with it a fine of up to $20,000 and/or imprisonment of not less than ten years up to life (99 years).
- Consider both options.

Whatever the choice, one should consider that a rapist rarely rapes once. You may be just another link in a long chain of events.

Sexual assault, specifically date/acquaintance rape, is a violent crime that invades a person. This situation does occur on college campuses. It will be up to you to make yourself as well as others around you more aware of the issue. It is just as important to know what to do as a victim or as a friend if rape does occur. You can make a difference.

■ Sexually Transmitted Diseases

If you are between the ages of 15 and 24 and sexually active, you are more likely to catch a sexually transmitted disease (STD) this year than a common cold.

STDs do not spontaneously generate. One or both sexual partners must be infected with at least one disease causing agent. The agent may be a bacteria, virus or parasite. Individuals can be infected with multiple STDs simultaneously.

Table 3	
Most Common STDs	**Disease Causing Agents**
Chlamydia	Bacteria
Genital Warts	Virus
Gonorrhea	Bacteria
Genital Herpes	Virus
Trichomonas	One-Cell Organism
Crabs	Organism (Louse)
Human Immunodeficiency Virus (HIV)	Virus

Although sometimes difficult to treat, it is possible to cure STDs resulting from bacteria and/or parasites. While viral STDs are also treatable, they cannot be cured. That is, once infected with a virus, the person will always be infected and potentially capable of passing the disease on to others.

Quite often STDs produce few, apparently insignificant or absolutely no symptoms, especially in women. However, if left untreated, STDs can cause devastating disease and disability, even death.

> ### Possible Problems Stemming from STD Infections
>
> | | |
> |---|---|
> | ▪ Chlamydia | Infertility in Women & Men |
> | ▪ Genital Warts | Precancerous Cervical Changes |
> | ▪ Gonorrhea | Arthritis, Heart Disease & Infertility |
> | ▪ Genital Herpes | Cervical Cancer Risk, Death in Babies |
> | ▪ Trichomonas | Bladder & Urethra Infections |
> | ▪ Human Immunodeficiency | AIDS Related Cancers, Disease & Death |
> | Virus (HIV) | |

Different sexual behaviors carry various degrees of risk. The most dangerous activity is anal intercourse, followed by vaginal intercourse and then oral intercourse. However, some STDs do not require penetration in order to be transmitted, merely proximity to susceptible mucous membranes such as external genitalia.

The only way to ensure 100% protection from STDs is to abstain. Couples who are monogamous, those who have had sex with only one partner and mutually exclude all other partners, are not at risk. Of course, this situation requires considerable trust which may be unwarranted.

The only way to remain sexually active and reduce your risk of acquiring a STD substantially is to use latex condoms consistently and correctly, either with or without spermicide, depending upon the type of sexual activity engaged. This must be done each and every time you have sex.

To practice safer sex, you must become a savvy consumer. Be certain to read all instructions and labels carefully before use and hopefully before purchase.

Safer sex requires good communication between partners, a shared commitment to risk reduction and some planning.

> ### Seek Medical Attention If You Experience . . .
>
> | | |
> |---|---|
> | ▪ Skins rashes | ▪ Aches and pains in the joints |
> | ▪ Spiking fevers | ▪ A run-down feeling |
> | ▪ Itching or burning upon urination | |
>
> ▪ Learning your sexual partner has tested positive for a STD
> ▪ Blisters or sores, with or without pain, in or around the penis/vagina
> ▪ Profuse vaginal/penal discharge that is yellow or greenish in color and/or foul smelling
> ▪ For women, abdominal cramps more or less severe than menstrual pain

Contraception

If 100 sexually active couples use no method of contraception, 85 will become pregnant within the first year. Choosing a method of birth control is imperative if you are sexually active and heterosexual.

Features of Safer Sex Products

■ *Latex condoms made in America*

■ *Spermicides containing Nonoxynol-9 or Octoxynol*

■ *Lubricants compatible with latex such as saliva and/or silicon or water soluble lubricants like KY Jelly*

Generally, females of child bearing age (usually between 12 & 52 years of age) are fertile only 48 hours each month. This usually occurs mid-cycle and is known as ovulation. Ovulation occurs when an ovary releases a mature egg into the fallopian tube. If not impregnated, some two weeks later the woman loses her uterine lining and thus has a menstrual period. A woman's fertility is said to be cyclic.

On the other hand, male fertility is said to be constant (from about age 13 until death). The male's sperm can remain viable within the female's tract for five to seven days. If she ovulates during this time, fertilization can occur. Because the need for and knowledge of intervention is well defined in the female, most methods of birth control focus upon female fertility.

Regardless, men can play a significant role in the couple's selection and continued use of contraceptives. It is in the male's best interest to ensure that his female partner is using an appropriate form of birth control. With DNA tests, paternity can be established. Increasingly, the financial responsibilities of fatherhood are being enforced by the courts.

Methods of birth control generally can be grouped according to how they work by: (1) forming a barrier (physical and/or chemical) or (2) altering the endocrine system through artificial hormones.

Approximately 85% of all child-bearing age women can safely use any form of birth control with no ill effects. Some medical conditions, however, preclude safe usage. For instance, women diagnosed with liver disease should not take "the pill," and "the shot" is not recommended for women who suffer from migraine headaches. Together the woman and her health care provider can explore which options best suit the woman's health care needs. Ultimately, however, only the woman and her partner can decide whether to use a particular method as directed or not.

Products That Do *Not* Reduce the Risk of STDs

■ *Natural or lambskin condoms*

■ *Novelty condoms such as glow-in-the-dark or camouflage varieties*

■ *Latex condoms that "snap, crackle or pop" when opened*

■ *Lubricants containing oil—whether animal, vegetable or mineral (e.g., baby oil, petroleum jelly, body lotion, etc.)*

■ *All hormonal means of birth control such as birth control pills, contraceptive implants and/or injections*

All contraceptives have negative as well as positive aspects. For instance, some methods interrupt lovemaking more than others. The expense of certain methods may fit one person's budget better than another's. While effectiveness is probably very important to singles, it may not be that crucial to married couples. Circumstances and health needs change over time. Thus, couples and individuals tend to change methods several times during their reproductive years.

One critical factor that should be kept in mind when choosing a birth control method is sexually transmitted disease (STD). Only barrier methods can reduce the risk of acquiring a STD from a sexual contact. Only a combination of latex condoms and additional spermicide offer significant STD risk reduction during intercourse. Remember, pregnancy can occur only if sperm are present during ovulation. STDs, however, can be transmitted ANY TIME one or both of the partners are infected.

Believe It or Not, You Can Get Pregnant Even If . . .

- the woman is on her period (it's possible to ovulate).
- the woman does not have an orgasm.
- the couple has intercourse standing up.
- the woman is on the pill (especially in the first two weeks).
- the male withdraws from the vagina prior to ejaculation.
- a douche is used following intercourse.
- ejaculation occurs on the female's external genitalia.
- a contraceptive is used (nothing is 100% effective).

Table 4. Appropriate Contraception for Most College-Aged Couples			
Method (Type)	Failure Rate	Cost	Most Pronounced Side Effects
Pill (Hormone)	.3%	$15–$25/month	First 3 months
Implant (Hormone)	.1%	$1000+/up front but good 5 years	First 12 months
Injection (Hormone)	.1%	$40/3 months	First 12 months
Latex Condoms (Barrier)	10%	$.50 each	None
Latex Condoms + Spermicide (Barrier)	.3–1%	$1.00 each use	None
Diaphragm/Cap (Barrier)	15–20%	$22/good for 2 years & $.50 each use	None
Female Condom (Barrier)	15%	$2.50 each	None

Student Diversity and Social Awareness

■ Introduction

Welcome to a preview of the 21st century! Look around you. Have you noticed that in the last 10 years the face of America has changed dramatically? People don't look the same as they did when you were in grade school. Chances are the students in your college classrooms represent many different ethnic groups, religions, social-economic classes, ability levels, ages, etc. The population of the whole United States will be very different in the beginning of the 21st century than it was 100 years ago at the beginning of the 1900's. What do you think the reasons are for such a major change? What implications will all of these changes have on your future? Will you be affected? If you think you won't be, you'd better think again.

Before we get started, let's see what you already know, think you know, or don't know about diversity.

1. Based on the 1990 census, what percent of the current population of the United States is African/American? Hispanic?

2. What percent of the people in the United States are of the Jewish faith?

3. How many of the Fortune 500 corporations (top grossing companies in the United States) are headed by a woman as their CEO (chief executive officer)?

4. What is the average life span for citizens of the United States?

5. What percentage of Americans have or will develop a disability at some point in their lives?

6. The richest 10 percent of people in the United States control what percent of the nation's wealth?

■ The American Population

When we look at the United States today we see the results of hundreds of years of history. Who runs the country politically and economically, who gets along with whom, what actions receive what kinds of reactions all come from the foundations that were laid when this nation was formed.

Let's go back 150 years. What did the population of the United States look like? Where did all these people come from? Other than the Native Americans and Mexicans (a blend of Native Americans, Spanish, and Africans) most people were coming from the countries of western and northern Europe. What brought them here? Basically, there were two types of immigrants that entered this land: the voluntary and the involun-

From *The Community College: A New Beginning*, Second Edition by Aguilar et al. © 1998 by Kendall/Hunt Publishing Company.

tary. Those who came voluntarily did so in hopes of a better life, to take advantage of the "land of opportunity." They came to escape poverty, to seek jobs, to find a place where individual freedoms flourished, and to give their children something they didn't have in their homelands.

Involuntary immigrants were brought to this country to be slaves. Taken from their homes where they were free people, they arrived here as property. Their experience as newcomers to America was very different from other groups. They were separated from their families. If they established new families those, too, were subject to being sold apart. Husbands and wives could never be sure of a life together. Parents had no control over the fate of their children. They could not teach them the languages, cultures, and customs from their former lives. For most, there was no hope that hard work would bring a better way of life or prosperity to their loved ones. The vast majority were not allowed to be educated, and they received no direct benefit from their labors.

By the early 1900's the migration of people from western Europe gave way to an influx of people from eastern and southern Europe. As wars and famines made living difficult in their homelands, they found a place where property was affordable and available. In addition, the labor demands of this newly industrialized nation made earning a living possible if one had a good work ethic and a strong back. On the opposite coast, however, a different picture was emerging. Immigrants from China were populating the Pacific coast states, especially California. Originally recruited by the owners of the railroad system as a convenient and inexpensive labor source, they soon became the object of prejudice and discrimination. Americans who had come to the United States the century before seemed to forget that they, too, had been foreigners at one time. They feared that this new wave of immigrants would take their jobs, intermarry with their children, speak languages they didn't understand, or bring strange, "unAmerican" ways of doing things to their communities. Laws were passed to limit the number of people from certain "undesirable" countries who could move to the United States.

A study of the immigration laws of the late 1800's and early 1900's is quite revealing. The Chinese Exclusion Act, the Japanese Exclusion Act, and the National Origins Act were the first of many laws that effectively blocked Asian people from entering this country for more than 75 years. Most of the laws were not repealed until 1965. Throughout that time selective immigration was allowed based on social status, income, education, profession, and existing family members living in this country who were already citizens (though many groups were not yet allowed to become naturalized citizens). Also, certain countries were given more favored status for immigration. For example, when Hawaii became a U.S. territory, the doors were opened for its people to move to the mainland. When the Philippine Islands were needed to establish military bases in the Pacific, the doors opened for their people to come. Ironically, Mexicans were heavily recruited at that time to come to the United States to work in agriculture and for the railroads. Until 1965 the Mexican border was not patrolled to keep Mexicans out, but rather, to prevent Chinese from entering the U.S. through Mexico.

Still, despite the restrictions, political and economic factors around the world continued to make the United States a viable option for those wanting to start over. By the mid to late 1900's wars in Southeast Asia and revolutions in many parts of Central and South America created a whole new group of immigrants—the political refugees. Motivated by a desire to right some of the past inequities, as well as feelings of responsibility for protecting people whose lives had been jeopardized by U.S. wars, new faces were allowed to join the American mosaic. Their struggles to become a part of mainstream society mirror those of the voluntary and involuntary immigrants who came before them.

Immigration, of course, is only one way people come to this country. Birth rates are equally important as we tally the numbers of those living in our nation at the end of the 20th century. A look at the census data comparing population growth in the United States from 1980 to 1990 reveals that Asians and Hispanics are increasing at much faster rates

Population Census Data and Projections

Percent of Total

Group	1980	1990	2000	2020
White (Non Hispanic)	79.9	76.0	71.9	64.9
Black	11.7	12.1	13.0	14.0
Hispanic	6.4	9.0	10.8	14.7
Asian/Other	2.0	2.9	4.3	6.4

than ever before. Because of these trends, we're starting to see more of the "others" who make up this nation. In fact, if the population growth continues in its current pattern through the middle of the 21st century, the United States will achieve a balance similar to the world population.

So what does all of this mean to you? How will the population growth trends affect your life? They probably already have. The influences of our diverse society are all around you. If you travel, read, watch TV, go to the movies, listen to music, work, shop, eat, attend school, or interact in society you have no doubt encountered people who are different in some way from yourself and your family. What you need to understand is that the population will continue to become even more diverse in the future. How well equipped do you feel to handle the problems of living and working with these "others?"

■ Civil Rights in the 20th Century

Let's take a look at some of the gains made in civil rights through the last century. In 1900 if you were a woman you could not vote or hold political office. Jim Crow laws kept blacks and Asians (considered at that time to be black) from having much opportunity to participate in mainstream society. If you were a Native American, you were not allowed to become a naturalized citizen until after 1924 (never mind that your ancestors had lived in this country for centuries before it was the United States). If you immigrated from Asia, it would take even longer to gain the right to become a citizen. People with disabilities were routinely sterilized to prevent them from having children. In many states they weren't allowed to marry. Incidentally, most of those laws stayed on the books until the 1950's and in some states they are still state law! In Virginia, for example, people could be sterilized for any of the following reasons: being feeble minded, epileptic, an inebriate (meaning someone addicted to alcohol or other drugs), diseased (imagine how that one was interpreted!), blind, deaf, deformed, dependent (which meant an orphan, homeless person, ne'er-do-well(!), criminal, or insane person). Unbelievably that practice wasn't stopped until the mid 1970's. (Pfeiffer, David, "Eugenics and Disability Discrimination" from *Disability & Society*, Vol. 9, No. 4, 1994, pp. 481–499.)

It was a struggle for people throughout the 20th century to gain the rights that we take for granted today. The biases and discrimination that existed had to be overcome by each new group entering this country. For ethnic Europeans to blend in they often had to set aside their cultural identity, sacrifice their language, customs, traditions, etc. in an effort to become more American. Many changed their family names, or at least the spelling of

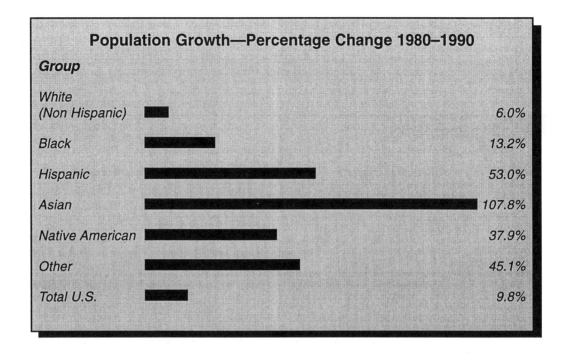

Population Growth—Percentage Change 1980–1990

Group	
White (Non Hispanic)	6.0%
Black	13.2%
Hispanic	53.0%
Asian	107.8%
Native American	37.9%
Other	45.1%
Total U.S.	9.8%

their names. Once they did this, though, it became easier to be assimilated and to take advantage of the opportunities of the mainstream culture.

On the other hand, it was not as easy for people from non-European cultures who immigrated here. They had the same problems as Europeans in giving up their cultures of origin, but also had the added burden of physical characteristics that could not readily be adapted. They faced a long and perilous struggle to gain the rights to participate fully in our society. You may or may not have learned about this in your history books. If not, think about why not. Regardless of who you are, your privilege is owed to the efforts of those who went before you to make this country more just and fair.

Despite all these gains, though, a major carryover from the 20th century is the difficulty this nation has in dealing with the issues of race, class and gender. We have made tremendous progress, as evidenced in the changing face of America, but there are still major inequities and problems. Your turn at the wheel of responsibility has come. What contributions will you make to insure that this country continues to grow toward equity and becomes a better place for your children, grandchildren, and future generations?

■ The Question of Race

How many races do you think there are? If your answer is more than one, we all have a problem. How did this notion that there is more than one race, the human race, come into existence? What purpose do you think it served to create a system that divided people into separate races? Who gained and who lost with such a system?

If you see yourself in the white race, you are in the smallest minority of people populating the earth. At some time during the 21st century this will be true in the United States, too. The projected population growth indicates that the "minorities" will be a numerical majority within the next 40 to 50 years. Does that idea bother you? Will you be able to live and work comfortably with a diversity of people? If the large numbers of people of color becomes a geographical (who controls the land) or political (who runs the country) issue, what are the implications? Do you form white supremacist groups? Do you create apartheid? Do you start the war of Armageddon?

If, on the other hand, you view yourself as a member of the human race, then you see the differences between human beings as being between your brothers and sisters. Eye color, skin color, and hair texture are all just surface variations. This world could be a better place if we treated each other as family, neighbors, and friends.

Social Class

One characteristic that has made the United States such a great nation is that most of its population is middle class. We don't have a large peasant class ruled by an aristocracy. However, in the last half of the 20th century some of the progress made by the middle class has been lost. Although there was a steady increase in the per capita income of Americans, when the figures are adjusted for inflation there has actually been a decline in quality of life and income of the middle class. The gains reflect an increase in the incomes of the upper class. If we were to illustrate the distribution of wealth in the United States, it would look like an inverted pyramid with the wealthiest 10% of the population controlling 80% of the country's monetary resources. So, the rich really are getting richer, and the poor really are getting poorer.

This is a cause for concern because the middle class is the only one that cannot pass its class status to the next generation. Children of upper class parents can inherit the family fortune. Poor parents have little material wealth to leave their children. That's why the middle class has to value education as its only means of holding on to its position or getting ahead. The following table shows how much income goes up as education level goes up.

With an increase in income level and social class comes better access to health care and thus, longer life expectancy. The opportunities available to you are also affected by income. Even personal safety is determined to some extent by where you can afford to live. So it is obvious that in this country your quality of life is greatly determined by your socioeconomic status.

Gender

Historically, the first discrimination was probably between men and women. This phenomenon was already present at the beginning of our great nation. It is evidenced in the preamble of the Constitution of the United States, when our forefathers emphasized that all men were created equal. That is literally what they meant—all **men**. (However,

Average Annual Earnings by Education	
without a high school diploma	$14,391
with a high school diploma	$20,036
with a bachelor's degree	$34,096
with a doctorate	$54,982
with a professional degree	$74,725

remember that in 1776 all men really meant all white, educated, male property owners.) The inequity was also evidenced by the more than 140 years it took women to finally get the right to vote and hold public office. This second class status is socialized within the very fabric of our nation and its people. We are still trying to overcome the notion that women are the weaker gender. It is very apparent when one looks at the inequities found within careers and salaries. If you take women in business as an example, we find that of the top 500 CEO's (chief executive officer) of the Fortune 500 companies, only two are women. That means that the other 498 are men. Males still make more money than women for the same jobs, with the same education level. Even though it's illegal to actively discriminate in this manner, it is still done. It is carefully concealed, but in jobs where there is not a straight scale, where negotiation is part of the starting salary process, men negotiate better deals than women. Why? It could be socialization, it could be women lack the confidence to drive the hard bargain, or it could be the person who does the hiring. More often than not the person in charge of personnel selection is a man. Plus, even today there is still the perception that men are the breadwinners, and therefore, should earn more. Think of how many men you know that feel threatened when their wife's salary is higher than their own. Are they proud of her, or do they become intimidated? How many couples would move to a new city because the wife was offered a better job?

Yet, although they earn less, women pay more for goods and services. When women buy cars, they pay inflated prices compared to men. They are charged more for services such as dry cleaning clothes, alterations, haircuts, and car or home repairs. Women are also more likely to be victims of domestic violence and physical assault.

In government we still see these inequities, despite all of our progress. Today there are four or five governors, a couple of United States senators, and two women on the Supreme Court. However, since women make up 51% of the population that's still gross underrepresentation. Women win elections at about the same rate as men when neither is an incumbent (person currently doing the job). But incumbents (male or female) win elections at a much higher rate than challengers. The few women in elected positions show, not that people won't elect women, but that women are still playing catch up for all the years they were prevented from holding such a position. There are far more male incumbents today because there have always been more males in office.

In the career arena we find that the major professions traditionally held by women do not have the earning power of male dominated occupations. I've heard the argument that women tend to work at less demanding, less difficult occupations; that their jobs take less skill and expertise than male dominated occupations. Is it really true that the person who cares for your child (or teaches your child to read) is worth less per hour than the person who unclogs your sink? In almost every occupation, though, you will find a wage gap between men's salaries and women's. The February, 1997, issue of *Working Woman* lists the differences in average salaries for men and women in the same occupations. Here are some examples from their 1997 Salary Survey:

Profession	Women	Men
accountant	$28,496	$38,844
computer systems analyst	$40,716	$47,320
university professor	$57,790	$65,080
elementary school teacher	$32,604	$37,076
food service supervisor	$14,872	$20,020
lawyer	$49,816	$60,892
registered nurse	$36,036	$37,180
orthopedic surgeon	$254,138	$305,453
real estate salesperson	$26,832	$33,800

What do you see when you look at these comparisons? We could try to explain this by saying that men have worked longer in these occupations, and therefore, have more experience. But that won't explain why men in traditionally female occupations such as nursing and elementary school teaching still have higher salaries.

Sometimes the issues are not as obvious. Bias can be found in something as subtle as providing less funding for medical research to cure breast cancer or other "women's diseases." Or, it can be a teacher giving the girls in class less encouragement to pursue higher levels of math and science. In fact, studies done by Drs. David and Myra Sadker showed that elementary and secondary school teachers gave more instruction and attention to the boys in their classes than the girls, even when the teachers were aware that they were being studied and were trying to be equitable. Girls were praised more often for their appearance and the neatness of their work. If they made mistakes, they were told that they were incorrect, but not given further instruction. Boys in the same classrooms were praised more for the quality of their work, and when they made mistakes were retaught the concept. The Sadkers also studied the students' self concepts. They found that girls had higher self concepts and expectations of success than boys in elementary school and junior high, but by the time they reached high school the boys far outpaced the girls in those same areas. They concluded that the socialization process still tells girls that there are limits to what they can achieve.

The Intersections of Race, Class, and Gender

Now that we've looked at these components separately, we have to examine how they overlap. One of the biggest areas where this overlapping is evident is income level. Your chances of being poor are increased by multiple factors:

Chances of Being Poor In America

	White		Black	
Economic Status	male & female	female head	male & female	female head
Poverty Near Poverty	1 in 9 1 in 6	1 in 4 1 in 3	1 in 3 1 in 2	1 in 2 2 in 3

From the table it is clear that for black females the poverty rate is much higher than for other groups in our society. The reasons for this are complex. The negative historical, political, and socioeconomic forces of this society place many black females at a very real disadvantage in regards to their access to education, health care, job opportunities, child care, etc.

Because we know from government census data that Native Americans have the highest poverty rate of **all** ethnic groups, if you are an unmarried, Native American female your chances of living in poverty are much higher than for any other combination in our society. That is not to say that Native Americans cannot overcome this barrier, but the speed they need to reach escape velocity is much greater than for any other group. How fast do you need to travel to insure that you escape poverty?

Yet we must be sensitive to the issues raised here. What constitutes success? We should be careful lest we in our arrogance try to put everyone in the same value system mold.

Sometimes the values of groups differ with the typical American notions of success (i.e., a big house, fancy cars, exotic vacations, six figure income, etc.). For some people self sufficiency and a peaceful life is better than the materialistic trappings of affluence. Acquiring more money is not necessarily the goal of all peoples.

History has shown that we have not been very successful in accepting people of different cultures and values. Perhaps in the 21st century we will be able to find a better way to accomplish this. We could not resolve this problem in the 20th century. An industrial society could not and did not coexist with a naturalistic society. It consumed all of the hunter/gatherer cultures and almost completely annihilated them. That is still happening around the world today as rain forests are being cut down to make way for industrialized farming, mining, manufacturing and housing. The consequences of these activities have long-range ramifications for our earth in terms of global warming, lack of oxygen being produced, etc. It also goes full circle in its effects on populations. As indigenous people (those who have been living there for centuries) are forced out, where will they go? Many will immigrate to the United States and start the cycle all over.

Will a post industrial society based on information and technology be able to find a way to accommodate people who do not value wealth and power? What do you think? What will happen to those people whose cultures differ from the norm? Will they be labeled "insane," and institutionalized? Will that make it easier to take their land and force them to relocate? One of my colleagues and I do an interesting class activity in our general psychology classes. We give the students a case study that describes a person's behavior. They are to decide whether or not to commit this person to a mental institution, and are given typical criteria for judging whether a person is insane. Although one of the choices is to ask for more information, few students in any of my classes select that response. The majority of the students always choose to commit the person. Those who do ask for more information are given a second sheet that explains the behavior in a cultural context as part of a centuries old religious experience. It is made clear that the person poses no threat to society. Yet even after this further information is revealed to the class, many still think the person should be institutionalized for believing in a religion with such "weird" rituals. Does that mind set help explain why history tends to repeat itself in terms of our dealing with people who are different?

■ Diversity Issues Today

Considering all of the changes that are taking place in the population of the United States, how are we going to get along better? Looking back at our track record from the 20th century, it wasn't great. It wasn't all bad, either. More progress was made between 1900 and the 1990's than in any of the previous centuries. But, then, it depends on whose perspective you take. If you were advantaged and now have to share that advantage, you might feel that you've given a lot! If, however, you've been struggling, trying your hardest and still find yourself hitting your head against the "glass ceiling," the progress doesn't seem to be enough. If it seems that others only have to put forth effort to succeed, and you not only have to put forth effort, you have to overcome the obstacles of race, class, and/or gender, you may still find the system very unfair.

I often hear comments from students who think that there is true equal opportunity in this country today. They say things like, "Slavery ended over a hundred years ago. Why don't *they* get over it?" or "Affirmative action gives all of *our* jobs to *them*. It isn't fair." First, we have to realize that although slavery became illegal in the 1860's, it wasn't until the 1960's that there were many attempts made to provide equal opportunities for African Americans and others. That wasn't so long ago! Some of you were not born yet, but most adults today can remember when separate and unequal was the norm. Affirmative action programs were an attempt to make career opportunities available to those who previously had been denied access to higher paying jobs. To some extent they were successful, to some extent they weren't. What kind of system would you devise if you were trying to overcome the effects of hundreds of years of discrimination?

Although we don't buy or sell people any more, we can still "enslave" them with our attitudes and actions. We pre-judge people based on some very flimsy external factors. Sometimes it seems that no matter what education or social class level a person of color achieves, they still face blatant discrimination. You'd have to get tired of people assuming you must be the chauffeur or the doorman because you are dressed nicely, but your skin color is dark. In many U.S. cities it's difficult to get normal services such as having a taxicab stop to pick you up or finding a place to get your hair cut/styled. An African American female administrator on our campus relates a common reaction from people meeting her for the first time. When they find out she works for the college, they immediately assume she must be a cook in the cafeteria. Why isn't their first impression that she has an advanced degree and is highly successful in her field? It isn't the way she dresses, speaks, or walks. Those cues would all point to a middle class, professional person. I could tell hundreds of such stories from people of ALL ethnicities. Unfortunately, no one group is free from showing prejudice and having an us/them attitude toward people who are different. To the extent that we cling to our ethnocentrism (the belief that MY group or culture is the best and the only one of value), we limit our own opportunities and those of others. What most of us really want is to be able to accomplish our goals based on our own effort, and not to be judged by external factors.

■ Perceptions Are Powerful

Sometimes our perceptions (the way we see and think about things) limit us. How do we perceive ourselves and other people? When you look at someone else, what do you see? When others look at you, what do they see? Is it the same as your perception of yourself? Consider the following discussion questions and be prepared to give your responses in class.

1. How are my perceptions of other people different than their perceptions of themselves?

2. How do my perceptions affect the way I behave around those I consider "different?"

3. How will my attitude and behavior affect my ability to work and communicate with others?

4. What changes do I need to make to help me work and communicate better with others?

5. What can I do as an individual to make positive changes in my world with regard to respecting other people?

Because perception is at least a two way mirror, it reflects how we see ourselves inside as well as how we are seen on the outside. We don't exist in a vacuum. We find ourselves in the crossroads of society and culture, shaped by those like us in the past, present, and future. We are the image of how we respond to the external world. Our self image is formed, in part, by the responses we receive from the external world.

Today, one of the challenges is that people's appearance is no longer consistent with their internal state. For example, we see people who do not dress or behave according to traditional gender types. We have fashion models, such as RuPaul, who make close to a million dollars a year cross dressing. If you did not know RuPaul was a man, you would assume he was a woman because he is strikingly beautiful. Our notions of beauty are being challenged. So too, our notions of femininity when we see women body builders who develop their muscles and physical strength. Such things cause us to adjust our perceptions.

People have different, and sometimes very curious perceptions about race. For example, the popular singer Mariah Carey has a triple heritage. She has, because of her parents' ethnicities, African, Hispanic, and European (Irish) roots. So, how do you perceive her? She seems to have the luxury of being able to shift her identity. Because of her fame and international celebrity, Mariah is a heroine to Hispanic Americans, White Non-Hispanics, Black Non-Hispanics, Irish Americans, and people from Ireland. At what point does this luxury become a conflict, though? Does a person of mixed heritage lack a true identity? What line should someone like Ms. Carey check when asked on a form to indicate her race? How much African blood do you need to be Black? One drop? If one of your parents is White and the other is Hispanic, are you White Non-Hispanic or just Hispanic? Which parent's heritage should you claim? Is there an American identity, or do people who can't trace their roots have an ethnic identity? Sometimes students in my classes don't know what to call themselves if they're "generic" White American. They don't feel they have a true ethnicity.

■ Ability Issues

What do you think when you see someone in a wheelchair? Do you think of them as less intelligent? Do you speak to the person they are with instead of directly to them? Do you act like they are also hard of hearing or cannot speak? Only as recently as 1990 have people with disabilities been given a chance for equal opportunities. If you have ever had to use crutches or a wheelchair (or travel with someone in a wheelchair), you may have a slight appreciation for what persons with physical disabilities experience on a daily basis.

What if the disability is not obvious? What about someone with a learning disability? Do you think it is a waste of taxpayer money to fund special tutorial programs for people with learning disabilities? What if you are the person with the learning disability? Many students with learning disabilities have had to endure years of suffering because parents, teachers, and classmates didn't understand or accommodate their disability. Schools today try to do a better job of identifying these students at an early age, but if you are an adult, you may not have been so fortunate. Our culture seems to value people according to two main criteria: physical attractiveness (beauty/youth) and intelligence. Psychologist and best selling author Dr. James Dobson calls them the gold and silver coins of self worth. Those people blessed with the golden coin of beauty don't have a problem finding friends and getting positive attention from other people. From the time they are a cute baby through their high school years when they are the most sought after boy/girl to date, they seem to draw people in with their good looks and charming smiles. Those with the silver coin, intelligence, may not be as popular as their golden classmates, but they, too, are recognized as possessing something of great value. Their parents and teachers are proud of them, they win awards, they feel good about themselves and what they can accomplish. Let's turn the picture over, though, and look at some of those other children. Imagine the child with a learning disability who cannot understand the lessons the way the teacher explains things. S/he receives no awards for outstanding performance. What is done to rescue the self esteem of this student? The child with a physical disability is often made to feel less than adequate in a society that worships perfection. Do we contribute to these problems with our perceptions of people with disabilities? Do we limit the things we think they can accomplish?

This is another area where we really might need to make some adjustments in our thinking. Sometimes life has a way of forcing us to rethink and readjust our attitudes. People who are able bodied and perfectly healthy one day can, through an accident or illness, become disabled in a matter of minutes. Your chances of developing some kind of disability in your lifetime are 50/50. What will you do then? Will you give up on life and wait to die, or will you continue to achieve and excel?

We have many examples of people who have overcome even extreme disabilities and accomplished great feats. Some have done more with their lives because of their disabilities than they would have had they stayed able bodied. One example is a woman named Joni Erickson Tada. As the result of a diving accident when she was a teenager, Joni became a quadriplegic who has no control over her body from the neck down. During rehabilitation therapy she learned to draw and paint by holding the paintbrush with her teeth. After she became well known for her art, she decided to tell her story in a book. That was the beginning. Today she has written several books, has had two movies made about her life story, has become an international authority and advocate for the disabled, is invited to speak at conferences around the world, runs her own corporation, and has a daily radio program.

We can probably all think of someone we know who has not let a physical or learning disability keep them from achieving success. I've listed a few well known people with disabilities. How many more can you add to this list?

Albert Einstein (scientist, inventor)—learning disability

Robert Dole—(politician)—physical disability

Cher (singer, actress)—learning disability

Whoopie Goldberg (actress)—learning disability

Franklin D. Roosevelt (President of the U.S.)—wheelchair user as a result of polio

Mary Tyler Moore (actress)—chronic illness: diabetes

Stevie Wonder (singer, songwriter)—blind

Ray Charles (singer, songwriter)—blind

Christopher Reeve (actor)—paraplegic, wheelchair user as a result of an accident

Heather Whitestone (Miss America, 1995)—deaf

Ludwig Von Beethoven (composer, musician)—deaf

Agatha Christie (writer)—learning disability

_____

_____

_____

_____

_____

_____

■ The "Isms" That Separate Us

Another step on our journey toward making this nation a more perfect union of peoples is to rid ourselves of the "isms." We've taken a look at the big three—racism, classism and sexism. We've also discussed discrimination against people with disabilities. Unfortunately, there are still more dragons out there to slay. So pick up your sword and let's go get them!

What are some of the "isms" that you've encountered? You may not be able to label them with snappy, one word descriptions, but you know when you've observed or experienced them. Perhaps it is prejudice because of religious beliefs. Perhaps it is related to a person's age. As a culture (and as individuals) we seem to have lost respect for our elders. We're too busy today to sit and talk with them and learn from their wisdom. Their slowness interferes with our fast pace and irritates us. Of course, ageism can go the other way, too. Sometimes teenagers are the targets of negative stereotyping. Or, what about discrimination based on a person's size? Have you ever noticed how people treat someone (especially a woman) who is very large, or someone (especially a man) who is very short? Those who don't fit the "norm" are likely to be ridiculed and rejected for being different. Whenever we put another person into a category labeled "other" or "not like us," it increases the chances that we will treat them differently than we would like to be treated. It makes it easier to rationalize away behavior that we would immediately recognize as wrong if it happened to someone in our family. Watch for other examples of the "isms" as you interact with people. Then, resolve to become part of the solution, not part of the problem. Be an advocate for justice, fairness, and equality through your own words and actions.

■ Diversity and Intelligence

Since this is a college textbook, let's talk about one of those fundamental educational concepts—the intelligence quotient or IQ. What is your IQ? Have you ever been given an intelligence test? What does your score mean to you? How do you perceive yourself intellectually? What is intelligence? Is an intelligent person someone who does well in school and who gets a high score on the ACT or SAT test?

People who have studied intelligence have different ideas about it. For example, Dr. Howard Gardner of Harvard University thinks that there are seven types of intelligence. Here is a brief description of each type:

1. Verbal/Linguistic—relates to written and spoken words. This form of intelligence dominates our educational systems. Most of what we learn in schools comes in the form of reading or writing. People who are high in this intelligence do well on tests and fit our typical notion of "smart."

2. Logical/Mathematical—has to do with reasoning, deductive thinking, problem solving, recognizing patterns, and working with abstract symbols such as numbers or geometric shapes. This intelligence is associated with "scientific thinking" and is a top priority in our educational system.

3. Visual/Spatial—relies on eyesight and also the ability to visualize things/places. It is valued in our culture by those who appreciate the visual arts such as painting, drawing, sculpture. It is useful in situations where you need to be able to use space or get around somewhere, such as in navigation, map-making, architecture, computer–aided drafting, graphic arts, etc. It is also an ability that is used in games or puzzles where you need to see things from different angles, and is often considered synonymous with a good imagination.

4. Body/Kinesthetic—the ability to express oneself through movement, do things using the body, or to make things. This intelligence is highly rewarded in successful athletes, dancers, and inventors. The ability to use the capabilities of the body, sometimes even without conscious thought, is another characteristic of this intelligence.

5. Musical/Rhythmic—being able to "tune in" to sounds and rhythms and use them to create mood changes in the brain. For example, creating soothing melodies, stirring marches, or stimulating raps requires strong use of this intelligence. Expressing yourself with sounds from nature, musical instruments or the human voice, or being able to differentiate tone qualities are more examples of this intelligence.

6. Interpersonal—the capacity to communicate effectively with others through verbal or nonverbal expression. Persons who have a high degree of this intelligence can work effectively in groups. They notice things about other people such as their moods, facial expressions, posture, gestures, inner motivations, and personality types. They can listen to others and make them feel valuable and understood.

7. Intrapersonal—probably the least understood and valued in our educational system, this intelligence deals with knowing and understanding oneself. It involves being able to analyze our own thinking and problem solving processes; being aware of our inner thoughts, feelings, and internal state. It is also a sensitivity to and understanding of spiritual realities, and experiencing wholeness and unity. Being able to perceive the future and contemplate our unreached potential requires use of this type of intelligence.

When you read through these descriptions, could you pick out your strongest type of intelligence from Gardner's list? Though all are valuable, why do you think the educational system only focuses on two of these types? When we look at the basic school curriculum, the only courses considered "academic" are those that rely on verbal/linguistic and logical/mathematical skills. The other intelligences might be addressed with a few electives or extra curricular activities, but those don't generally count heavily toward your GPA. What would happen if schools really made an effort to develop the other types of intelligences?

It is interesting to note that the types of intelligence least emphasized by schools in the United States, when developed fully, provide the greatest income potential and social status. Stay with me here and think about this for a moment. Actors, actresses, musicians, entertainers, world class professional athletes, those in the performing arts such as dance, or figure skating can make a **lot** of money in our society. In addition, people with some of these intelligences have demonstrated a capacity for greatness that extends far beyond their lifetimes. Let's consider a few examples.

OPRAH WINFREY is a successful talk show hostess who uses her interpersonal intelligence to make over $100 million per year.

MICHAEL JORDAN is a Chicago Bulls basketball player whose highly developed body/kinesthetic intelligence has brought him worldwide fame. He earns over $30 million a year in salary and even more for product endorsements.

KRISTI YAMAGUCHI is an Olympic gold medalist and world champion figure skater. She has perfected her body/kinesthetic intelligence and can earn over $200,000 for winning a single competition.

MICHAEL JACKSON has become one of the most famous and highest paid singers this country has ever produced. His use of musical/rhythmic intelligence from a very young age made him a multimillionaire before he was even in high school.

GLORIA ESTEFAN is an award-winning singer/songwriter who through her musical/rhythmic intelligence appeals to people of all cultures. She inspired many with her courage and strength when she returned to the entertainment world after a tragic accident and injury.

BILL COSBY has been on the top ten list of highest paid performers for years. His success is due to his well developed interpersonal and verbal/linguistic intelligences.

BILL GATES used his visual/spatial intelligence to develop a totally different concept for using computers. His Windows software programs revolutionized the computer industry and made him one of the richest people in the world. His net worth is reported to be $40 billion.

FRANK LLOYD WRIGHT was perhaps the most influential and imaginative architect from the United States, who used his visual/spatial intelligence to create some striking (and now famous) homes and buildings.

MAHATMA GANDHI is honored and revered in India as the father of that nation. Although he excelled in several areas of intelligence, he is best known for his intrapersonal intelligence that changed the course of history for his own country and had far reaching influence even in this country.

MAYA ANGELOU has achieved national acclaim for her work. She uses her verbal/linguistic intelligence to express what she experiences through her well developed intrapersonal intelligence.

While our culture values medicine and science, those occupations won't pay you a salary of $100 million per year. On the other hand, this country doesn't need more than one or two Oprahs. We do need thousands of doctors in every state, though. So how do you decide which intelligence to develop to its fullest potential?

An interesting pattern seen in these examples of the five intelligences not stressed by academia is that they provide a desirable path for minorities in this country to achieve great success. That's why a young person in the inner city will practice basketball for hours every day, aspiring to be the next Michael Jordan, rather than sit in the library doing homework. For many children the possibility of becoming a rap artist, baseball player, movie star, or TV personality is far more real than trying to become a famous surgeon, rocket scientist, or Supreme Court Justice.

The choices you make regarding your career and your future will depend on the intelligences that you have. Think about your particular strength. How have you been encouraged to develop it? Your decisions may be limited by the encouragement you receive and the role models you follow. Regardless of your gender, ethnicity, or social class you can overcome the barriers and obstacles in your path. Do it for yourself, and do it for all of your children, grandchildren, nieces, nephews, cousins, friends and loved ones who will come along behind you.

■ Summary

Diversity is a complex and multifaceted issue. Hopefully, this brief look has piqued your interest to explore the topic further. In closing, let's return to the questions asked at the beginning of the chapter and fill in some of the blanks.

1. When I ask my classes this question, the usual response is 35% to 40%. Despite what many people believe, though, African Americans make up only 10% to 13% of the general population. African American leaders have been advocates and spokespersons in the quest for civil rights and equality in this nation for over a century.

   About 8% of the population is Hispanic or Latino/Latina. Obviously, certain parts of the country have larger Hispanic communities, and thus more visibility, than others. Their numbers are increasing at a much higher rate than either African Americans or Euro-Americans. Their influence, politically and socially, is beginning to be felt with greater impact.

2. This is another question where people's perception is usually quite inflated. Students typically guess around 15% to 20%, but in reality less than 2% of the population are of the Jewish faith. It makes one wonder why so small a minority of people have been the objects of so much persecution and discrimination throughout history.

3. Linda Wachner, President, Chief Executive Officer (CEO) and Chair of Warnaco, a corporation that makes women's intimate apparel, was the only woman until this year to head a Fortune 500 company. January 1, 1997, a second woman joined the "club." Jill Barad is the new CEO of Mattel, making the toy manufacturer "the largest corporation, by far, to be headed by a woman—and Barad only the fourth woman to become CEO of a Fortune 1000 company" (Greene, Katherine and Richard, *Working Woman*, January, 1997, page 28). Wachner simultaneously heads Authentic Fitness, a sportswear company best known for making Speedo swimsuits. With her combined salaries, stock awards, bonuses, and other compensations she earns over $11 million. Barad, the first woman to make it to the top by climbing the corporate ladder, earns a total of $6.17 million including salary, incentives, stock options, and bonuses. These two head the list of top paid women in corporate America in 1997 according to *Working Woman*.

4. Your life expectancy is probably somewhere near 85 if you are a typical "white" female. It's one of the few places in our culture where women have the distinct edge over men. Men live to an average age of 80 years. If you are African American you can subtract about 10 years for males or 7 years for females.

5. By the year 2000, fifty percent of the population will have some sort of physical or mental disability due to the aging of the baby boom generation. Twelve percent of all people become disabled before age 55, and the numbers increase with age. Of course, at any age you have a 50/50 chance of becoming disabled due to an accident or illness.

6. The nation's wealth is controlled by a very small minority of its citizens. The top 10% have 80% of the resources, which leaves 20% of the wealth to be shared by 80% of the population. One cause of division among groups in this country is the fierce competition for that remaining 20%. The middle class is being squeezed, making its members less willing to share their limited resources with the poor. Because there is very little left for the lower classes, they have nothing to lose by seeking alternative (illegal) methods of getting ahead. This trend cannot continue without serious social consequences. Education continues to offer the greatest hope for escaping poverty and for maintaining the middle class.

■ Journal Assignment

Choose one of the following topics and write in your journal about it:

1. Think about an incident of discrimination or harassment that you experienced or witnessed. (The discrimination may have been based on race, ethnic group, religion, sex, physical disability or age.) How did the experience affect you and the other people involved? Discuss your feelings, values, beliefs, and actions after the incident. What actions can you take to reduce the occurrence of such incidents?

2. Reflect upon sex discrimination in our society. How has it affected you or a person who is important to you (e.g., your spouse, child, friend, or relative)? Write about the effect of sex discrimination on self-esteem, education, career choices, relationships, and leisure activities. What are your feelings about sex discrimination?

3. Write about the experience of someone you know who has a physical or learning disability. How has that person coped with the challenges of daily life, pursuing his or her education, participating in leisure activities, establishing a social life, or finding a job?

4. If you are a non-traditional student (more than 25 years of age), write about the sources of support that have encouraged you to attend and succeed in college (e.g., your family, a mentor, a friend, your own inner strength and motivation). What additional resources might you tap to help you succeed in college? How have you coped with the challenge of juggling the many roles in your life in addition to your role as a student? How do you feel about being an older student on campus?

5. If you are a traditional college student (less than 25 years of age), write about your experiences with non-traditional students. How have they enhanced your college education? Are there any disadvantages to having non-traditional students on campus?

■ Exercise 1. How I See Myself

Divide the circle graph below into wedges illustrating the various groups with which you identify. Make the wedges proportionate to the importance a particular identity is to you. For example, you may make pieces to show gender, ethnicity, religion, lifestyle choice, career choice, age, etc. The largest piece of the pie should reflect the main way you perceive yourself. If you would like you may color code your graph and include a key.

College Experience for the Nontraditional Student

What makes us think that we know anything about this experience? Well, actually, I (Joann) returned to college at the age of 38 to complete my Bachelor's degree after 18 years out of full-time college. I was a package deal with a 13-year-old child, house payments, and a LOT of anxiety. I was afraid my brain had turned to concrete. I was terrified that as sole support in my household, I was making a critical error in quitting my job to return to school. (What if I couldn't cut it and ended up jobless *and* without the education?) How would I manage my finances while in school? Would students be accepting of such an old lady? Could I conscientiously take care of my responsibilities as a mother while also being a student? And, my *biggest* worry of all: Would I be able to fit into those desks? (Childbirth and 20 years of ice cream have made me much more of a woman than I was the last time I was in college.)

The anxieties I had are common to students returning to college or attending for the first time. The "official" government definition of a nontraditional student is an undergraduate who is 25 years old or older. As I looked around me in college, I am happy to report I wasn't the only person in my class with grey hair and an intimate understanding of hemorrhoids. In fact, there are growing numbers of middle aged and older Americans entering college. Some colleges and universities have enrollments of over 50 percent of their student body made up of undergraduates 25 or older. Many institutions have a nontraditional student body that is larger than their minority student body. But there are others where the fact that you KNOW where you were the moment you learned that John Kennedy was shot means you're old enough to be the professor, because few of your student peers were born yet!

No matter what kind of institution you attend, there IS a place for you . . . it's the place you make for yourself! When I decided to return to college after almost two decades away from full-time scholastic pursuits, I was encouraged because the college catalog assured me that there were support systems in place to help nontraditional students adapt and cope with the challenges of college. I felt good going into this experience knowing that my college would be there for me, right? Well, I discovered an interesting thing about two weeks into my educational journey. I discovered that when I quit my job, I also ended up quitting many of my friends. My friends were almost exclusively connected with my work, and though I could still call them and talk to them, it just wasn't the same. I had lost an important support network. Never fear, however, I could go to the Student Development Center and they'd help me connect with new folks. That's what my college catalog said. So, I went. The teen-aged student assistant answering the phones and acting as receptionist briefly paused in her conversation with her boyfriend, just long enough for me to ask my question, "Who do I see about the services for nontraditional students?". As she popped her bubble gum, she not so politely informed me, "Oh, they had a group or something they used to do, but it's not active any more." I walked away stunned. My safety net was only a marketing tool!

The reason I tell you this story is not to evoke your sympathy, but to tell you that after that encounter, I went away . . . and got angry. I got angry enough that several weeks later, I put on my best business suit, and a pair of closed-toe pumps, and put my hair

From *Learning for the 21st Century*, Fifth Edition by Bill Osher and Joann Ward. © 1998 by Bill Osher and Joann Ward.

up in my best businesslike bun. I visited the Dean of Students and systematically out-lined why services to nontraditional students were important. I had gathered statistics about my particular institution, including the fact that we represented slightly more stu-dents than the identified minority populations, which received substantive special ser-vices from the college. I was nice. I was polite. I was assertive. I got shuffled off to someone else. BUT, because I'd persuaded the Dean of Students of the importance of some sort of support network, the delegated individual worked hard to help implement some new programming oriented towards the concerns I and other nontraditional students had.

The moral of this story is, if you don't like the way things are, change them. You can be the instrument of change at your college or university. You can also take advantage of the programs and services that may already be there for you.

Study and Learning

Just like younger students, you can also use the Learning Resource Center, tutoring ser-vices, and other centers devoted to assisting you academically. Had my brain turned to concrete? Well, no. I do think and process learning material differently now than I did at 18 when I was last in college full-time. I did need to obtain the services of a tutor to help me in a couple of subjects. The first thing you must do is accept the fact that you need help. The second thing you must do is go find it. Our large colleges and universi-ties have many programs available to help students be successful, but oftentimes you have to be a detective with the skills of Sherlock Holmes to find them. So, ask around. In some colleges, they're in the library. In some they are in the Counseling Center or Student Development Center. In others, you may find them located in learning centers in the dorms. Still others may have a stand-alone center designated for this purpose. If it's important for the young students to take advantage of this, it's doubly important that you do so. By the time you get to college, you've forgotten a lot about the "how" of how to study. The tutors at these centers will clue you in to systematic ways to approach studying so that your study time is spent as efficiently as possible. The effort you ex-pend is genuinely rewarded through good grades.

Studying and learning have been different this time around. At 18, I could shuttle infor-mation into short-term memory and take an exam and ace it. It's been different in my late 30's and 40's. Not bad; just different. The down side has been that I do have to study longer and with more systematic approaches. The up side has been that I learned the material, really learned it. What I studied in my teens has long since trickled away. What I've learned in the last six years is with me for all time.

Approaching studying has been different, too. Using distributed study (review, review, review) is the most beneficial approach. When did I do my studying, you ask? Well, I think it's important for you to solve this problem creatively yourself, according to your body clock, your responsibilities, your school hours. I am a morning person (yes, I wake up cheery) and perform best after having had some sleep. My brain doesn't take in ANY new information after 3 o'clock in the afternoon. So, I arranged morning classes as much as possible. I worked in the afternoon and was home with my child in the evenings. Study time: I woke at 4:00 or 5:00 AM to study. The house was quiet. I could throw in a load of laundry, sit down with a book or notes, and polish off assignments without any distraction from phones or kid(s). Is this the right schedule for you? Probably not. I think there are few individuals that would identify this as the "right" schedule for them. The point is to think creatively about how your biorhythms work, how you prioritize your responsibilities, and how to put it all together in a schedule that's a good fit for you. Experiment a bit until you find the combination that works best.

It's also important for you to sit down and develop some realistic goals. If you plan to have a perfectly immaculate home, attend every special event at your child's school, con-tinue to help with scouting, continue your volunteer work at the church or hospital, work part-time, be a stimulating and interesting spouse, and make straight "As," you are setting yourself up for less than success, and probably a "nervous breakdown." It is not humanly possible to do all that. (Although, in my experience, there are just enough superwomen and supermen around to make you feel inferior.) Before attempting classes, and after you start them, you must prioritize, eliminate, reduce, and consolidate so that only the essentials require your attention. I had to cut back on many of my previous outside interests. The house, though never a candidate for *Better Homes and Gardens*, dropped low enough on the priority list during the quarter that by the quarter break, a small backhoe seemed like a good idea. Meals had to be simplified. Schedules for my child as well as myself had to be adjusted constantly around study groups, project meetings, and library visits. I believe there is an unquestionable drop in the quality of your life while you are in school and working intensively on your studies. That's why it's important to use your quarter breaks to refresh yourself. Be selfish enough through the quarter to make time for yourself occasionally.

No one in my house died from malnutrition because we ate out more often or had more sandwiches at home. My house *still* isn't destined to appear in *Better Homes and Gardens* but no burglar nor any of the occupants of our house ever was killed or maimed by tripping over dirty laundry. And, I got to some, but not all, of my child's special events at school. I think she's smarter and better off for having come to class with me now and again. She certainly formed a more realistic concept of what kind of energy is required to be a conscientious student, for when she entered college herself. Remember, you can only approximate perfection; you can't have it. So, don't kill yourself trying for a goal that isn't even possible.

Remember too, that even when you try your hardest, even when you do everything the instructor asked for, even when the sun and stars are perfectly aligned, sometimes, you'll meet an instructor that just doesn't see things the way you do. You CAN personalize it and obsess about it endlessly. You can eat away the majority of your stomach lining with unending ruminations about how to handle a certain class situation or alter a professor's opinion about your grade. This can happen to anyone. Grades are not who you are. You are not a "B" or a "C" or even a "D." If you feel that you have genuinely been treated unfairly by your professor, or that you have been subjected to some sort of discrimination, then clearly others, such as the Dean of Students or department chair, need to be made aware of your concerns. However, sometimes there just is a problem with personality and you may have to "build some character." These are moments where you will have to decide how much energy you want to invest in "fighting" the problem. Talk to your professor first. Attempt to calmly straighten out any inequities you perceive. There are weights and balances in any educational institution, but think carefully before using them. My point here, however, is that you may have a whole string of "As" and "Bs," only to meet Professor Death, who hates nontraditional students, especially you (because you remind him of his mother/father). When that kind of chemistry occurs, it is sometimes best to "gut it out" and know that you are still a good person, despite the personal views of this one individual. Perfectionism in grades is a sure passport to ulcers. You are no smaller in stature for accepting the fact that there was no way possible to completely satisfy this particular professor. You just pick up, go on, and do the best you can in the next classes. It's not a good feeling at all, and there is no comfort in all that "character" you built, but sometimes reality is cruel. As Lilly Tomlin's character, *Edith Ann*, would say, "And, that's the truth!"

Finances

It helps if you are independently wealthy going into this venture. However, if you're not, you can still survive with good planning. Talk to your financial aid counselor or director BEFORE you begin your educational journey. They can give you vital information about how much you can earn in a year before you become ineligible for govern-

196 ■ RELATIONSHIPS AND DIVERSITY ON THE COLLEGE CAMPUS

ment grants and so forth. If you plan to work a part of a tax year before beginning college, you'll want to get as much information as possible to ensure your application for aid will be granted.

If you are planning on going to school part-time, there are still programs available. With luck, your college/university financial aid office will have some evening hours available for students such as yourself. If they do not, and you must take time off of work to visit them, be sure to let them know that it would help you and other students to have that office open at least one evening each week. As long as you are perceived as someone who is not being critical, but merely mentioning something you'd find immensely helpful, your comments are more likely to be heard. Once again, I encourage you to consider yourself as an instrument of change. You can encourage others to understand your perspectives and respond to them. Just don't expect the response to occur overnight!

You can also be a financial aid officer of your own. You can go out and find scholarships. I was alert and listened all the time for opportunities. I overheard some students in a hallway saying, "I could never accept money from an organization like that!" I interrupted and asked what organization it was. Then I went right over to Financial Aid and applied for that scholarship. I could accept their money. And I did get a scholarship from (of all organizations) my state's Beer and Wine Wholesalers Association. While one student had an ethical problem accepting money from these folks, I didn't. I knew I was using it to further my education. I did not have to drink to get the scholarship. I only had to endorse a check.

I also applied for and got a substantive scholarship from an honor society that inducted me. I got money from an organization that I belonged to. I got scholarship money from an organization called The Philanthropic Educational Organization (PEO) that specializes in scholarships for single women returning to college as nontraditional students (For more information about how to get in touch with a local group, write to: PEO Sisterhood, 3700 Grand Ave., Des Moines, IA 50312). I had never heard of PEO until a friend mentioned that I might qualify for one of their scholarships. I made it a point to follow up on it and did get support for graduate school. I got money from my college's scholarship foundation.

The point is, while there is little scholarship funding for graduate students, a substantive portion of my two graduate degrees was financed through scholarships. I was able to do that because I made good grades, was active in leadership positions, and constantly nosed around to see what opportunities there were for scholarships. So, being your own advocate is important to your financial success in college.

Jobs

Keep in mind that even if you don't work full-time you might have to work part-time while in college. I did. I was an administrative office manager making close to $13/hour in my full-time job. Even though I'd quit full-time work to return to college, I still needed some money for pocket change . . . lunch money, if you will. I decided I wouldn't mind being a student assistant if I could just go in, do a job, and get out without someone feeling like they had to stand over me and give me close supervision. So, I walked up to the professor I most liked and felt I'd probably get along with and said, "Could you use a student assistant, if that student assistant could type 80 words per minute?". Amazingly, he could. Don't tell Bill (my co-author), but it's the best job I ever had. I washed rocks. Yes, you read that right, I washed rocks. I worked in the Geology Department and as a part of a research project, I systematically prepared an acidic broth which I submerged rocks in, and then when they'd partially dissolved in a day or so, I'd go back and rinse the acid off, sieve the residue, save some, and throw the rest in to sit in the acid for another few days. I often typed proposals, ran errands, or simply babysat my professor's children. There was no pressure. He understood when I needed to take a day off to study for mid-terms, and no one hassled me about anything. It was great! I had no clothing expense because what do you need to wear special to wash rocks? Certainly not business attire. I didn't have to commute to anywhere across town; I was already there on campus. I earned something just over the minimum wage, but it was a low stress job with an understanding boss. For me, that was just what I needed. Don't overlook such opportunities even though the wage rate is much below what you are used to. When you consider the "commute" time, the fact you can report to work in cutoffs, and that your boss will be understanding when you have a big test coming up, the benefits can outweigh the underwhelming salary.

Keep in mind that your college/university probably also has a placement or career office. Jobs for part-time positions are often posted in a common area so that you can review opportunities. Even if jobs are not available in an area you have interest in, go in and ask one of the career counselors. Recently, my daughter, who is now in college herself, went in to talk to her placement counselor to help her get a summer job or internship in her particular field. While there wasn't anything available on the posted positions, her counselor was able to network her to local resources who have jobs in her field. Never underestimate the power of networking with college professionals AND your student peers. Don't forget that they are sources of information about career opportunities and part-time jobs, too.

Student Peers

When I entered college for my second time as a full-time student, I was afraid that I'd be alone in a sea of acne and raging hormones. I wondered if I was going to be able to have any friends at school. I should not have worried. Despite the fact that I am an EXTREME introvert, I still had many young people and other nontraditional students as friends. Yes, it was important for me to have the support and encouragement of the other nontraditional students, but don't rule out the support and encouragement you can get by befriending young people. Many of them are serious about their studies and are very willing to be a part of a study group. They will work with you on class projects and barter skills (like typing for auto work). Serious students will be happy to collaborate with you because your life skills put you closer to understanding the professor. You have access to resources they do not. For instance, I had good ideas about how to make a business presentation for a Mass Communication class, because I'd already done and seen many more such presentations than my younger cohorts. I also discovered that young people away at college sometimes like being around someone they can talk to about college issues, and get an older person's perspective. Basically, they sometimes want a little mothering or fathering from someone that isn't in a position to judge them or make them feel inadequate or inferior or as if they might be disappointed. Friendship is a two-way exchange. And there are ways that you can assist your younger student peers just as much as they can help you. Be open to those opportunities. Make them yourself by asking others to join you in group study to review for tests or to brainstorm for class projects. The payoff is worth it.

Children

I say children, because it's not always a simple case of child care, although that can be a lot of a nontraditional student's challenge. Children will influence your college experience tremendously. Is there any other aspect of your life they don't?! So, you will have to take your child(ren) into account as you move through your college experience.

Some colleges and universities have on-site child care centers. Most do not. Some ways to get around the hassles of child care are to trade child care with another student. Post signs around campus immediately following your next quarter registration. If you get all your classes in the morning, you could babysit a classmate's progeny while they take afternoon or evening classes. A better plan is to find someone before registration, and to approach signing up for classes as a logistics problem so that you can be certain one or the other of you is home to take care of the children.

Some parents with older children are more interested in being home to put their child(ren) on the school bus in the morning and greet them as they get off in the afternoon. Sometimes you can arrange a trade-off with someone so that you can see their child(ren) off in the morning, if they can greet your child(ren) in the afternoon. Networking is the solution to this, and the only way to approach it is to talk to everyone, post signs in approved campus locations, and perhaps even take out a small ad in the college paper. Most college papers have very inexpensive ad space, especially for their own students. Be certain you interview any prospective person carefully so that you are certain you feel comfortable and safe about them being with your child(ren).

Some parents worry about what to do when a child is ill or if you have a teacher's work day. My child was 13 by the time I went back to school, but I saw many other moms and dads with younger children accompanying them to class. If you have an understanding instructor, and your child can play QUIETLY at a desk with an Etch-a-sketch™ or color, you may be able to take them with you. I saw many moms and dads who packed Cheerios™, some raisins, and a banana or two, along with Matchbox™ cars and Barbies™, so that they could still attend their classes.

Obviously if your child is too ill for school, (s)he probably shouldn't be with you at college. In cases like this, call your professor. Explain the problem—prior to class time, if at all possible. There are certainly a small proportion of insensitive individuals out there that "accept no excuses," but you will find that the majority of professors will help you in your efforts if you are honest with them, and don't use this kind of situation as a convenient excuse for turning in work late. Sometimes your grades will suffer because you have to make choices between home and school. Sometimes you might end up making a "B" instead of an "A" because you missed a test the prof wouldn't let you makeup. Those instances are rare in my experience. And, ultimately, children are our treasures. The time you invest in taking care of them will be more important than any grade you may earn.

Older children may actually enjoy hanging out with mom or dad. Mine was able to see the show-and-tell slides in my Human Sexuality class as a by-product of a teacher work day. Now she knows a lot more than I ever did about sex at her age! She also got to have quiet time to read in the college library, hang out at the pool, and bowl her way to perfection. Many of the recreational resources open to you as a student are also open to your children and spouse.

Your example to your child(ren) of the importance you place on your education is a powerful educational tool in and of itself. Not only will your child(ren) respect you more, but they will see, firsthand, the importance and purpose of attending college as they watch you work toward your own life goals. Yes, it's a bit funny sounding the first time you tell your child(ren)'s coach, "Sorry, we can't stay and chat. I have to get home to do MY homework." In the long run, the struggle will be worth it.

■ First Generation

There is another aspect of going to school that I think it is helpful to talk about. Students who are the first in their family to attend or complete a college program, are often referred to as first generation students. While my mother was college educated, I was the first person in my father's family to ever complete college, and I was the first person on either side of my family to get an advanced degree. I had not anticipated this could create problems in family relations, but it did.

I am proud of my blue collar roots. My father worked a variety of jobs but the last 15 years of his work life, he was a security guard. My brother drives an 18-wheeler. We've never been affluent or traveled in high socio-economic status circles. My relationship with both my father and brother suffered after I went back to college.

The television show *Frasier*, gives us a peek at two brothers who grew up to be affluent psychiatrists. Presumably they were put through medical school by their hard-working father, a beat-pounding cop. Frazier and Neils have sophisticated tastes, a home and apartment straight out of *Architectural Digest*, and Italian-designed suits. In Frazier's beautifully, and artfully appointed apartment sits his father's old, polyester-upholstered, plaid recliner. It sits there, held together affectionately with duct tape and perfectly formed about the elder Crain's anatomy. The contrast between the apartment furnishings and the recliner are the perfect metaphor for what can happen in family dynamics. It is important to remember that the elder and junior Cranes do coexist happily, if with some hiccups. Everyone's family situation is different and college is not a recipe for disaster within your family. Just be aware that you and your family might experience some hiccups too.

You will be exposed to a breadth of ideas that no one in your family has perhaps ever examined in quite the way you are now. You will mingle with people who are drastically different than the people you came from. You will look at social and political issues, informed through the lenses of history glasses. You will immerse yourself in a community where being open is preferred to being closed . . . where new ideas and new concepts can be genuinely examined before adopting or discarding them. You are likely to learn about the earth, physical principles, and biological functioning in ways that sound bazaar and foreign to your family.

For some, this will not be a bad thing. For others, family members may make value judgments. For example, my father has uttered these words, "College ruined you." My brother has said, "You're not one of us anymore." My father's dream was that his son would go to college. He hasn't valued his daughter getting an education. And, because I do see the world differently than he does, he feels I've been ruined by all those "liberal educators." (Ruined means I didn't vote the same ticket he did.) For my brother, my expanded vocabulary, and differing values about people, culture and ethnicity mean that we don't share the same value system anymore. He is right. I am not one of them in quite the same way.

First generation can also refer to students who are the first generation in the U.S. My mother was an immigrant to this country, and my father is the first generation born here on his side of the family. So, I come from people who came from somewhere else. There are important issues around that which you need to be conscious about.

For example, if you are Hispanic the good news is that the rates of Hispanics who have completed college has grown over fifty percent. The bad news is that it means instead of Hispanics graduating from college as 2.5 percent of the total numbers enrolled, you've risen to 3.4 percent. It means that depending on where you are, you may look around and not be able to see many people who look like you or share your holidays and customs. A 1993 study (Chahin, J. *Educational Resources Information Center*, Hispanics in Higher Education: Trends in Participation, ED357911, Mar.93.) points out the sad reality that Hispanics have not participated in higher education in anything like their proportional representation in the general population.

Laura Rendon of Arizona State University in Tempe, now with a Ph.D., talked to me about her first generation experience. She is the first generation in this country, and as you can see in the story, the first in her family to enter higher education.

"My parents never got beyond the second grade. They understood the value of education, but they never thought higher education was for us, for working class Chicanos whose lives had nothing to do with the world of college.

"I remember when I was getting ready to leave my hometown of Laredo, Texas to work on my doctorate at the University of Michigan. A few weeks before I left, my mother developed an intense pain in her chest, accompanied by a fever. I took her to a number of doctors, and even to a hospital in San Antonio, but test after test revealed no serious problems. In angst, I left for Michigan thinking that if she got seriously ill, I would come back to Laredo and enroll at the University of Houston, where I had also been accepted.

"My mother had one more pain episode after I left and it has not reappeared since then! One time I asked her why she cringed at the idea of me leaving. 'Tengo miedo, hija.' ('I'm afraid.') she replied. Knowing nothing about the world of college, my mother was afraid I would come into harm's way and there would be nothing she could do to help me. Today, both she and my father are very proud of me. They get a kick out of introducing me to their friends by saying: 'This is my daughter. She's a doctor.'"

The anxiety and worry that both Laura and her Mother experienced are very real and very difficult issues to work through and every family does it differently. If your family dynamics are changing, sometimes the best thing you can do is to wait it out like Laura did, and just see if things sort themselves out.

Many first generation students find that whether they are African-American or Latino/a or Vietnamese, education has a different meaning for them and their families than it does for an Anglo. Education is not as valued in many ethnic communities. For example, some African-American students find it difficult to obtain family support for their educational goals, because the family feels they are shirking responsibilities . . . hiding in academe when they need to be out working and contributing to the family income. When you feel this happening, it is important for you to find a support system that does act as your cheering section. If your family has their doubts, or even downright discourages your ambitions, find a cheerleader who will urge you onward.

■ Cheerleaders/Mentors

My cheerleader and mentor was an instructor who expressed confidence in my ability from the first time I ever met her. I was filled with doubts and anxiety. Anne, however, has been a stalwart help to me. She has listened to me cry when the chips were down, and she has rejoiced in the triumphs of both myself and my child. I have celebrated the holidays in her home and shared the warmth of her hearth, when my family situation became too complex to contemplate spending the holiday with them. This person pushed me upward when I didn't know for sure what direction to move in. She gave me opportunities to test myself, and guided me through them. Without her confidence and urging I would have still made it through school, but I am definitely a richer person for having had her support and encouragement, and I hope that in some small way I have enriched her life too. You need to find your own cheerleader(s). It might be another student, an instructor, coach, even your boss, but don't turn away from those who reach out in small ways to pull you up. When you do reach the top, you can, in turn, turn around and pull another up to pay the debt.

Sometimes we need our school lives enriched by a cheerleader, and sometimes we just need a cheerleader for helping us keep our home life intact. For a non-traditional student with family responsibilities or working obligations, you may need to find a cheerleader who will support you not necessarily in your school efforts, but in keeping your home life intact. The person who comes over before mid-terms and feeds the kids so you can sleep or study would be one example. Maybe you have a friend or family member who cooks you an occasional meal and drops it off, or invites you over. Sometimes it is just a friend you can call at any hour of the day or night and moan about bills and school. Some years back another couple were the cheerleaders for me and my husband. We lived very frugally and often by the end of the pay period the kitchen cabinets were pretty empty. Joe and Rada would have beans and we'd have ground beef, and together we could all play chess and have chili. Together we supported one another by having some fun and sharing what we had in the way of foodstuffs. More than food was on the table. Encouragement, a common bond, was there too.

Stereotypes continue to attribute negative characteristics to some populations, undermining self-confidence. If you don't believe you're college material, you may give up too soon when you encounter difficulties. Your cheerleader can help you through the rough periods.

■ A Word About Developmental Classes

Many non-traditional students have to take developmental studies before they are permitted to attempt for-credit course work in mathematics or English. This can be very discouraging and frustrating. First, it is somewhat galling to have to pay to take classes that will not count towards your degree. Courses that can be very rigorous and very challenging at that! Second, these are courses that often test the metal of non-traditional students, and temper them with the fire of frustration. Some issues to remember if you are caught in this situation are: (a) you have to take the classes; there's no way around it. You have to do it and do it successfully; (b) there are usually campus resources in place to assist you. If you are taking a developmental class and are not performing up to your expectations, it is important to talk to the instructor frequently. Use *every* resource at your disposal to help you. If your college/university has a learning resource center, use it. If there is tutoring through your Student Development Center of the Student Affairs office, use it. If you must pay for tutors to help you, do it. It is part of getting through.

Make sure you thoroughly understand your college/university policies regarding developmental course work. Often there are requirements you must meet within certain time limits. There can be limits about taking a "W" in a class. There are sometimes requirements about completing the course work before you reach a certain number of quarter/semester hours. Don't get in trouble by being naive. Ignorance of the law is no excuse, and ignorance of your college/university regulations will only cause you headaches.

Language skills may inhibit success, but they don't ensure failure either. You can compensate for inadequate language skills in many ways. First and foremost, find an ally, someone who is your friend and who does have good language skills. Have that person proof all your assignments before you turn them in. Many colleges have language labs where students are employed to help you with papers and proofing. Use those services. Sometimes a professional staff person will help you even though it is not technically their "job." You might, for example, talk to someone in Student Affairs, or a graduate student in the English department office, or even an interested instructor in your major, and see if they will help you or assist you in finding someone who will help you.

You are not stupid or ignorant because you need to take developmental classes or use the language or math labs. You are savvy to use these resources. They are provided to help you succeed. The only stupid thing is not to use these resources because of pride. Pride never got someone an "A" if they were struggling. Pride contributes to many individuals' downfalls though because they don't want anyone to perceive them as stupid or inadequate. Don't let pride be the stumbling block that stands between you and success. If you need a tutor, get one. If you need someone to proof your writing, ask someone to help you. Ask several someones if you must to find the person who will take the time to critique your style and grammar. It is important to have confidence in the work you turn in. Neatness counts, but so does accuracy, and your grades will shoot up if you can turn in work that is not only neatly typed, but grammatically correct and free of misspelled words.

Reading speed can sometimes be a problem too. Slow readers are not anxious to run right out and get *War and Peace* to read. And, in fact, in some literature courses you can end up reading *War and Peace*—or a similar number of pages! And you have to do it in a week or two! This can be very daunting if your reading speed is slow, and if you have any problems with comprehension. The first thing you can do to improve your reading speed is this: read. Yes, it is an awful remedy for slow readers. But the more you read the faster you will get. Subscribe to a popular magazine like *Newsweek* which has easy flowing writing, coupled with attractively illustrated and interesting articles. Read it every week. It will increase your vocabulary and you will become an expert in world affairs. It will broaden your knowledge horizons, while giving you practice in reading.

Students that have a hard time with comprehension sometimes can do better if they listen to the text. You can read a text once into a tape recorder. You'll retain some of the material, but then you can go back and listen to what you read, and for some people that will increase their ability to recall the details of the material.

If you have excessive difficulty and you believe that your reading comprehension and speed are excessively below the ability of your peers, you might approach your Disability Student Coordinator, Counseling Center, or Student Development Center to see if they can screen you for a hidden learning disability. Many people do not discover their learning disabilities until their college experience. And, while you will still have to successfully complete the requirements for a course, if you are discovered to have a learning disability, there are accommodations the college can provide for you to reduce your stress, and increase your chances for academic success.

■ Full-Time/Part-Time or No-Time?

Everyone has differing levels of ability and energy. At different points in my life I (Joann) have also had more and less in the way of energy and ability. I have worked three part-time jobs and gone to graduate school full-time. I have also found that full-time work and full-time undergraduate school was incompatible for me. I know that many people can and do accomplish this successfully. It just wasn't for me.

You have to look at your life, your job and your family situation to determine how to approach school. One reason that non-traditional students are considered at higher risk is because they are more likely to go to school part-time and part-time students are less likely to graduate than full-time students. If it is practical and possible, you are better off attending full-time.

I started college full-time in 1970 and went to school for one year as a full-time student. After that I went to college off and on for twenty years. I heard many people tell me, "If you ever quit, you'll never go back." But I did go back. Over and over and over again I went back. I have decided that when people say that, they are really expressing something about themselves. They quit and they never went back. This doesn't mean that you can't or won't. I have had to take time off to rest. College is exhausting if you are also the head of a household. I have taken off years because I had challenging jobs that precluded me from attending school. I have taken off time because I was discouraged. But I always went back, and you can too. I got my Bachelor's degree in December of 1990. I quit my full-time job to go back to school full-time and finish my degree. That may or may not be possible for you to do. But persistence is possible in all of us.

I have gone full-time, part-time and no time. But I always went back, and I eventually finished what I started. I do not believe that I am exceptional, special or gifted in any way. I do believe that if I could do it, so can you.

■ Doing the Dream

And, oh, about that last, and the biggest worry: Will I fit in those desks? The answer is: not very comfortably, but, definitely yes! Don't let such details keep you from showing up and attempting school. It has been one of the most satisfying and wonderful experiences of my life. If I could afford to be in school forever, I'd be there. I'm doing the next best thing by becoming an instructor. I still get to be in the school environment, but now I don't have to TAKE the tests; I GIVE them!

Going back to school is scary. It provoked a lot of anxiety in me. I had many doubts and worries. However, I found out that you can live fairly comfortably on very little money, IF you have planned ahead well and you've covered as many options as possible. I found many good friends, young and old(er). If necessary, go to the college counseling or student development center. There are professionals there skilled in helping you adjust to the situation.

I have never remotely done anything as satisfying as college except for the birth of my daughter. College has been a special experience. It wasn't all triumph, some of it was a trial. It hasn't been all book learning and theory, a lot of it was also applied and practical. If you have a college degree as your dream, then *do it!* Keep at it until you succeed. It *is* worth the energy and effort you sink into it. Don't listen to all those pessimists that tell you, "If you ever quit, you'll never go back." I did. In fact I went back over and over and over again until I got my degrees. So can you. And, remember the very best advice I got as I progressed through my programs: "You only have to do this for 10(16) weeks." (Depending on whether you're on a quarter or semester system, you only have to do THIS for 10 or 16 weeks.) You don't have to do it forever. You don't have to do it for a year or three or four years. You only have this particular schedule, and this particular set of headaches for just 10(16) weeks. "You can do *anything* for 10(16) weeks!" The quarter/semester you are presently in is the only one you can care about at any particular time. Do that one, and do it well, and eventually when you collect enough of them successfully behind you, they *do* give you a diploma. Don't allow yourself to become overwhelmed. As a professor once told me about a class, "The bad news is you do have to eat an elephant this quarter. The good news is, I'll feed it to you a bite at a time." Well, the bad news is you do have to collect four or so years of education. The good news is, you only do it 10(16) weeks at a time.

CHAPTER 7
A Student's Healthy Lifestyle

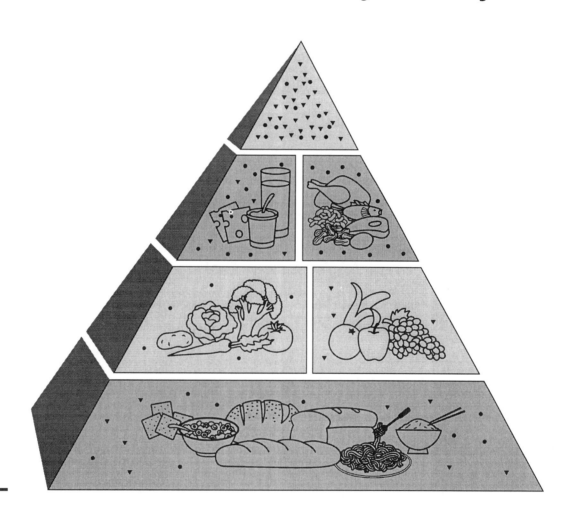

Maintaining a Healthy Lifestyle

■ Healthy Lifestyles through Wellness

How are you? You probably answered "fine" without really thinking. But, how do you **really** feel . . . about yourself, your life, your lifestyle, your health? Chances are that you may not have considered all of the many facets that constitute your true well-being. Do you eat well? Do you exercise regularly? Do you smoke or drink? Do you have close friends with whom you can share your experiences, both good and traumatic? Are you under extreme stress to get good grades, perform well on the job, or be a good parent? Do you get regular medical checkups and do you practice self-care? Are you aware of safety and environmental factors that contribute to your health? This chapter will help you develop important strategies that will enable you to live life to the fullest, both physically and emotionally.

Traditionally, health was simply defined as the absence of disease or symptoms. This concept has gradually evolved over the past fifty years so that health is now defined by the World Health Organization as a continuous and harmonious balance of physical, mental, spiritual, intellectual, and social well-being. This continuum of a "balanced," healthy lifestyle has been defined as **wellness.** True wellness involves contracting with yourself to engage in healthy behaviors and attitudes that enhance the quality of your life and personal performance.

To achieve this state of wellness, you must maintain a balance of six continually changing dimensions that affect your overall health. These components of wellness are:

Physical

Physical wellness is the ability to maintain positive lifestyle habits to enable you to perform your daily tasks. Such components of the physical dimension of wellness entail eating healthy foods, maintaining appropriate weight and body fat, performing regular exercise to maintain cardiovascular fitness, and avoiding the abuse of tobacco, alcohol, and other drugs.

Emotional

Emotional wellness is the ability to manage stress and express your emotions appropriately by recognizing and accepting your feelings about the events in your life. Stress is part of everyone's life, but your ability to properly manage life's stressful events can greatly influence your overall health potential.

Spiritual

The belief in an abstract strength that unites all of your internal energies. This strength can include religion and/or nature, but also includes your values, ethics, and morals.

From *The Freshman Year: Making the Most of College* by Glenda A. Belote and Larry W. Lunsford. © 1998 by Kendall/Hunt Publishing Company.

Your personal sense of spirituality provides meaning and direction to your life, enabling you to learn, develop, and meet new challenges successfully.

Social

The skill to interact successfully with other people at work, school, and the community. This dimension of wellness encompasses your ability to handle relationships, both intimate and casual.

Intellectual

The ability to learn and use your knowledge effectively to enhance your overall health. Knowledge of self-care techniques, disease risk factors, as well as your family history of disease, are all important components to achieving intellectual wellness.

Environmental

The physical and social setting that influences your lifestyle. This dimension includes your personal safety practices, such as wearing seat belts, to your efforts to help promote a clean environment.

These six dimensions of wellness overlap, and components of one often can directly or indirectly affect factors in another. Some health parameters are under your direct control and some are not. For example, your lifestyle behaviors (diet, exercise, habits) constitute the greatest percentage of influences on the quality of your life.

Relationships involving family, friends, and the community are also important, as are factors pertaining to the quality of health care you receive by physicians and health care facilities. Approximately 85 percent of the factors influencing your health are within your control. The remaining 15 percent are beyond your individual control and consist of heredity predispositions. If your medical history reveals a family tendency toward a specific disease, such as heart disease or cancer, your lifestyle decisions can delay the onset, minimize the disease's effects, or possibly even prevent the disease from occurring. This is why a good knowledge of preventive medicine becomes so important.

Health Benefits of Wellness

You can achieve wellness through improving your knowledge about health, eliminating risk factors, practicing good self-care habits and preventive medicine, and maintaining a positive attitude. Some of the benefits of wellness include:

- a decreased risk of developing chronic diseases;
- a decreased risk of accidents;
- a decreased recovery time after injury and illness;
- an improved cardiovascular system function (heart efficiency and blood vessel diameter both increase);
- an increased muscle tone, strength, and flexibility;
- an improved physical appearance—less fat, greater muscle tone;
- an increased ability to manage stress and resist depression;
- proper nutrition for optimal growth, repair, immune function, and development;
- a higher self-esteem;
- an increased energy level, productivity, and creativity; and
- an improved awareness of your personal needs and the ways to achieve them.

■ Wellness as a Challenge

Your belief in your ability to perform healthy behaviors will influence your actual choices, your degree of effort to make the change, your persistence, and your emotional reactions to the new lifestyle. Your ability to turn your health-related goals into reality is dependent on formulating a plan of action. This lifestyle modification has several steps:

> **Step 1. Evaluate your personal health habits.** Make a list of your behaviors that promote health and make another list of your behaviors that are harmful. Once you have compiled both of your lists, note which behaviors present the greatest threat to your overall well-being. These behaviors should be targeted for change first.
>
> **Step 2. Set realistic, specific, observable, and measurable goals.** Don't expect miracles. Setting goals that are too ambitious leads to failure; the fear of failure may discourage future efforts. View lifestyle change as a lifetime change. Strive for moderation rather than striving for complete behavior reversal or abstinence. Behavior changes that are "slow-but-steady" are the ones most likely to result in permanent success.
>
> **Step 3. Formulate a strategy for success.** Most people want to make positive changes, but too often find reasons why they cannot make changes. They may not have the time, are too tired, or simply feel embarrassed. What are some of your reasons? These barriers to change must be avoided if you are to achieve your healthy goals.
>
> **Step 4. Evaluate your progress.** How well are you doing? The only way to consistently stick with your new healthy behavior is to receive feedback by monitoring your progress. This evaluation allows you to modify the program, enabling you to better achieve your goals. Initially, the evaluation periods should be frequent, such as daily or weekly. After periods of consistent success, the time interval between evaluation sessions could be lengthened to, perhaps, monthly.

Success does not have to be all-or-nothing. This manner of thinking can be detrimental to your overall motivation to change. When your goals are not fully realized, simply reshape your goals, set a more realistic time schedule, or formulate different intervention strategies, and **TRY AGAIN**. More importantly, answer these questions:

"What did I learn from this experience?"

"What can I do differently?"

Based on your answers, make a revised contract and begin immediately. Remember that lifestyle change is never easy but its rewards will last a lifetime. The exercise on the next page will assist you in planning for a healthier lifestyle.

■ You Are What You Eat

Dietary habits play a key role in both how long we live and how well we feel. A healthy diet is one that features a proper variety and balance of foods to supply our body with nutrients, essential dietary factors required for growth, energy, and repair. There are six nutrients: proteins, carbohydrates, fats, vitamins, minerals, and water.

Protein is necessary for growth and repair, forming the basic building blocks of muscles, bones, hair, and blood. Meat, poultry, fish, eggs, milk, cheese, dry beans, and nuts are excellent dietary sources of protein.

Carbohydrates provide the body with glucose, its basic fuel. There are two types of carbohydrates: simple and complex. Simple carbohydrates are sugars, which are responsible for providing short bursts of energy. Examples of dietary sugars include glucose, sucrose (table sugar), fructose (the sugar found in fruits), honey, and syrup. Complex carbohydrates consist of starches and fiber, important ingredients of cereals, breads, rice, pasta, fruits, and vegetables. Soluble fiber, found in oats, beans, apples, and citrus fruit, has been shown to lower blood cholesterol levels and decrease the risk of heart disease.

Fats are high calorie nutrients that come in two primary types: saturated and unsaturated. Saturated fats, found in animal products such red meat, egg yolk, and butter, have been shown to increase the blood cholesterol levels and increase the risk of heart disease. In contrast, monounsaturated and polyunsaturated fats are found primarily in foods of plant origin and have been shown to lower blood cholesterol levels. Polyunsaturated fats are found in safflower and corn oils, whereas canola and olive oil are monounsaturated fats. In contrast to protein and carbohydrates, which contain four calories per gram, fat contributes nine calories per gram when metabolized in the body. For this reason, a simple way to lose weight is to decrease the amount of dietary fat.

Vitamins are organic nutrients which work with the body's enzymes to enable biochemical reactions to take place. Vitamins C and E, as well as beta carotene, serve as antioxidants, substances that protect cells from dangerous free radicals produced by normal metabolic processes. Antioxidants have been shown to reduce the incidence of heart disease and certain types of cancer.

Minerals are inorganic substances found in food that are also essential for proper metabolism. Macrominerals (sodium, potassium, calcium, phosphorus, and magnesium) are required in larger amounts than are the trace minerals (iron, zinc, selenium, iodine, chromium, and fluoride). Calcium is the most abundant mineral in the body, responsible for bone integrity and prevention of osteoporosis, as well as for conduction of nerve impulses and cardiac contraction.

Approximately 60% of your weight consists of **water**. Water helps to digest foods, maintains proper body temperature, lubricates joints, and eliminates the body's waste products via urine. Water is necessary for survival, as we would die after only a few days without water. In contrast, we could survive for several weeks without food. You should drink at least eight glasses of water a day, not counting alcohol and drinks that contain the diuretic caffeine, such as coffee, tea, and certain soft drinks.

■ How Much Should I Eat?

According to the American Dietetic Association, 12% of your daily calories should come from protein; 58% from carbohydrates (of which 48% should be complex carbohydrates and only 10% simple sugars); and a total of 30% from fats (10% saturated fats, 10% monounsaturated fats, and 10% polyunsaturated fats). In contrast, the typical American diet consists of too much saturated fats and simple sugars, and lacks sufficient amounts of complex carbohydrates. To best help you determine what your daily nutrient intake is, you need to understand the food pyramid.

■ The Food Guide Pyramid

In 1992, the United States Department of Agriculture published the Food Guide Pyramid, a guideline to simplify the selections of foods that constitute a healthy diet. As shown in Figure 3, the Food Guide Pyramid incorporates five food groups plus fats, oils, and sugars. Foods in one category cannot replace those from another.

Exercise:

Do aerobic exercises (walking, jogging, swimming, cycling, etc.) for 30 minutes three to four times a week.

Incorporate exercise into your daily activities (e.g., take the stairs).

Always do warm-up and cool-down exercises and stretch before and after your aerobic session to improve flexibility and decrease risk of injury.

Nutrition:

Eat foods high in complex carbohydrates (breads, cereals, fruits, vegetables, pasta) to constitute 48% of your total daily calories.

Limit simple sugars (table sugar, soft drinks, candy); consume only with meals.

Limit saturated fat intake (animal fats, whole milk, etc.); consume more fat calories as monounsaturated (canola and olive oil) and polyunsaturated (vegetable oils) fats.

Drink at least eight glasses of water daily.

Stress management:

Improve your time management and organizational skills (set priorities, don't procrastinate, make a daily schedule with flexible time and follow it).

Practice progressive muscle relaxation, meditation, yoga, and deep-breathing exercises.

Self-care:

Don't smoke.

Only drink alcohol responsibly ;(e.g. don't drink and drive, no more than two or three drinks in one sitting, etc.).

Perform breast or testicular self-exams monthly.

Have regular medical screenings and physical exams.

Know your blood pressure and cholesterol numbers.

Practice abstinence or safer sex (always use condoms).

Sleep at least seven to eight hours daily and develop a regular sleep-wake cycle.

Read about current health topics and medical discoveries; check the Internet.

Safety:

Always wear a seat belt.

Learn cardiopulmonary resuscitation (CPR).

Check smoke detectors in your home annually.

Figure 1 ■ Wellness Strategies for Top Performance: Academically and Athletically

I, _____, pledge that I will accomplish the goals listed below.

—Personal Goal: Improve my fitness level.

—Motivating Factors: I want to have more energy and feel better.

—Change(s) I Promise to Make to Reach This Goal: Jog for 20–30 minutes at least three times a week.

—Start Date: January 1

—Intervention Strategies:

1. I will walk early in the morning before classes.
2. I will walk after classes on days when it is raining in the morning.

Plan for Making This Change:

First week: walk for 10 minutes three times a week.

Weeks 2 to 4: Increase the amount of walking time by five minutes every week until I walk for 20–30 minutes each session.

Week 5: Evaluate my progress.

Weeks 5 to 9: Gradually increase my speed.

Week 10: Evaluate my progress.

After the first 10 weeks: Continue my morning jogs three times a week.

—Target Date for Reaching Goal: March 15

—Reward for Reaching Goal: Buy a new, expensive pair of jogging shoes.

—If I Need Help: I can call my friend _____ to walk or jog with me.

Signed: _____

Witness: _____

Date: _____

Figure 2 ■ A Sample Contract for Lifestyle Change

The foods at the base of the Food Guide Pyramid form the foundation of a healthy diet and consist of foods high in complex carbohydrates—breads, cereals, rice, and pasta. The foods at the Pyramid's base are high in fiber, iron, protein, and B vitamins, and should be consumed in the largest quantities, namely six to eleven servings daily. The second tier of the Food Guide Pyramid consists of vegetables and fruits—foods that are high in fiber, low in fat, and high in vitamins A and C. Scientific studies have revealed that vegetables and fruits may prevent cancers of the lung, colon, stomach, bladder, and breast. According to the Food Guide Pyramid, three to five servings of vegetables and two to four servings of fruits are recommended daily. Foods in the "Milk, Yogurt, and Cheese" group are high in calcium, protein, and vitamins A and B-12. Two servings per day are recommended. Foods in the "Meat, Poultry, Fish, Dry Beans, Eggs, and Nuts" group are excellent sources of protein, iron, zinc, phosphorus, and B vitamins. These foods are also high in fats and cholesterol; thus, you should choose low-fat varieties. Finally, foods at the apex of the pyramid (the smallest part of the pyramid) should be consumed in very small quantities. Fats, oils, and sweets are high in calories but supply little or no vitamins or minerals. Select foods from this category that are high in monounsaturated fats, such as canola or olive oils.

◼ Using Your Resources

Visit the campus health center, a primary care physician, or a registered dietician to receive a personal nutrition consultation. A licensed health professional can help you lose weight or gain weight; prescribe a diet to help control blood pressure, diabetes, or high cholesterol; or provide guidance concerning dietary supplements.

◼ Responsible Drinking

According to a number of studies, abuse of alcohol is the number-one problem facing college students today. Although more students are choosing to abstain, approximately 85 percent of college students use alcohol. A small percentage of these students drink irresponsibly, either binge drinking (drinking five or more drinks at one sitting), drinking while under the legal drinking age, or driving under the influence of alcohol. The leading cause of death among college students is alcohol-related automobile accidents. The use and abuse of alcohol is also associated with most cases of campus violence, arrests, vandalism, rape, accidents, homicides, unwanted sex, sexually transmitted diseases and HIV/AIDS, unwanted pregnancies, poor grades, and drop-outs.

Alcohol can also impair your judgment. You may actually have sex with someone whom you would normally not even go out to lunch with! However, the consequences of your decision, such as an unintended pregnancy, a sexually transmitted disease, or an accident resulting in a lifelong disability, may last a lifetime.

By definition, any drink containing 0.5% or more ethyl alcohol by volume is an alcoholic beverage. However, different drinks contain different amounts of alcohol. For example, one drink is defined as any of the following:

- ◼ one 12 oz can of beer (5% alcohol);
- ◼ one 4 oz glass of wine (12% alcohol); or
- ◼ one shot (1 oz) of distilled spirits, such as whiskey, vodka, or rum (50% alcohol). The alcohol content is expressed as **proof**, a number that is twice the percentage of alcohol: 80-proof gin is 40% alcohol, etc.

Food Guide Pyramid

A Guide to Daily Food Choices

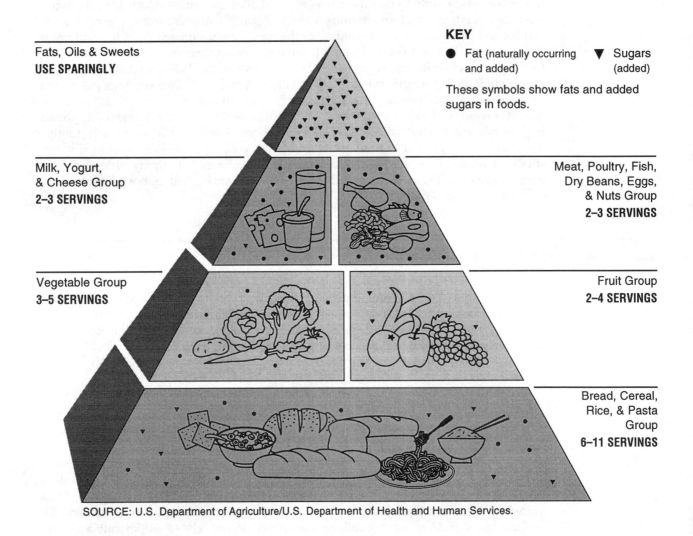

KEY

● Fat (naturally occurring and added)

▼ Sugars (added)

These symbols show fats and added sugars in foods.

Fats, Oils & Sweets
USE SPARINGLY

Milk, Yogurt,
& Cheese Group
2–3 SERVINGS

Meat, Poultry, Fish,
Dry Beans, Eggs,
& Nuts Group
2–3 SERVINGS

Vegetable Group
3–5 SERVINGS

Fruit Group
2–4 SERVINGS

Bread, Cereal,
Rice, & Pasta
Group
6–11 SERVINGS

SOURCE: U.S. Department of Agriculture/U.S. Department of Health and Human Services.

What counts as one serving?

Bread, Cereal, Rice & Pasta Group	Vegetable Group	Fruit Group	Milk, Cheese Group	Meat, Poultry, Fish Group	Fats, Oils, Sweets Group
1 slice of bread	1 cup raw leafy veg.	1 medium fruit (apple, orange, banana)	1 cup nonfat milk	3 oz cooked lean meat+	butter, margarine*
1/2 cup of rice	1/2 baked white potato	3/4 cup juice	1 cup nonfat yogurt	3 oz sliced turkey+	corn, safflower oil
1/2 cup of pasta	1/2 baked sweet potato	1/2 cup canned fruit	1.5 oz natural cheese*+	3 oz chicken breast+	olive oil
1 oz of dry cereal	1/2 cup steamed veg.	1/2 cup grapes	1.5 oz processed cheese*+	1.5 cups kidney beans	canola oil
1/2 cup oatmeal	1 cup lettuce	1/2 cup melon chunks	1/2 cup low-fat cottage cheese*+	3 eggs	palm, coconut oil*+
1/2 bagel	1/2 cup carrot sticks			6 tbsp peanut butter	cakes, pies, cookies
				1.5 cups lentils	sugared drinks

* = foods that are high in fat
+ = foods that contain saturated fat or cholesterol

Figure 3 ■ Food Guide Pyramid

To determine the amount that you can safely drink, you need to determine the blood-alcohol concentration (BAC), the percentage of alcohol in the blood. The BAC is usually measured from your breath. Most people reach a BAC of 0.05% after consuming one or two drinks; at this level, they do not feel intoxicated. If they continue to drink past this BAC level, they start to feel worse, with decreased reaction times, slurred speech, and loss of balance and emotional control. The legal BAC in most states is 0.08%. Persons driving a motor vehicle with a BAC of 0.08% or greater are cited for driving under the influence and are subject to severe legal penalties and fines. At a BAC of 0.2%, a person is likely to pass out and at a BAC of 0.3%, a person could lapse into a coma. Death is likely with a BAC of 0.4% or higher.

These factors will influence your BAC and response to alcohol:

- **How much and how quickly you drink.** If you chug drink after drink, your liver, which can only metabolize 0.5 oz of alcohol per hour, will not be able to keep up, resulting in a rapidly rising BAC.
- **The type of drink.** The stronger the drink, the faster the rise in BAC, and the consequent symptoms. If the drink contains water, juice, or milk, the rate of absorption will be decreased, slowing the rate of BAC rise. However, if you mix an alcoholic drink with carbon dioxide (e.g., champagne or a cola), the rate of alcohol absorption will increase.
- **The temperature of the alcoholic drink.** Warm drinks result in a faster rate of absorption.
- **Food.** Food slows the rate of absorption by interfering with the intestine's absorptive membrane surface. Certain high-fat foods can also prolong the time it takes for the stomach to empty its contents, resulting in delayed absorption times.
- **Your size.** Large people who have excessive fat or muscle tend to have a larger water volume, which dilutes the alcohol consumed. Therefore, large people can drink more alcohol and will get drunk more slowly than small or thin people.
- **Your gender.** Women tend to get drunk more quickly than men. Women possess smaller quantities of a stomach enzyme that metabolizes alcohol. The hormone estrogen also plays a role, as women are more sensitive to the effects of alcohol just prior to menstruation and when they are taking birth control pills that contain estrogen. One drink consumed by a woman will produce roughly the same physiologic consequences as two drinks consumed by a man.
- **Your age.** The older you are, the higher the BAC level will be after consuming equivalent drinks.
- **Your ethnicity.** Certain ethnic groups, such as Asians and Native Americans, are unable to metabolize alcohol as quickly as others including Caucasians and African Americans.
- **Other drugs.** Mixing alcohol with certain common medications, such as aspirin, acetaminophen (Tylenol), and ulcer medications can cause the BAC to rise more rapidly.

Prolonged alcohol consumption can lead to physical tolerance, as your brain becomes accustomed to a certain level of alcohol. You need to consume more alcohol to achieve the desired effects. This could lead to abuse and alcoholism.

■ Alcoholism

Alcoholism is a chronic disease with genetic, physiologic, and psychosocial consequences. Like other addictions, alcoholism is characterized by the following: drinking more alcohol than intended; persistent desire but unsuccessful attempts to stop drinking; frequent withdrawal and absenteeism; decreased performance at school or work; continued drinking despite the realization that his/her drinking is causing physical, social, or psychological problems; the presence of withdrawal symptoms when not drinking; and the need for increasing amounts of alcohol to achieve intoxication.

■ Drinking Responsibly

Abuse of alcohol is no longer the cultural norm, even in many segments of the college student population. Responsible drinking is always up to you. Alcohol does not need to be present to have a good time with friends. However, if you choose to drink alcohol, it is imperative that you also eat, to slow the rate of alcohol absorption into your body. Set a limit in advance on how many drinks you are going to have, and stick to it. Always go to a party with a designated driver, a friend who, in advance, commits to not drinking. Do everything possible to prevent an intoxicated friend from driving.

Don't rely on alcohol or other drugs as a means to relax; find alternative measures such as exercise, listening to music, reading, meditation, yoga, guided imagery, biofeedback, and hobbies to help you unwind.

Finally, don't drink alcohol just because you observe others drinking or because you believe "everyone else is doing it." According to national surveys, more students **believe** that others are using alcohol (95%) than what is actually reported (85%). Students who choose not to drink excessively report "second-hand" effects of the irresponsible use of alcohol by their friends. These non-drinking students are more likely to be physically abused or assaulted by their drinking friends, or become a victim to sexual harassment or assault. Academic performance may also suffer because of time spent caring for a roommate who had too much to drink; decreased study time, lack of sleep, and poor concentration may also be "second-hand" effects when friends or roommates drink irresponsibly.

■ Using Campus Resources

The health center on most campuses sponsors student organizations which provide information and consultations concerning alcohol and drug abuse prevention. BACCHUS (Boost Alcohol Consciousness Concerning the Health of University Students) is a national student organization that provides programs on responsible alcohol use, including National Collegiate Alcohol Awareness Week and the Safe Spring Break campaign. To find out more information, contact your campus health center or counseling center. They may have physicians or mental health professionals who can assist you or refer you to a community organization for treatment.

HIV Infection and AIDS

We are experiencing an epidemic in the United States that is actually a worldwide pandemic. Infection with the Human Immunodeficiency Virus (HIV) has become the number-one challenging public health problem today, with far-reaching medical and psychosocial consequences. It is estimated that over 30 million people worldwide are infected with HIV, with approximately 16,000 new infections occurring daily. In the United States, it is estimated that over one million people are living with HIV infection, with about one-third having Acquired Immunodeficiency Syndrome (AIDS), the terminal phase of the continuum of HIV infection. States with the highest incidence of HIV and AIDS are California, New York, Florida, and New Jersey. The incidence of HIV infection is highest in individuals between the ages of 20 and 29 years, with the incidence of AIDS highest during the fourth decade of life (i.e., between 30 and 39 years of age). In the United States, AIDS is now the second leading cause of death among people aged 25 to 44, and in many parts of the country, AIDS is now the number-one cause of death among men in this same age range. Although the rate of infection is still highest in men, the incidence of infection is steadily rising in women. HIV infection is disproportionately higher among African Americans and Hispanics, when compared to Caucasians.

Epidemiology

The Human Immunodeficiency Virus is difficult to acquire. It is not spread through respiratory droplets or through casual contact, like the common cold or influenza viruses. You cannot acquire HIV by touching, simple kissing, hugging, or sitting next to someone who has the infection. HIV is not transmitted by sharing eating utensils, handshakes, using toilet seats, donating blood, or by mosquitoes.

There are only a few modes of HIV transmission. The virus is present in significant amounts only in blood, semen, vaginal secretions, and breast milk. The virus is present in very small concentrations in saliva, but there is essentially no risk of transmission via deep kissing. Transmission of HIV can occur as a result of:

- **Sexual activity.** HIV can be spread in semen and vaginal fluids during unprotected anal, vaginal, and oral sexual contact with an infected partner. Transmission is more likely to occur during anal intercourse than vaginal intercourse, and more likely to occur during vaginal intercourse than oral sex. Women are more likely to acquire HIV from an infected male partner than are men acquiring HIV infection from a female partner. The largest number of cases (55%) of HIV transmission involves homosexual sex, usually unprotected anal intercourse, between men; however, the incidence of heterosexual transmission has risen steadily over the past seven years, and is currently at 18 percent.
- **Injections using shared needles.** Any contaminated needle can transmit the virus, making steroid use, tattoos, and body piercing potentially risky unless sterile needles are used.
- **Perinatally.** A baby may **acquire** the virus before birth via the mother's circulation through the placenta, during the birth process via vaginal secretions, or after birth via infected breast milk. Mothers who are HIV positive have a 25 percent chance of infecting their unborn baby; this number decreases to less than 10 percent if the mother receives treatment during pregnancy.

■ **Transfusions of blood, blood products, or organ transplants from HIV-infected individuals.** Since March 1985, the blood supply has been tested for the presence of HIV, significantly decreasing the incidence of HIV transmission via this means. Changes in the methods of screening blood donors have also helped with this decline. However, the risk still is present albeit very small.

■ Testing for HIV

The most widely used tests to determine the presence of HIV infection actually do not detect the virus itself, but measure the presence of antibodies that are formed in response to infection with HIV. The standard laboratory blood tests that are most commonly used are the Enzyme Linked Immunoassay (ELISA) and the Western Blot. The Ora-Sure is a type of ELISA test that detects the presence of HIV antibody in the mouth mucosa rather than in the blood; the accuracy of the Ora-Sure test is about the same as for the blood test.

The Western Blot is a more specific and expensive test and is therefore primarily used as a confirmatory test when the ELISA comes back as positive. The Western Blot is performed on the same blood specimen which resulted in the positive ELISA. If the ELISA is positive and the Western Blot is negative, the person does not have HIV infection. If the ELISA and the confirmatory Western Blot tests are both positive, then the person is diagnosed as having the HIV infection.

Since it takes at least two weeks to six months for the body to produce enough HIV antibodies to be measured by the tests, a negative result obtained on a test done too soon after the last risky behavior may not be accurate. It is imperative, therefore, that the ELISA be performed at least one additional time, preferably about six months later. Approximately 95 percent of people who have been infected with HIV will have positive blood tests within the first six months.

Anyone who feels they may be at risk should be tested for HIV. Early testing is important because treatments with AZT, ddI, ddC, and the powerful protease inhibitors suppress proliferation of HIV and, in most cases, lower the number of viruses in the bloodstream to undetectable levels, leading to a delay in the onset of AIDS symptoms. The use of AZT and the protease inhibitors, however, does not represent a cure. To date, there is no cure for HIV, and education remains the key ingredient in prevention.

■ *Always use a latex condom rather than a natural membrane condom.*

■ *Store condoms in a cool, dry place; never store them in the car or in your wallet.*

■ *Do not use condoms beyond their expiration date.*

■ *Only use water-based lubricants, such as K-Y Jelly; oil-based lubricants will break down the latex.*

■ *Use spermicide containing nonoxynol-9, as this compound inactivates HIV.*

■ *Know how to use a condom properly; practice if necessary.*

■ *Do not reuse a condom.*

■ *ALWAYS use one!*

Figure 4 ■ Guidelines for Condom Use

■ Limit Your Risk

NO ONE IS IMMUNE! Your risk of acquiring HIV infection is not dependent on who you are, but is dependent on your behaviors. The only absolutely safe way to protect yourself is by reducing or eliminating risky behaviors. If you do choose, for example, to have sexual intercourse, you should ALWAYS use a condom, even if you think that your partner is not infected. You can never be certain of your partner's past sexual history or drug use history, because he/she may have acquired HIV from a previous partner several years ago. Unknown to both of you, your partner may have slept with someone who slept with someone who once secretly abused injection drugs. Remember, once individuals become infected with HIV, they can remain completely asymptomatic for many years and may not even know that they have the infection! Next to abstinence, the safest way to protect yourself is to always use a latex condom with the spermicide nonoxynol-9. How confident do you feel that you will practice safer sex? Complete Exercise 2 to find out.

■ Summary

We discussed several important ways to enable you to live a balanced, healthy life. Health is something to be cherished. A healthy student is one who will excel academically, be more productive, and have time to pursue recreational pursuits and spend quality time with family and friends. A healthier student is a happier student, a happier employee, and a happier member of the community. Healthy decision making while in college will pay big dividends, with many benefits that will last far after you graduate.

■ Exercise 1. Wellness Lifestyle Assessment

DIRECTIONS: Using the following scale, answer each statement by placing the number that most closely corresponds to your lifestyle and feelings in the space preceding each statement.

KEY: 1 = "no/never" or "don't know"
2 = "rarely" or "1–6 times a year"
3 = "occasionally" or "1–4 times a month"
4 = "often, frequently" or "2–5 times a week"
5 = "yes/always" or "almost daily"

A. Physical Assessment

_____ 1. I perform aerobic exercises for twenty minutes or more per session.

_____ 2. When participating in physical activities, I include stretching and flexibility exercises.

_____ 3. My body fat composition is appropriate for my gender. (Men: 10–18%; Women: 16–25%)

_____ 4. I have appropriate medical checkups regularly and keep records of test results.

_____ 5. I practice safer sex or abstinence. I never have sex when intoxicated.

B. Nutritional Assessment

_____ 1. I eat at least 3 to 5 servings of vegetables and 2 to 4 servings of fruits daily.

_____ 2. I eat at least 6 to 11 servings daily of foods from the bread, cereal, rice, and pasta group.

_____ 3. I choose or prepare foods that tend to be lower in cholesterol and saturated fat.

_____ 4. When purchasing foods, I read the "Nutrition Facts" labels.

_____ 5. I avoid adding salt to my food.

C. Alcohol and Drugs Assessment

_____ 1. I avoid smoking and using smokeless tobacco products.

_____ 2. I avoid drinking alcohol or limit my daily alcohol intake to two drinks or less.

_____ 3. I do not drive after drinking alcohol or after taking medications that make me sleepy.

_____ 4. I follow directions when taking both prescription and over-the-counter medications.

_____ 5. I keep a record of drugs to which I am allergic in my wallet or purse.

D. Emotional Wellness Assessment

_____ 1. I feel positive about myself and my life. I set realistic goals for myself.

_____ 2. I can effectively cope with life's ups and downs in a healthy manner.

_____ 3. I do not tend to be nervous, impatient, or under a high amount of stress.

_____ 4. I can express my feelings of anger.

_____ 5. When working under pressure, I stay calm and am not easily distracted.

E. Intellectual Wellness Assessment

_____ 1. I seek advice when I am uncertain or uncomfortable with a recommended treatment.

_____ 2. I ask about the risks, benefits, and medical necessity of all medical tests and procedures.

_____ 3. I keep informed of the latest trends and information concerning health matters.

_____ 4. I feel comfortable about talking to my doctor.

_____ 5. I know the guidelines for practicing good preventive medicine and self-care.

F. Social and Spiritual Wellness Assessment

_____ 1. I am able to develop close, intimate relationships.

_____ 2. I am involved in school and/or community activities.

_____ 3. I have recreational hobbies and do something fun just for myself at least once a week.

_____ 4. I know what my values and beliefs are and I am tolerant of the beliefs of others.

_____ 5. My life has meaning and direction. I have life goals. Personal reflection is important.

◾ Analyzing Your Wellness Assessment

For each of the six wellness sections, add the total number of points that you assigned to each question. Place the totals of each section below:

TOTALS for each of the six sections:

A. Physical Assessment   _____

B. Nutritional Assessment   _____

C. Alcohol and Drugs Assessment   _____

D. Emotional Wellness Assessment   _____

E. Intellectual Wellness Assessment   _____

F. Social and Spiritual Wellness Assessment   _____

TOTAL POINTS   _____

Then, divide the Total Points by six to get the
"Average Wellness Score" =   _____

What do your results mean? The results apply to each of the six individual sections, as well as for determining your overall wellness assessment (after dividing your total score by six).

Total for each section (or Average Wellness Score)	RESULTS (for each individual section and for the overall assessment)
23–25	Excellent Your lifestyle choices and attitudes can significantly contribute to a healthy life. You are to be commended!
19–22	Good You engage in many health-promoting behaviors and attitudes. You care about your health. However, there are some areas that you could improve to provide optimal health benefits and wellness.
11–18	Average You are typical of the average American who tends to not always practice the healthiest of behaviors, despite having the knowledge which would suggest the contrary. Now is the time to consider making changes in your lifestyle to foster a healthier future.
5–10	Needs immediate improvement You are to be commended for being concerned enough about your health to take this assessment, but your behaviors and attitudes may be having a detrimental effect on your overall health. Now is the time to take action to improve your health!

◼ Exercise 2. Can You Practice Safer Sex?

Most people know how HIV is transmitted and what behaviors are necessary to reduce their risk of acquiring the virus. However, some of these behaviors are not always easy to do. Your confidence in yourself to perform these protective sex behaviors is as important as simply knowing what the behaviors are. Assess your safer sex confidence level by answering these questions honestly, according to the key below:

KEY: A = I always could do this in all situations.

B = I could do this occasionally.

C = I could not do this.

_____ buy condoms at a store.

_____ discuss using a condom with a new sex partner before having sex.

_____ refuse to have sex with a person if he/she did not want to use a condom.

_____ talk to a new sex partner about his/her past sexual experiences and number of sexual partners.

_____ ask a new sex partner whether he/she has ever had sex with another person of the same sex.

_____ ask a potential sex partner about the use of intravenous drugs and sharing of needles.

_____ be able to avoid using alcohol on a date to help make a decision about sex easier.

_____ be able to clearly express what my sexual expectations and limits are before beginning any sexual activity.

_____ be able to resist an unwanted sexual advance or stop sexual activity if a condom wasn't available.

_____ be able to resist an unwanted sexual activity even when slightly intoxicated after a few drinks.

What do my results mean?

1) Multiply the number of responses you answered with "C" by 2.
2) Add to the result, the number of responses you answered with "B."
3) Responses answered with "A" do not count as points.
4) Add the answers from 1) + 2) above to get the "Confidence Score."
5) Circle your overall confidence score on the continuum below to determine your risk.

| 0 | 2 | 4 | 6 | 8 | 10 | 12 | 14 | 16 | 18 | 20 |

LOW RISK   HIGH RISK

If you scored between 10 and 20 points, you tend to doubt your ability to behave in a way that would protect you from acquiring HIV. You should evaluate your own beliefs and attitudes concerning safer sex in the four areas assessed: condom use, self-protection, sex under the influence, and sexual limits.

Wellness

■ Exercise 1. Wellness Awareness Check

DIRECTIONS: Place a check mark in the appropriate "yes" or "no" box and see how you rate yourself on "wellness."

	Yes	No
Regular exercise can reduce stress and prolong life.	☐	☐
Sports and school performance can be affected by the kind of foods you eat.	☐	☐
Nutritionally good foods cost more than nutritionally inadequate foods.	☐	☐
A college student should eat two to four servings of fruit every day.	☐	☐
Carbohydrates are the body's most important source of energy.	☐	☐
The substance most abused by college students is marijuana.	☐	☐
One alcoholic drink is equal to two beers.	☐	☐
College students need to know how to use stress management techniques.	☐	☐
Of all infectious communicable diseases, sexually-transmitted diseases rank highest with students of college age.	☐	☐
Many communicable diseases can be prevented by immunization.	☐	☐
A regular systematic program of exercise increases your total blood cholesterol which aids the body's cardiovascular system.	☐	☐

From *Keys to Excellence*, Fourth Edition by Cooper et al. © 1997 by Kendall/Hunt Publishing Company.

■ Introduction

Positive
lifestyle
practices

Active participation in a Wellness Program can positively affect the length and the quality of your life. This participation includes a combination of sound nutritional habits, stress management techniques, ideal body weight maintenance, avoidance of substance abuse, knowledge of disease prevention, and a regular systematic program of combined aerobic exercise, resistance/strength/training, and flexibility training. Adopting these positive lifestyle practices while in college will help make you responsible for your own health care. Developing intelligent and lifelong wellness practices is what this chapter is all about.

■ Nutrition

College students have many demands placed on them. Performance in school, athletics, work and leisure time activities can be affected by foods eaten or not eaten. Only YOU can control the amounts and types of food you consume. Just as a car won't run well with poor quality fuel, your body will eventually suffer if you deprive it of essential nutrients.

Nutritionally good food costs no more than nutritionally inadequate food and can sometimes actually cost less. Having a thorough knowledge of nutrition can enable you to choose foods which enhance your diet and give you the best food value for your dollar. Following the seven recommendations of the U.S. Department of Health and Human Services will help you improve your nutrition and can help prevent dietary problems.

1. **Eat a variety of foods.**

	Number of Daily Servings
Vegetables	3–5
Fruit	2–4
Grains (cereal, bread, pasta, rice)	6–11
Milk, Yogurt, Cheese	2–3
Meat, Poultry, Fish, Dry Beans, Eggs, Nuts	2–3

2. **Maintain a healthy weight.**
   Evaluate your weight as it relates to your body fat percentage, blood pressure (leading value) and blood cholesterol level. It may be necessary to reduce your weight if any of these measurements is high. Consult your physician first for advice regarding a weight-loss program. You may be referred to a registered dietitian by your physician if you require a nutritional program.

3. **Choose a diet low in fat, saturated fat, and cholesterol.**
   Limit your fat intake to 25% to 30% of your total caloric intake. A maximum of 10% of total calories should come from saturated fats. Saturated fats are found in foods such as whole milk, butter, ice cream, meats, and hard cheeses which tend to raise the blood cholesterol level. Only foods from animal sources contain cholesterol; thus, consuming fewer high cholesterol foods such as eggs, shrimp, red meat, and organ meats can help lower/control the total cholesterol level. Approximately 15% of the total daily caloric intake should come from protein. Good sources are beans and peas, non-shell fish, skinless poultry, and lean meat. Practice broiling, baking, or boiling rather than frying food. Trim all the visible fat and skin from meat prior to cooking.

4. **Choose a diet with plenty of vegetables, fruits, and grain products.**

   Carbohydrates, primarily found in plants, are the body's most important source of energy. Simple sugars such as those found in fruits, candy, donuts, and jellies are quickly broken down and absorbed by the body. Complex carbohydrates (starches) such as whole grains, cereals, vegetables, and beans are more slowly broken down and thus provide a more stable form of energy over time. They also supply the body with other necessary nutrients such as vitamins, minerals, and fiber. This is why it is especially important to eat complex carbohydrates and a sufficient amount of protein such as orange juice, cereal and skim milk rather than a sugary donut for breakfast.

5. **Use sugars only in moderation.**

   An excessive intake of refined sugar can contribute to obesity, tooth decay, and hypoglycemia. Hypoglycemia occurs when rapid elevation of blood sugar is followed by a period of lower-than-normal level of blood sugar caused by the release of insulin into the bloodstream. This condition may make you feel lightheaded, weak, and/or dizzy. Many refined foods such as candy, baked goods, and soft drinks contain high amounts of "hidden" sugar. If the label on a food product lists sugar as one of the first or second major ingredients, avoid or cut down on that food. Be aware that sugar comes in many forms such as corn syrup, honey, molasses, dextrose, fructose, maltose, glucose, sucrose, lactose, and sorbitol. Often several of these forms of sugar are listed as ingredients on a single label.

6. **Use salt and sodium in moderation.**

   Most people consume much more salt (sodium chloride) than is needed by the body. Reduction of salt intake in a diet may help to lower high blood pressure. The body needs about 220 mg. (about 1/10 of a teaspoon) daily, but the average American eats 10 to 20 grams (2 to 4 teaspoons) per day. Processed foods in particular are high in salt content. Much of this salt is hidden in processed foods. Reduce the amount of salt used in cooking and at the table; cut down on foods containing visible salt such as chips, pretzels, and salted nuts; and reduce consumption of canned vegetables, frozen dinners, and other processed foods.

7. **If you drink alcoholic beverages, do so in moderation.**

   One alcoholic drink is equal to one beer, a five-ounce glass of wine, or 1 ounce of distilled spirits such as gin, rum, or vodka. Moderate drinking is defined as a maximum of two drinks per day for men and one drink per day for women. Pregnant women or persons on any kind of medication should not drink alcohol.

■ Stress

Stress—without it, life would be boring! Stress is the body's response to demands made upon it by physical or psychological stimuli. Positive stress, called eustress, results in better health and improved performance. Winning the lottery, receiving a promotion at work, or becoming engaged are examples of eustress. Distress, which occurs when responding to negative stressors such as a failing grade, loss of a job, death of a loved one, or a divorce can be accompanied by deterioration in health and poor performance.

Your body responds to eustress and distress in a similar manner. You may experience some of the following temporary effects of stress on your body:

- increase in heart rate
- rapid breathing and/or shortness of breath
- constipation or diarrhea

- lower back pain
- tiredness
- headaches and/or dizziness
- sleep problems
- irritability and/or moodiness
- inability to concentrate

If you are unable to deal with stress for a prolonged period of time, serious physical and mental problems such as stomach ulcers, heart disease, severe headaches, hypertension, depression, weight problems, and drug and/or alcohol abuse may develop. Research indicates that people who are very stressed seem more likely to catch the common cold.

Managing Stress

You must recognize that stress is a problem in your life before you can deal with it. Life is full of daily hassles such as misplacing your keys, getting stuck in traffic, waiting in lines, and experiencing other minor annoyances at school, work, and home. When you realize that these situations are not worth getting upset over, you will learn to put up with them and be proud of the fact that you have control over your emotions.

Sometimes stress is difficult or not possible to control. In those cases, you must learn to cope with the stress.

Managing Stress Techniques

- Participate in activities which are enjoyable for you. This is important to your well-being. Make time each day in your life for fun. Laughter is also a great stress reducer.
- Exercise can be a great stress-reducer. People who exercise regularly are able to handle stress better.
- Release emotions in a positive manner. Crying is a very healthy way to release emotions, as long as it is not excessive.
- Practice good time management techniques. Organize your time by keeping an appointment calendar indicating important dates, events, and assignments.
- Set reasonable goals for yourself. Challenging but realistic goals will help you stay on track. Goals which are too difficult will only add to your frustration and stress.
- Talk with someone such as a counselor, teacher, family member or friend whom you trust. Sharing your problems and concerns with another person helps, and he/she may offer another view of the problem. If you feel very distressed, overwhelmed, or depressed, possible sources of help are your doctor, school psychologist or counselor, and local health agencies.
- Practice techniques such as deep breathing, meditation, yoga, massage, imagery, or progressive muscle relaxation.

Remember that the way in which you react to the stressor, not the stressor itself, is the cause of many stress-related illnesses. Take the time to learn which stress-reduction techniques work best for you.

■ Communicable Diseases

Ways to decrease chances of contracting communicable diseases

College students should become informed about the many different kinds of communicable diseases that exist in the world. Attending college for the first time translates into more independence for the student and, consequently, less observation and monitoring by parental authority than in the past. Additionally, frequenting a new environment populated by a great number of human beings will generally increase the chances of contracting a communicable disease. Obtaining booster shots and various immunizations, following good personal hygiene practices, and maintaining high personal sanitation standards are ways to decrease the chances of contracting a communicable disease.

Virus

Communicable diseases are caused by microorganisms called germs. Fortunately, very few microorganisms are disease-producing in humans. Besides, germs must find a way to be transmitted and find entry into a human being to be pathogenic (disease-producing). Disease-producing germs come in various sizes from microscopic sizes to almost visible forms. Viruses are the smallest germs while Rickettsia are barely detectable under a microscope. Bacteria germs come in three micro shapes: rod, spherical, and spiral. Fungi germs include molds and yeasts, and other plantlike microorganisms. Protozoa are single-celled parasite germs while worms are larger, multi-celled animals.

Transmission of communicable diseases

Communicable diseases can be transmitted by several common ways: respiratory discharge, discharges from the intestinal tract, contaminated water or soil, contaminated food or milk, association with animals, insect bite, intimate contact, and sexual activity. Some communicable diseases can be prevented by artificial immunization (inoculations), but many more cannot be controlled by this means. Being alert to the danger signals of the onset of various diseases and seeking early medical treatment are prudent practices to follow. Avoiding the causes of such diseases is also an important practice.

Improved environmental sanitation conditions help to decrease the number of communicable disease cases. The development of antibiotic drugs and penicillin with its derivatives has improved the treatment of individuals who have symptoms or have been diagnosed as having a communicable disease.

Sexually Transmitted Diseases

Of all the infectious communicable diseases, sexually transmitted diseases (STD's) rank highest with students of college age. STD's are caused by sexual contact or intercourse when one person infects the other(s). The five most common STD's are chlamydia, gonorrhea, syphilis, genital herpes and Acquired Immune Deficiency Syndrome (AIDS). Three other STD's are hepatitis, genital warts, and trichomoniasis.

Chlamydia

Chlamydia is a bacteria-like microbe with some characteristics of a virus. It can be mistaken for gonorrhea. Chlamydia must be treated with tetracycline rather than penicillin.

Gonorrhea

Gonorrhea is caused by a bacterial infection. Painful urination and pus discharge from the penis in males, and possible minor urinary discomfort and/or vaginal discharge in females are the typical symptoms. Treatment of choice for gonorrhea is penicillin. Females often cannot detect gonorrhea in its early stages. It is common for gonorrhea and syphilis to be contracted together, so be aware!

Syphilis

Syphilis is a four-stage disease caused by spirochetes. In the initial stage, a lesion appears on the genitals while a genital rash is common in the second stage. The third stage is one of latency with no symptoms; however, syphilis remains highly contagious. The final stage is one of tissue destruction and possibly death. Treatment includes maintaining high levels of penicillin, erythromycin or tetracycline in the blood stream for a specified period of time until all spirochetes are dead.

Genital
herpes

Genital herpes is caused by a virus which promotes sores near the infected genitals (type 1) or on the labial area (type 2). Herpes simplex virus type 1 or type 2 can be treated without drugs. However, herpes cannot be cured or completely eradicated unlike most other STD's.

AIDS

Acquired Immune Deficiency Syndrome (AIDS) caused by the Human Immunodeficiency Virus (HIV) can be transmitted during sexual contact, via body fluids, or by sharing needles. The HIV attacks white blood cells in the human blood, weakening the immune system and damaging one's ability to fight off other invading diseases. Currently, there is no vaccine to prevent AIDS; nor is there any proven AIDS cure. In the early stages of AIDS, there are no physical symptoms or signs that indicate a person has been infected. With a weakened immune system, individuals are subject to infection by various other diseases or to damage to the nervous system and brain by the AIDS virus itself. Death will eventually occur.

Consider some of the situations which may cause a high number of STD's among college students. Do college students know much about STD's? Do parents, and society in general, overemphasize the moral implications of STD infections? To avoid embarrassment, do infected persons try self-medication or receive "quack" treatment? Has the effectiveness of antibiotic drugs used to treat STD's been overrated? Has greater sexual freedom and/or relaxed restrictions by parents contributed to the spread of STD's? Are college students who do not practice "safer sex" uninformed regarding the transmission of STD's?

Safer Sex

Control of certain human behaviors is essential to the prevention of the spread of STD's and AIDS. Abstinence from sexual intercourse and/or intravenous drug use are preferred behaviors. Faithful monogamous relationships and "safer sex" practices—use of latex condoms combined with the spermicidal chemical Nonoxynol-9 from the beginning to the end of sexual intercourse—are desirable behaviors. Oral sex should not be performed when either partner is considered at high risk. College students must understand and put into practice sexual behaviors which are prudent, conscientious, and healthful.

■ Substance Abuse

Influence of
friends

Admission to and attendance in college is a new and exciting experience for students. New friendships and acquaintances are formed. Time is spent on campus, in the classroom, and at organized activities where students are faced with the many influences of campus life which can result in either positive or negative impacts. The use of drugs, steroids, alcohol, or tobacco is a dangerous practice for college students. Research indicates that the influence of friends is the most-cited reason for experimentation in substance use among college students.

Will power

The most important factor regarding substances is not the question of legality, but rather the effect a substance or combination of substances has on the mind, body, and life of a college student. The key to abstaining from the use of substances is to develop sufficient will power rather than to rely on imposed external forces. Will power can be developed just as one develops sound study habits. However, a genetic predisposition to substance abuse may overwhelm an individual's will power. In these instances, external safeguards may be helpful in substance abuse control for certain individuals.

Knowledge, emotional maturity, and will power are qualities which will help students avoid harmful substances whether the substances are considered to be prescription, illegal, addictive, synthetic, natural, dietary, or social.

Alcohol College students should keep in mind that alcohol is the most abused of all the substances. Its low cost, legal status and easy availability make it popular among college students and, therefore, subject to abuse.

Steroids Steroids are synthetic derivatives of the male hormone testosterone. In particular, male students take steroids to help produce large muscles. Steroid-takers are subject to aggressive behavior, high blood pressure, cardiovascular disease, cancer and a long litany of other side effects. The irony is that the intended larger muscle tissue that is produced is highly susceptible to injury by the steroid-taker.

Remember—your heart is a muscle too! Steroids are taken in series that are ingested and/or injected. Steroid use is illegal and is a felony.

Drugs Drugs can enter the body by injection, inhalation, ingestion, and topical application, or through the mucous membranes. Review the following list of classifications and examples of drugs to become familiar with and to avoid use of these substances.

■ Classification of Drugs

1. **Inhalants**
   Airplane glue
   Amyl nitrite (poppers)
   Nitrous Oxide
   Cleaning fluids
   Hair sprays
   Paints

2. **Barbiturates and Methaqualone**
   Sedatives
   Sleeping pills
   Depressants
   Quaaludes
   Phenobarbital
   Valium

3. **Amphetamines**
   Stimulants
   Uppers
   Speed
   Diet pills
   Dexedrine

4. **Narcotics**
   Opiates
   Morphine
   Codeine
   Methadone
   Heroin

5. **Hallucinogens**
   D-Lysergic Acid (LSD)
   Phencyclidine (PCP)
   Mescaline (Peyote Cactus)
   Psilocybin (Mushrooms)
   Marijuana (THC)

6. **Cocaine**
   Cocaine Hydrochloride

7. **Alcohol**
   Beer
   Wine
   Liquor
   Rubbing alcohol

8. **Tobacco (nicotine)**
   Smokeless tobacco
   Cigarettes
   Cigars
   Pipe tobacco

9. **Anabolic Steroids**
   Winstrol
   Deca-Dianabolin
   Depo-Testosterone

■ Exercise—Nature's Tranquilizer

Aerobic Exercise

Aerobic exercise is continuous and rhythmic exercise performed for a minimum of twenty minutes, three to four times a week. Using the larger muscles of the body, beginning aerobic exercisers raise their heart rate to a training zone which is between 60 and 85 percent of their maximum heart rate (MHR).

■ Exercise 2

Calculating Your Training Zone

1. Subtract your age from 220 = MHR

2. Multiply your MHR × .60 = lower limit

3. Multiply your MHR × .85 = higher limit

   Your training zone is _____ to_____

#2	#3
lower	higher
limit	limit

In order for a training effect to occur during your workout, you must bring your heart rate over the lower limit of your zone (60%—answer 2) and maintain it throughout your exercise bout. However, it would be very **unsafe** for you to exceed the upper limit of your zone (85%—answer 3). Fit aerobic exercisers train in a 70% to 85% zone and the very fit between 75% and 90%. Sustained aerobic exercise such as swimming, walking, cycling, jogging, and aerobics works to improve your cardiovascular efficiency, increase your muscular endurance, and expend calories to promote weight loss.

Your physical education instructor can assist you in monitoring your pulse and/or heart rate before, during, and after exercise. He/she can also demonstrate safe body alignment during performance and assist you in understanding the scientific principles involved in selecting and performing the appropriate exercise program for your particular body shape, size, and needs.

Resistance/
Strength
Training

Resistance/strength training programs are designed to increase the strength, size, and endurance of fibers that make up muscles. Utilizing all the major muscle groups of the body, resistance weight trainees perform eight to 12 repetitions per set on 12 different exercise machines with proper form and with a full range of motion during workouts two or three times per week. A variety of different training methods can be developed. Combining aerobic and resistance weight training with a daily regimen of stretching movements is recommended for a total training program for college students. Aerobic exercise, resistance weight-training, and flexibility training are for almost everyone. Students with high blood pressure should participate in weight training only with the consent of their physician. Beginning or accomplished exercise enthusiasts can improve their flexibility, balance, strength, endurance, and respiratory/circulatory systems as well as maintain a lean body.

Staying strong and flexible is the key to staying active in later years. Basic everyday movements such as getting up from a chair require muscular strength. Strength is a benefit at any age and any level of fitness. The development of muscle mass is important in losing and maintaining weight. Lean body tissue (muscle) expends calories at a faster rate than fat tissue. Certain chronic problems such as lower back pain are often related to poor abdominal muscle strength and inflexible posture muscles (hamstrings). Getting stronger and maintaining flexibility can improve your performance in sport, exercise, and dance activities.

Other specific benefits of a regular systematic program of exercise include:

- Increased self-confidence and self-esteem
- More energy
- Improved circulation and lower blood pressure
- Reduced tension and assistance in stress management
- Lowered resting heart rate (aerobic training)
- Decreased total blood cholesterol (aerobic training)
- Maintenance of proper weight.

■ The Importance of Sleep

You will probably spend about one-third of your life sleeping. During sleep, the regeneration of body cells accelerates; thus, young people who are growing and older people who need more time to recuperate often require more sleep than others. Most college students find that six to eight hours of sleep per night is sufficient, but some require more or less.

Insomnia can be caused by many factors:

- stress brought about by physical, social, psychological or economic problems
- excessive fatigue
- excitement or anticipation of a trip or event
- intake of caffeine or other stimulants late in the day
- eating or drinking too much.

If you experience occasional problems in falling asleep, try any of the following:

- Sleep in a dark, quiet room.
- Go to bed at approximately the same time each night.
- Keep the room temperature comfortable.
- Sleep in a comfortable bed.
- Drink warm milk or eat a high carbohydrate dessert just before bedtime.
- Take a warm bath just before bedtime.
- Listen to relaxing music.
- Have a good day, free of stressful situations.

■ Journal Questions

1. What did you learn from this chapter?

2. What improvements can you make in your diet?

3. How can you better handle stress?

4. How can you improve your exercise program?

5. What other changes can you make to improve your health?

6. List at least two things you learned about yourself from this chapter.

7. Did this chapter give you what you expected? What more do you need?

■ References

American College of Sports Medicine. *Guidelines for Exercise Prescription*, Fourth Edition. Philadelphia: Lea and Febeger, 1991.

Anspaugh, David et al. *Wellness Concepts and Applications*. St. Louis, MO: Mosby, 1991.

Byers, Curtis and Shainberg, Louis. *Living Well*. New York: Harper Collins, 1991.

Jones, Kenneth; Shainberg, Louis U. and Byer, Curtis O. *Health Science*. New York: Harper and Row, 1968.

Santiago-Ramos, Patricia. *Acquired Immune Deficiency Syndrome (AIDS) Report FEA/ United AIDS Task Force*. July, 1987.

Selye, Hans. *The Stress of Life*. New York: McGraw Hill, 1956.

U.S. Department of Health and Human Services. *Surgeon General's Report of Acquired Immune Deficiency Syndrome*. Washington, D.C.: 1989.

U.S. Department of Agriculture and U.S. Department of Human Services. *Dietary Guidelines for Americans*, Third Edition. Washington, D.C.: 1990.

■ Exercise 3

DIRECTIONS: Answer the following questions.

1. Why is it important to eat breakfast?

   _____

   _____

2. What types of food should be included in breakfast?

   _____

   _____

3. List three ways to reduce the amount of fat in your diet.

   _____

   _____

4. List three stressors in your life and ways that you can deal with them.

   _____

   _____

5. List two ways that communicable diseases can be prevented.

   _____

   _____

6. How can sexually transmitted diseases (STD) can be transmitted.

   _____

   _____

7. Name the substance that is most abused by college students.

   _____

   _____

8. Why do students use steroids?

   _____

   _____

9. Define aerobic exercise.

_____

_____

10. What is the purpose of resistance/strength training?

_____

_____

11. Why is body joint flexibility important to maintain?

_____

_____

12. What is wellness?

_____

_____

CHAPTER 8
Self-Esteem and You

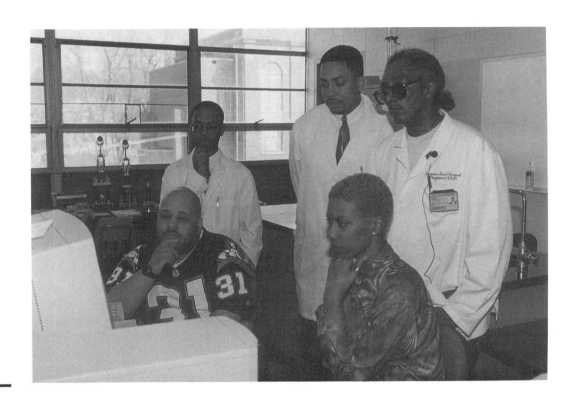

What Makes Achievers Tick?

Successful people are achievers, but what makes them go? Great **tomes** have been written on the psychology of achievement. We believe all this material can be boiled down to one short sentence: achievers are goal directed. Goal and Direction. Let's take a look at each.

■ Goals

1. **Achievers set goals.** They aim for excellence: building a better "widget," writing an A term paper, instilling a love of learning in first-graders.

2. **Achievers set *clear* goals.** There is a difference between dreams and plans. Anyone can fantasize about fame and fortune, but a plan requires concrete, specific objectives to shoot for. The most effective people take the trouble to make their goals clear. Too many students say, "I'm going to get a lot of studying done this weekend," or "I want to make it big in the business world." The true achievers more likely say, "I'm going to study history for two hours Saturday morning and work math problems for two hours on Sunday afternoon," or "I'm going to major in electrical engineering so I can eventually develop computer hardware." When you set clear goals, you can tell whether you're really making progress. If you are, success is a powerful motivator. If not, you can adjust your plans.

> **A**nyone can fantasize about fame and fortune, but a plan requires concrete, specific objectives to shoot for.

3. **Achievers set *realistic* goals.** Their goals demand talent and effort, but they are doable. The most successful people don't generally take long shots. They don't depend on luck. Achievers like a challenge with some risk, but not the probability of failure.

   One way psychologists have studied achievement is to watch subjects compete at a ringtoss game. If points are awarded based on distance from the target, players who throw from medium range almost always win the most points. They also reveal the highest drive for success on other measures. And, most importantly they tend to be the best students, the most effective salespeople, the most successful entrepreneurs.

   Underachievers go after ridiculously easy goals or impossibly difficult ones. Achievers like a challenge, but they don't want to be overwhelmed. They aim for goals of moderate difficulty. Then, as soon as they reach them, they set their sights one notch higher.

4. **Achievers set long-term, intermediate, and short-term goals.** Successful entrepreneurs often have five-year plans, quarterly goals, and a weekly calendar. The best students operate similarly.

■ Direction

Direction implies action, movement, getting things done, making things happen. The director of a movie, more than anyone else, determines the quality of the film. A director is in charge.

Achievers are also in charge. They don't wait passively for success to come their way. They strive to reach their goals. Here's how:

1. **Achievers think a lot about their goals and how to reach them.** They daydream about them, juggling strategies and weighing alternatives. Since they think about how to reach their goals so much of the time, they come up with a lot of shortcuts, improvements, and better methods.

   Just about everyone dreams of success. The true achievers go one step farther—they dream how to make it happen!

2. **Achievers plan.** They're more time conscious. They set objectives and deadlines on paper and keep score of how they're doing. This is why we urge you to use daily to-do lists and to map out your assignments for an entire semester.

3. **Achievers prioritize.** Working hard and getting lots of things done may not be enough if you neglect something important. It's getting the most important things done that makes you truly successful.

4. **Achievers take it step by step.** They implement the good plans they make. They break up large tasks into smaller ones. A year-long project can be divided into a series of shorter deadlines. A college education can be divided into four years, each year into semesters, each semester into weeks. A term paper can be similarly chopped up into manageable tasks.

5. **Achievers overcome barriers.** When they run into roadblocks, they keep trying till they find a way to get around them. Naturally, they can get discouraged too, but they bounce back from defeat rather than letting it keep them down. If personal shortcomings hold them back, they find a way to compensate or they change. They never wait to be rescued. They actively seek out expert help whenever it's needed to get the job done.

One of our greatest satisfactions is watching college students develop. We've seen country bumpkins overcome their lack of sophistication. We've seen shy students join clubs so they can learn to conduct a meeting. We've known premeds who managed to eke out Bs in calculus because they studied overtime and hired a tutor.

Successful people come in all shapes and sizes. One thing they have in common is that they don't easily take "no" for an answer. They're not quick to throw in the towel. They encounter their share of setbacks, but they keep on keeping on.

We recall one young woman from a rural background whose father had died when she was a child. Her mother discouraged her from applying to a competitive college. She filled out the forms by herself and also applied for financial aid. When she arrived on campus, she felt out of place, and she had to struggle to survive in class. Her boyfriend kept after her to transfer to the junior college in her hometown. Besides, who needed a college degree? She could always clerk in the local dime store. With some difficulty, she broke things off with her old boyfriend. She joined a study group, and that helped her with her grades. She got counseling to improve her self-confidence. She had to work part-time to make ends meet. At first, she waited tables, but eventually she did drafting for a small engineering company. She finally managed to graduate and began working full-time for the same firm.

It wasn't a very good job. Her attempts at finding a better one didn't lead to much, so she got help from her college's career planning center. She developed a better job search plan and improved her resume. She was discouraged to discover she was no longer eligible to set up interviews through the campus placement center. But she didn't give up. She began dropping by the placement office at noon and started having lunch with the corporate recruiters. Within a few months she had been invited to interview with several companies. She received several offers and accepted the one she felt was best for her.

We are proud to know this woman who was born into near poverty. Her family and friends advised her against pursuing her dreams. She made mistakes, and she encountered innumerable barriers to success. But she didn't give up.

Today, she is an engineer for a Fortune 500 corporation. She designs radar systems for supersonic aircraft.

■ It's All Up to You

There is a ten-word phrase which contains the secret of your success. Just to make it more challenging, each of the ten words is a two-letter word. The fifth and tenth words rhyme. Can you create the phrase? The phrase appears at the end of this chapter.

If you want success you've got to believe it's up to you to go out and get it.

Who determines your destiny? You? Or is your future controlled by forces outside yourself? Your answers to these questions have a powerful influence on what you accomplish. If you believe you control your future, psychologists say you have an internal "locus of control." If you believe you're a passive victim to what fate brings, they say you possess an external "locus of control."

We believe the foundation of all achievement lies in believing that planning and effort can influence the future. So, are you the kind of person who lays plans to open a business in five years? Or do you figure, "Why bother? Something will go wrong. It always does." Can you pass up the Monday Night Movie in order to fine tune your resume? Or do you think, "It's not worth it. You've got to have connections to work for that company." Do you study harder after a bad grade? Or do you say, "It doesn't do any good to prepare for that teacher's tests, anyway."

■ How to Get More Go

Chances are, you believe you can strongly influence your own future. You probably are the kind of person who is motivated to achieve or you wouldn't have read this far. But suppose you're not. You might be reading this chapter because it's required for a course. And now you're convinced that you're very externally oriented and have very little in common with achievers. Well, don't despair. You can change.

Research psychologist George Burris taught underachieving college students some of the same principles we've outlined in this chapter. In just one semester he got results. Achievement motivation scores went up, and so did grades. Another psychologist, Richard DeCharms, worked with teachers of disadvantaged children. He emphasized that they work to develop an internal locus of control in their students. And the students' grades improved significantly.

So what can you do if you want to achieve more? First, as simple as it sounds, you've got to believe that your own efforts make a difference.

DeCharms has developed an innovative way of thinking about power and achievement. He says people tend to be either Pawns or Origins. Pawns are passive, generally acted upon, and don't have much control over their future. Origins, on the other hand, actively determine what happens to them.

You can take the Pawn analogy one step further—individuals can be compared to the pieces in the game of chess. A pawn is the least powerful piece. Basically, a pawn can move straight ahead, one square at a time. It enjoys very little choice or power. When confronted with an obstacle, it can only wait until the obstacle is removed.

If, however, a pawn is passed all the way to the end of the board, it can be exchanged for a queen. A queen can move vertically, horizontally, or diagonally. It can go forward or backward for as many squares as there are on the board. Talk about controlling your own destiny! The queen has the whole board to play with. The pawn has just one square.

Suppose a queen mistakenly thought she was a pawn. Her choices would be drastically limited. Conversely, if a pawn started acting like a queen, the sky would be the limit.

Why do some people become pawns and others become queens? Why do some students feel powerless to influence their futures, while others are convinced their efforts can make a difference?

Any kind of oppression undermines the development of motivation. Oppression can be blatant, like racism or poverty. It can be as subtle as overprotective parents. But it's too late to change where you grew up or how your parents raised you.

So what can you do if you want to achieve more? First, as simple as it sounds, you've got to believe that your own efforts make a difference.

If we haven't convinced you, please talk to a counselor. Virtually all counselors are committed to helping their clients become more independent, more in charge of their own lives.

Second, follow the suggestions in this book. We didn't pull them out of a hat. Our ideas come directly from the experts on achievement motivation, such as Harvard's David McClelland. Look at the Table of Contents. Every chapter has to do with planning, organizing, developing skills, using resources, and setting goals.

We can't make you follow our suggestions, but we urge you to try them. They work. Your performance will improve. You'll taste success. And success breeds success. We guarantee it. Here's a way to assess your own motive to achieve.

The secret of your success: If it is to be, it is up to me.

Name: _____ Date: _____

◼ Quick-Scoring Achievement Motivation Quiz

Points   **Score**

1. <u>0</u> I have no clear goals in life.
   <u>1</u> I have a general idea of a career in which I want to succeed.
   <u>2</u> I set daily objectives which advance me toward my long-term goals.
   <u>3</u> I set daily, weekly, and quarterly goals which will advance me toward my long-term goals.   _____

2. <u>0</u> I'm too proud to accept help, no matter how stuck or lost I get.
   <u>1</u> I will accept help, but only when it's offered.
   <u>2</u> I actively seek out expert help whenever I get stuck or lost.
   <u>3</u> I am acquainted with most campus resources and regularly use them without becoming dependent upon them.   _____

3. <u>0</u> I tend to give up after the first setback.
   <u>1</u> I eventually bounce back from a setback after a period of immobilization.
   <u>2</u> I analyze my setbacks instead of kicking myself or blaming others.
   <u>3</u> A setback inspires me to try again, using new methods if needed.   _____

4. <u>0</u> My fantasies about career success are limited to scenes from "Lifestyles of the Rich and Famous."
   <u>1</u> My fantasies about career success include practical details of my future world of work.
   <u>2</u> My fantasies about career success include thinking about steps I can take on a daily basis.
   <u>3</u> My fantasies about career success include long-range, intermediate, and daily plans to reach my goals.   _____

5. <u>0</u> Most of my goals are so high that I seldom reach them or so low that I reach them with very little effort.
   <u>1</u> At least some of my goals are moderately difficult—high enough to challenge me but low enough not to overwhelm me with anxiety.
   <u>2</u> Most of my goals are moderately difficult.
   <u>3</u> Most of my goals are moderately difficult, and I increase their difficulty as I reach them.   _____

   TOTAL   _____

Scoring:

 0 Points   If you don't crawl out from under the doormat and start moving, you will be overwhelmed in the 21st Century.

 1–5 Points   You're taking the first steps toward success. Still a ways to go, though.

 6–10 Points   You're on the way, but watch out—success can be addictive.

 11–15 Points   The stuff of champions. You're on your way to succeeding in the 21st Century.

Motivate Your Way to Success

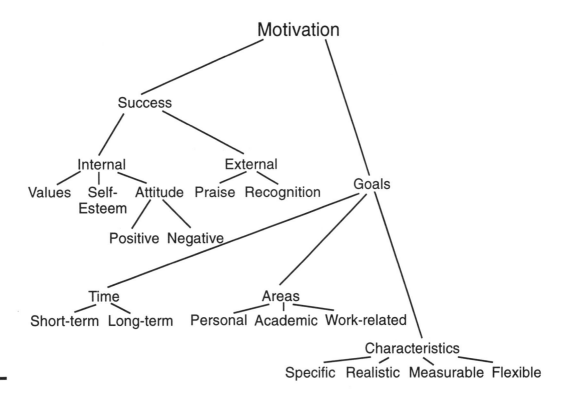

■ Welcome to College!

You have a lot of neat experiences ahead of you, some frustrating, and hopefully many rewarding. Are you excited about this new learning venture? Think back to your first day of elementary school. Do you remember how excited you were? Do you have that same enthusiasm today?

Unfortunately, many students associate learning with "school" and they don't have a lot of positive feelings toward school. Learning performance tends to drop as we go along in our academic pursuits. School is associated with "drudgery," and before we know it our attitude starts to be indifferent.

Let's try and start fresh with a good attitude like we had in first grade!

From *Practical Approaches for Building Study Skills and Vocabulary,* Second Edition by Funk et al. © 1996 by Kendall/Hunt Publishing Company.

■ Why Are You Here?

This is an important question for you to answer. There are several reasons why students attend college. Fill out the worksheet titled: Why Are You Here?

You need to stop and think about why you are in college. Are your reasons for being here due to others? Will these people be responsible for your success in life? Will they be attending class for you? Taking your tests? Receiving your diploma?

A recent study at a midwestern university revealed the top three reasons chosen for attending college were:

1. To increase the chances for a higher paying career

2. To expand knowledge

3. To help ensure success in life

This is a good time to examine your values and decide what you feel is important. Fill out the worksheet on clarifying your values. These values affect the choices you make in life.

The Coat of Arms Worksheet will help you think about your personal feelings. Fill in this worksheet and think about the priorities in your life.

The student who is "educated" is the one who has learned how to learn. It is important to be aware of your values and goals because that will help motivate you to do your best. You need to recognize what is important to you, and strive to reach your potential. A college education can help you develop a flexible and open mind, sharpen your ability, and enrich your life.

■ What Is a Successful College Student?

We all want to be successful. There is not one college student that attends college to be unsuccessful. How can we be successful? There have been numerous studies done in this area. Most of these studies show that successful students tend to possess the following characteristics:

1. *They have a definite reason for attending college.*

   You must decide what *you* want out of college. After completing the Worksheet, Why Are You Here, you have had the opportunity to think about what is important to you.

2. *They have selected a vocation and are pursuing this course.*

   Don't panic if you don't have a career chosen. But, be aware that it provides motivation to have a career goal. Spend this first year trying out several courses in varying fields. Maybe one will ring a bell! When you have chosen your career, you will be motivated by a clearer sense of direction.

3. *They realize the need for understanding the material in each class and envision the value of it.*

   A successful student does not study just to pass a test. They usually have a 3-pronged approach to the material.

A. They master the basic facts. Without doing this, there is nothing on which to build.

B. They take these basic facts and draw supporting details in for a total picture.

C. They learn to "think" with the subject. Once you are able to explain a concept in your own words—it's yours!

This approach allows them to "learn" the subject matter, not just memorize it.

4. *They have a desire for success.*

The more success you experience, the more you will want.

"Success Breeds Success"

"Success Creates Interest"

What a wonderful feeling accomplishment can bring! Have you ever failed a class that you really liked? Probably not. Success can create interest, which further ensures success. One way we have of achieving success is the attainment of goals. Much more about that later!

5. *They have the will to succeed.*

Abraham Lincoln loved to read. It was told that he walked 20 miles to borrow a book. Would you exert that much effort? If we can't park close to the library, we probably will not bother to check out a book!

How can we develop this kind of will to succeed?

GOALS $\longrightarrow$ SUCCESS $\longrightarrow$ STRENGTHENS WILL $\longrightarrow$ MORE SUCCESS

We can develop this will to succeed by the attainment of short-term goals. Small successes strengthen our will, and the strengthened will provides us with additional power to work even harder.

6. *They have developed good study skills.*

The definition of study skills is the efficient use of our mind and our time. The key word is "efficient." There are other phases of our life that need attention, and we need to develop study skills so we can accomplish the maximum in the minimum amount of time. Study skills are not instinctive, but something that we need to learn. The goal of study skills is independent learning. As long as you look to someone else for interpretation, you are not a free person intellectually.

7. *They know they must set priorities. "This is the time to learn"*

Rank your needs at this time. It is not necessary for school to be number 1, but it must be extremely high on the list.

Consider this scenario:

Greg was studying for a physics test. Doug and Jeff were on their way for pizza and a movie. They stopped by Greg's room and invited him along. Greg's decision could be crucial toward a high grade on his test the next day. What would you do?

■ What Is Motivation?

Webster's Dictionary defines motivation as the condition of being motivated; an incentive or drive. How do we apply this to ourselves? Let's think for a moment about ourselves.

How many brain cells do you have?

Hint: A lot more than you think!

You have 13 billion brain cells. Do you feel smarter already? One thing you should be thinking about right now is how to use these 13 billion cells to their fullest potential. In this book you will be able to find several effective ways to learn; ways that are the best for *you*.

Let's imagine that we have an assembled computer sitting in front of us. This computer contains one million parts.

What is the first thing we would need to do in order to use it?

Hint: Think electricity.

O.K., we should plug it in to the electrical outlet. What do we need to make *our* 13 billion part computer work? Our electric current is called *motivation*. Motivation is what makes learning come alive!

What Is Your Source of Motivation?

Our source of motivation is human needs. The psychologist Abraham Maslow believed that all human beings have a need to grow, to develop abilities, to be recognized, and to achieve. He viewed human needs in hierarchical order. Some needs take precedence over others. We need to satisfy the lower needs in order to achieve the higher ones (see Figure 1). If we don't take care of our fundamental needs which are our basic physiological needs (hunger, thirst, sex) and our need to feel safe, then we have difficulty proceeding to the next level which involves our psychological needs. These in turn need to be fulfilled in order to reach the top which is our self-actualization needs. For self-actualized persons, problems become a means for growth. Wouldn't it be nice to view problems in this manner?

What Is the Difference between External and Internal Motivation?

1. *Internal Motivation*—These are motivational elements that are within ourselves. We have feelings of pleasure or disgust as we meet or fail to meet our own standards. This is the reinforcement level we should all strive to meet. We should try to find value in our work, enjoy success, develop an appropriate value system, and thereby reinforce ourselves for our efforts. People differ in what they think provides reinforcement.

2. *External Motivation*—These are motivational elements that come from outside stimuli. Rewards in the form of material things, privileges, recognition, trophies, praise, or friendship. These are a "public" way of saying a job is well done.

Critical Thinking

Todd felt he had prepared for his first major exam in geology. Science was difficult for him. He had attended all lectures, revised his notes, and read the chapters. He made an appointment with his professor to clarify some points that he didn't understand. He felt he was ready for the exam. When Dr. Jones returned the test, Todd had scored 94%. The reward of the high score was a real high! He felt successful, and knew he could continue to do well in this course. He called his parents that night and they were elated. Their praise echoed their feelings. Todd had received internal and external praise. Do you believe the external or the internal motivation that he received from the test score was the best motivator?

As you progress through school, internal motivators should become stronger. We should not always feel the need for external motivation. This doesn't mean we don't want external rewards, but its value should begin to lessen.

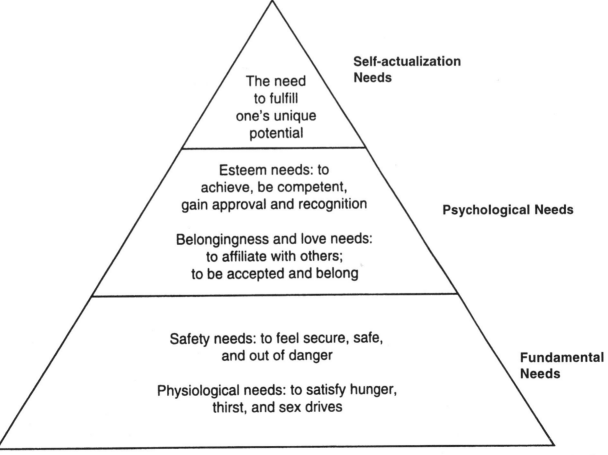

Figure 1 ■ Maslow's hierarchy of human needs. According to Maslow, it is only after satisfying the lower levels of need that a person is free to progress to the ultimate need of self-actualization.

■ What Are Your Goals?

Motivation is the first step in all goals. A goal should be something that you desire and that you will be motivated enough to try and reach.

Goals can be divided into three categories:

1. *Personal*—These will be determined by your value system. You have already filled out the value worksheet. This should give you an idea of what you feel is important to you. Personal goals can also include personal fitness, developing a positive attitude, and overcoming a bad habit.

2. *Academic*—You can be successful if you set your goals on what *you* want to get out of college. The worksheet on reasons to attend college should also include some academic goals.

3. *Work Related*—What do you want from your chosen field of work? Improving your performance? Changing jobs? Learning new skills?

Why Do You Need Short-term and Long-term Goals?

It is necessary to have short-term and long-term goals. It is easy to lose motivation with only long-term goals. Short-term goals are necessary to act as our motivational elements. The accomplishment of these goals give us the will to succeed. Long-term goals clarify our direction.

What Are Some Important Characteristics of Goals?

There are four characteristics of goals that we will discuss. While you are reading about these characteristics, think about how you can apply these points to your life.

1. *Goals should be realistic*—A realistic goal is one you can reasonably expect to achieve given your abilities. If your goal is too high and you don't reach it, it can certainly affect your self-concept. If your goal is too low, when you attain this goal there is no real feeling of success.

   Amy attained a 3.0 (out of a 4.0) in high school. Her college goal was to attain a 3.0 average. Is this a realistic goal? Is Amy setting herself up for failure, or is this a possible goal?

   Bill was valedictorian of his graduating class. His goal in college was to maintain a C average. His goal was not high enough to give him the sense of accomplishment that he would need to make him feel successful.

2. *Goals should be measurable*—A measurable goal establishes a time frame and it also has a foreseeable outcome. You should have daily and weekly goals. Attaining these short-term goals will give you the successful feeling that you need to experience to keep you going. Semester, yearly, and other long-term goals (college degree, marriage, family) are also vital because they clarify your direction.

3. *Goals should be flexible*—Decide what you want to do and be willing to change your plans if necessary. Rarely do we set goals and follow through to completion without any problems. You might change your major, withdraw from a class, or experience any number of setbacks. Reassess your plan for reaching your goal. You might

need to revise it or make a new plan. It's alright to change your goals if you make a mistake or decide to change your plans.

4. *Goals should be specific*—The purpose of goals is to make us "act." In order for a goal to activate us, we must have specific objectives in mind. If we are too vague, we never receive the satisfaction of success that we should feel when we attain the goal.

Nancy's goal this semester is to attain a 3.0 grade point average. Peggy's goal this semester is to "do well" in her classes. Who will receive the greater satisfaction if they attain their goal? Who will know if their goal is met?

Goals do not have to be major events. Your goal for today may include:

> Pick up cleaning
> Read chapter 3 in sociology
> Do math problems 2.1 through 2.6
> Clean the bathroom

These are specific goals. You will know at the end of the day if you have attained them. These are much more motivating than:

> Run errands
> Study
> Catch up on housework

■ Is There a Relationship between Setting Goals and Academic Success?

After what we have learned to recognize about goals, this is an easy question to answer—Yes—Yes—Yes. Goals are activators, they provide a successful background that enables you to continue to strive. They are like gas to a car, food to our bodies, and rain to the grass.

The attainment of goals is also related to a positive attitude and high self-esteem. When we attain goals, we feel successful!

■ How Can You Develop a Positive Attitude?

Visualize yourself being successful. Jeni Burnett, a Pittsburgh State University basketball player, relates her success technique at the free throw line:

> *First of all, I block out the crowd noise. I dribble a couple of times and feel the ball. During this time I visualize my entire body. I think about my legs bent properly, my arms' and hands' position, my release, the ball being "up," the correct spin, the right arch, my follow-through. I see the ball "swish" the net.*

It is amazing how powerful positive thinking can be! It is also very contagious. Of course, negative thinking is also contagious. It is unbelievable how a "down" person can pull others "down" with them. We all know some people that constantly dwell on the negative side of life. They sometimes do not even realize it—it has become a way of life.

> *Fred woke up with a headache. He had worked a double shift the previous day. His roommate, Jim, was on his way out the door to class. Jim had actually read his history chapter and he hoped it would help him take better notes. Fred noticed it was raining; he had worked a double shift the previous day. He rolled over and muttered that he wasn't going to fight the rain to listen to Dr. Smith's boring biology lecture. It was annoying enough that he had a headache. He could have gotten the notes from Sue, but he recalled after his remark about her sweater that she probably wouldn't share her notes. He told Jim that he couldn't understand why teachers always seem to enjoy frustrating students. There had to be more to life. Jim walked out the door to go to class. He was beginning to wonder why he got out of bed today.*

■ What about That Negative Voice?

Should we look at the negative side of a situation? We don't like to because being a "positive" person is crucial to our success. We also need to be realistic (unfortunately or fortunately—life is "real"). What are you going to do if you fail the first test in one of your classes? That is a possibility (distant, of course). What will your plan be? Inside we have two voices that are always screaming to get out of us. One is a positive voice, the other is the dreaded negative voice. Unfortunately, the voice seems to have more volume at the most inopportune times.

> *Jane came to college from a large high school. She took college prep classes and maintained a B average. She was active in a lot of social activities in her high school. Studying was a concern, but certainly not a major one. She kept up in her classes with very little effort. Jane came to college and since she had experienced success in high school with very little effort, why should this change? The social scene was important to her in college (that's o.k.) and she knew everything would just fall in place. In sociology and biology her first exams fell on the same day. (Don't teachers ever get together and try to avoid this?) The night before the tests (as in high school), Jane sat down and started digging. "Surely, I won't need to know all of this, so I'll concentrate on my notes," she rationalized. "The notes are obviously what the teachers will think is important. After all, that is what they talked about!" A lot of the information didn't seem that vital, so Jane picked*

out what she thought would be on the tests. About midnight, after telling at least twelve of her friends how hard she was studying, she was ready to call it a night. After all, her biology test was at 11:00 and her sociology was at 1:00. There was a mild panic at 9:30 the next morning when she realized she had slept through her alarm. But, not to worry, she had plenty of time to shower and review once more. Food could wait until lunch.

The biology test was given to the class. How could it be that many pages? Where did he come up with these questions? She found a lot of questions that she thought she knew, but the wording was ridiculous! What a relief when that was finished! On for a quick lunch and the sociology test.

She thought, "These teachers must get together and decide to ask weird questions." She wondered if there was an upper level education class for teachers that taught them to ask sneaky questions. "Why don't they ask questions that come directly from the book? After all, they wanted us to read it"—were two thoughts that Jane had. Jane definitely needed a nap after these two tests. She wasn't very concerned until the tests were handed back. There must be a mistake! She had never made a D in her life! How could she have made a D on both exams? She quickly folded back the corner of the tests so no one could see. What voices were screaming to be heard?

This could and might very well happen to you. It's not important that it happened, but it's how you are going to react that is important. You can turn this experience into a productive event. Before you throw this book in the trash, let's analyze the situation. Which voices will be dominant?

"I'm not smart enough to be here!"
"The teacher is a jerk—he didn't cover this!"
"He tried to trick us!"
"I hate this class!"
"At least I did better than Sally."
"I didn't really understand, I just memorized."
"I could have used the book to help me understand the notes."
"Now I know the type of questions that he asks."

High school students are usually concerned with the "literal" meaning of their textbooks. This means they are interested in the exact meaning—the words that are obviously stated. In college it is important to have an understanding of the material so you can *apply* the information. Concepts or ideas should be the result of studying your text. Maybe this means one of our *goals* should be the understanding of what the author is trying to say along with your teacher's interpretation. What do you think?

■ Summary

It is important to think about *why* you are attending college. You should recognize your values and goals because they clarify your direction. Your motivation is directly related to achieving your goals. Success in our endeavors strengthens our will to succeed.

A good positive attitude is vital in achieving success in college as well as in life!

Name: _____ Date: _____

■ Why Are You Here?

What are your reasons for attending college? Listed below are some reasons why some students attend college. Check those which are closest to the reasons why you are here.

_____ 1. I want to earn a degree.

_____ 2. My friends are in college and I want to be with them.

_____ 3. I want to please my parents.

_____ 4. I want to meet new people.

_____ 5. I want to prepare myself for a career.

_____ 6. College graduates make more money.

_____ 7. I want to broaden my knowledge.

_____ 8. College graduates have more status.

_____ 9. I don't want to work full time.

_____ 10. I want to improve my skills so I can get a better job.

_____ 11. My parents gave me no other choice.

_____ 12. I have a strong desire to achieve.

_____ 13. I want to become more independent.

_____ 14. I wanted to get away from home.

_____ 15. I want to participate in campus social life.

_____ 16. I have an athletic scholarship, veteran's benefits, etc.

_____ 17. College graduates have better jobs.

_____ 18. I couldn't go when I was younger.

_____ 19. I can advance to a higher level position at work.

_____ 20. To help ensure success in life.

_____ 21. I want to please my family.

_____ 22. I want to provide a good role model for my children.

_____ 23. I am being retrained because I lost my job.

List 5 of your reasons in order of priority (1 = highest priority)

1. _____

2. _____

3. _____

4. _____

5. _____

Values

In the first column check 10 of the values that are most important to you. In the second column, rank from 1–10 the order of priority of these 10 values.

A world without prejudice _____ _____

A satisfying and fulfilling marriage _____ _____

Lifetime financial security _____ _____

A really good love relationship _____ _____

Unlimited travel opportunities _____ _____

A complete library for your use _____ _____

A lovely home in a beautiful setting _____ _____

A happy family relationship _____ _____

Good self-esteem _____ _____

Freedom to do what you want _____ _____

An understanding of the meaning of life _____ _____

Success in your chosen profession _____ _____

A peaceful world _____ _____

Recognition as the most attractive person in the world _____ _____

A satisfying religious faith _____ _____

Freedom within your work setting _____ _____

Tickets and travel to any cultural or athletic
event as often as you wish _____ _____

The love and admiration of friends _____ _____

A chance to direct the destinies of a nation _____ _____

International fame and popularity _____ _____

The ability to eliminate sickness and poverty _____ _____

A month's vacation with nothing to do but enjoy yourself _____ _____

Write a brief paragraph describing what goals you are setting for yourself that reflects your top value choices.

_____

_____

_____

_____

_____

_____

_____

_____

_____

The Coat of Arms

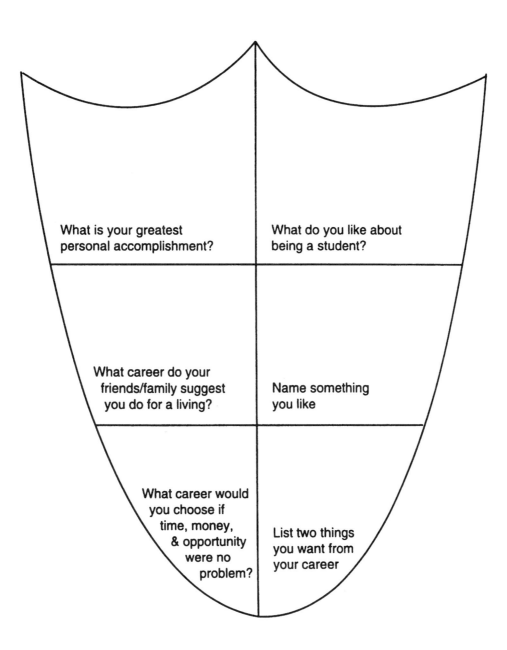

What is your greatest personal accomplishment?

What do you like about being a student?

What career do your friends/family suggest you do for a living?

Name something you like

What career would you choose if time, money, & opportunity were no problem?

List two things you want from your career

■ Personal Goals Worksheet

Your responses must meet the established criteria for goals!

Semester/quarter goals: _____

_____

_____

_____

Mid-term goals: _____

_____

_____

_____

One-year goals: _____

_____

_____

_____

Monthly goals: _____

_____

_____

_____

Name: _____ Date: _____

■ External or Internal Motivation?

Considering your experience in classes that you have taken, what has motivated you to learn, to work, to achieve?

In the first column, put a check mark if the experience has been used to motivate you. In the second column, decide whether the motivation was *E* (external motivation) or *I* (internal motivation).

_____ _____ 1. Teacher paying attention to me

_____ _____ 2. Not wanting to disappoint the teacher

_____ _____ 3. Getting on the honor roll

_____ _____ 4. Getting a job in the future

_____ _____ 5. Wanting to learn and understand

_____ _____ 6. Parents caring about me

_____ _____ 7. Teacher caring about me

_____ _____ 8. My satisfaction from receiving a high grade on an exam

_____ _____ 9. Not wanting to disappoint parents

_____ _____ 10. Being praised by classmates

_____ _____ 11. Finally figuring out the correct answer

_____ _____ 12. Putting words together that became concepts that made sense

_____ _____ 13. Helping other students

_____ _____ 14. Pleasing my family

List below the latest internal motivator that you have experienced.

_____

List below the latest external motivator that you have experienced.

_____

Write a brief paragraph describing how you feel you became motivated. Do internal or external motivation factors seem to be the most important? Do you feel motivated at this time of your life? Why?

_____

_____

_____

_____

_____

_____

_____

_____

_____

CHAPTER 9
Career Planning

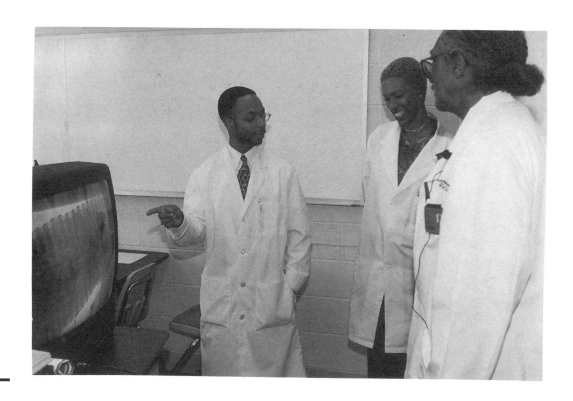

Career Planning for the 21st Century
Realizing the Dream

■ Introduction

Putting together the career puzzle

This chapter will help you understand and solve the puzzles of career planning. Also, this chapter will help show you that planning your future will aid you in achieving many things you want from life.

It's so easy to dream about many things in life. But, if you don't plan you may find that your dream has turned into a nightmare! Undue optimism characterizes many vocational ambitions. Unfortunately this results in a series of adjustments to reality. These adjustments can create disillusionment and disappointment.

You need a plan

Even those fun things like taking a trip need planning. If you don't plan your trip, you may never arrive at your destination.

Just as failure to plan for details can spoil the trip, failure to plan your life and career goals can keep you from being all that you are capable of becoming and from achieving those things you want from life.

Now is the time for you to begin planning your future in terms of realistic life and career goals.

You must decide what you want from life, determine the occupation necessary to support your lifestyle and decide if your are able and willing to get the education and training required for that career choice.

You must build your plan on a good foundation of information. The decisions you make are only as good as the information you base them on. Poor information—poor decision. Good information—good decision.

Students who focus on their career and select a major are more successful in college.

To solve the puzzle of career planning you need good information about three things:

1. Know yourself (self-awareness)

2. Career and job information

3. Educational and training information

These three parts of the puzzle will fit together to make your career decision and career planning easy.

■ Know Yourself (Self-Awareness)

(Who am I?) You need to know a lot about yourself before you can decide what type of career may be best for you. It is important that you consider many types of information about you!

My Interests

Ask yourself what you enjoy doing. You're the expert when it comes to knowing your interests. Do you enjoy working with people, data or things? Do you enjoy science, meeting people, selling, or music? Take the time to think about your likes and dislikes. Ask your instructor where you can go to look through an Occupation Outlook Handbook (OOH). Look at the occupational titles and carefully judge your degree of interest as you read the nature of the work for each occupation that catches your interest. Ask your instructor where you can take an interest test such as the Occupational Outlook Inventory.

My Abilities

Do you have the aptitude for the occupation? If you have the talents needed for the occupation you will find both the training and the job enjoyable. We all have strengths and weaknesses. You want your career choice to emphasize your strengths. Remember that you first must get through the training program. Don't only look at the career at face value. It may look easy to you. Look carefully at the training program. What courses must I complete? What skills must I master? Be realistic! But remember that you have potential abilities (aptitudes) which may not yet have developed into skills.

My Work Values

What do you want from your occupation? The things you get from the job that you value are what we call work values. Values are what is really important to you in your daily life. Think about the following ten work values and decide which are most important to you: (1) How much prestige do you want from the job? (2) Do you want a high degree of security on the job? (3) Is earning a high income important to you? (4) How much leisure time do you expect? (5) Is being in a leadership position important to you? (6) What about independence on the job? (7) Do you want variety? (8) How about employment outlook? Do you want a career that is growing? (9) Are you one that likes helping others? (10) Do you want to work in the field in which you are most interested?

All these work values may be desirable; however, no one occupation has all these desirable values. You must do some value clarification and decide which you can do without and which you need. You then must search for the career that best gives you those values. Of the ten values you just looked at, which three do you feel are most important. Also find two that you would like to have but are not a must.

My Work Patterns

Another part of the puzzle deals with your preferred work patterns. What are your thoughts on working weekends, overtime, shift work or irregular hours? Do you mind seasonal work or traveling? What about sitting for long periods? Do you mind working outside or in extreme cold or heat? What about noise, odors or dampness? These are only some of the work patterns you may encounter on the job.

My Personality

You may have considered some of the previous factors in helping make your career choice. But you never gave your personality a thought. It is found that personality is the most common factor for those individuals who don't seem to find job satisfaction. People many times adjust themselves or become something they are not, hoping to achieve some end. You may go to a job interview and pretend you love to work with people. After all the job is in sales and pays a high income. You get the job and soon you are being stressed due to the high amount of interaction with people. Actually you like working with things better than people. You have play acted yourself into being one of those unsatisfied with their career choice because you tried to adjust your personality.

Personality is a complex subject. However, over a period of many years researchers have accumulated a considerable amount of data that relates to personality and career choice.

By using information about your personality you can be matched with careers in which you can be comfortable being yourself.

You may want to read more about personality or ask your instructor how you can take a personality assessment such as the Myers-Briggs Type Indicator which is very popular with career counselors.

■ Career and Job Information

Now that you know yourself you will need to know about careers. Then you can put of the puzzle together. You must find out about different occupations and see where you fit in. You will be matching yourself and occupations.

This section will tell you how you can find the occupations that match your interest, abilities, work patterns and personality.

Use your campus career center or library to read printed material and get computer print-outs for occupational information. Use books and computer programs such as the Occupational Outlook Handbook. It is available in both book and computer form. The SIGI computer program, or other programs available, are excellent sources of current information. Talk to people in the field and visit job sites.

Remember, the decision you make is only as good as the information you base it on!

■ Educational and Training Information

The final piece of the puzzle is the training program. You must find the best one for you. Again you must find information about a number of things to make a good match.

Now that you know your major you must see which program suits you best. What length of program do you want? Do you want a certificate or occupational program that takes a year or less to complete? Are you interested in a two-year technical program or a two-year Associate in Science Degree? Does your career choice require a license, certification or internship? Can you meet admission standards? Is the program limited access (you compete with others to get one of the limited slots in the program) or have preselect classes (courses you must take and make good grades before you are allowed to apply)? Does your career choice require you to get a bachelor's, master's or doctorate degree? What are the required courses, or skills I must complete? What will it cost? Where is the training? Do your academic ability and interests match that of the program? Does the program match your major goals?

To search out this information you can visit your career center or library to find admission requirements. You can talk to advisors and talk to people who have gone through the program. Send for flyers and catalogs. Visit the school if you can.

■ Career Resources on Campus

Pick up pamphlets explaining these courses or just browse through the career books and college catalog collection. University transfer and scholarship information may also be found there. Your instructor may even take your class to the Center for more information.

■ University Transfer and Scholarships

Once you have decided on a career and choice of major you must decide if you are going on to a university. If the answer is yes, you must choose the right university for you. You must identify what you want from a university and then find those universities that match what you want. You will want to compare universities by getting information from various sources. Use their computers with scholarship information. You also can get information from your advisors. You may also be interested in the one-credit course that helps you with your transfer planning in a organized and systematic way.

■ Summary

This chapter helped you put together the very difficult puzzle of career choice. You have researched each piece of the puzzle and put them together. You now must outline your plan and follow it to be successful.

You found out about yourself by getting information about your interests, abilities, work values, work patterns and personality. Then you researched career and educational information to match to your personal characteristics. You have used a planned and organized way of making your career decision.

■ Journal Questions

1. What do you expect to learn from this chapter?

2. (a) What is your career goal?

   (b) What have you done to make this a reality?

   (c) What will you need to do in the future to make this goal a reality?

3. What values are most important to you in your career choice?

4. Give at least two things you learned about yourself or your career choice from this chapter.

5. Did this chapter give you what you expected? If not, what more do you need?

■ References

M-DCC Staff Career Exploration Center, North Campus, Miami, FL, 1995.

Lock, Robert. *Student Activities For Taking Charge of Your Direction.* 2nd ed. Pacific Grove, CA: Brooks Cole, 1992.

Sukiennik, Diane, et al. *The Career Fitness Program.* Scottsdale, AZ: Gorsuch Scarisbrick, 1992.

U.S. Department of Labor, Bureau of Labor Statistics. *Occupational Outlook Handbook.* Washington, D.C. 1994–1995.

■ Exercise 1. Career Choice Awareness Check

DIRECTIONS: Please place an "X" in the appropriate box.

	Yes	No
1. I should start planning for the future when I get out of school.	☐	☐
2. Many people lack enough information to make a good career choice.	☐	☐
3. My life goal is the same as my career goal.	☐	☐
4. Many people are in careers that do not ideally suit their personalities.	☐	☐
5. My abilities have little to do with my career choice.	☐	☐
6. Abilities and aptitudes are the same.	☐	☐
7. It will be easy to find many careers with work values such as security, high income, prestige, good future outlook, and a lot of leisure time.	☐	☐
8. The three parts of the career planning puzzle are: (1) knowing yourself, (2) knowing about careers, (3) knowing how to get trained	☐	☐
9. I can learn about various careers on campus.	☐	☐
10. Your career decision is only as good as the information on which you base it.	☐	☐

Name: _____ Date: _____

■ Exercise 2. My Dream Career

1. _____ Definite choice

2. _____ Leaning toward

3. _____ Undecided

■ Exercise 3. Identify Your Achievements and Aptitudes

1. For the last 2–3 years, list the subjects in which you got the best grades:

_____

_____

_____

2. List the subjects you like best:

_____

_____

_____

3. What are the subjects that you like best and in which you also receive the best grades?

_____

_____

_____

4. From your past experience, estimate your possible aptitude level for each of these work aptitudes.

	High	Medium	Low
a. Business Aptitude	_____	_____	_____
b. Clerical Aptitude	_____	_____	_____
c. Logical Reasoning	_____	_____	_____
d. Mechanical Reasoning	_____	_____	_____
e. Mathematical Aptitude	_____	_____	_____
f. Social Skills	_____	_____	_____

◼ Exercise 4. My Work Values

1. List your top 3 work values

_____

_____

_____

2. List 2 or more values that are not a must but would be nice to have.

_____

_____

_____

_____

_____

_____

■ Exercise 5. My Work Patterns

List the work patterns you want to avoid.

_____

_____

■ Exercise 6. Career Write-Up

Sources used _____

Job title _____

Nature of Work

Working Conditions

Employment (Where are the jobs?)

Training, Qualifications, and Advancement

Job Outlook

Earnings

Related Occupations

Name: _____ Date: _____

■ Exercise 7. Career Write-Up

Sources used _____

Job title _____

Nature of Work

Working Conditions

Employment (Where are the jobs?)

Training, Qualifications, and Advancement

Job Outlook

Earnings

Related Occupations

Name: _____ Date: _____

■ Exercise 8. Training Decision Chart

Rate each category listed below using the following scale:

2—very acceptable   1—acceptable   0—not acceptable

CAREER CHOICE	SCHOOL	COURSE OR TRAINING REQUIRED	LICENSE, CERTIFICATION, INTERNSHIP, OR DEGREES	COST	LOCATION	TOTAL
_____	_____	_____	_____	_____	_____	_____
_____	_____	_____	_____	_____	_____	_____
_____	_____	_____	_____	_____	_____	_____
_____	_____	_____	_____	_____	_____	_____
_____	_____	_____	_____	_____	_____	_____

Using the rating, choose the training programs that seem like the best choices.

1. _____   2. _____

Name: _____ Date: _____

 # Exercise 9. Matching Personal and Occupational Information

DIRECTIONS: Write the titles of two occupations you've explored (A and B) at the top of the columns. Read each statement under self-awareness. If the statement is correct for either or both occupations put a check on the line under that occupation. If neither occupation matches your personal traits put a check on the line under neither.

Self-Awareness	Occupation A	Occupation B	Neither
Interests My personal interests seem to match the interest areas related to this occupation.	_____	_____	_____
Abilities I have the abilities that this occupation requires	_____	_____	_____
My plans for future education or training are at least equal to the amount and type this occupation requires.	_____	_____	_____
Values (What's important to me) The employment outlook for this occupation gives me the job security I need.	_____	_____	_____
The chances for advancement in this occupation are good enough to satisfy me.	_____	_____	_____
The pay range in this occupation is high enough to satisfy me.	_____	_____	_____
Patterns My work patterns fit in with the working conditions typical of this occupation.	_____	_____	_____
Personality My personality seems to be right for this occupation and I can be myself on the job.	_____	_____	_____

Exercise 9: Matching Personal and Occupational Information

Directions: _____

Name: _____ Date: _____

■ Exercise 10.

DIRECTIONS: Please place an "X" in the appropriate box.

	Yes	No
1. I should start planning for my future right now and not wait until I am out of school.	☐	☐
2. Most people who chose their career usually based their choice on good information.	☐	☐
3. My career goal is a part of my life goal.	☐	☐
4. Many people are in careers that ideally suit their personalities.	☐	☐
5. My abilities have an important bearing on my career choice.	☐	☐
6. Aptitudes are potential abilities.	☐	☐
7. There are few careers with all the desirable work values such as security, high income, prestige, good future outlook, and a lot of leisure time.	☐	☐
8. The three parts of the career planning puzzle are: (1) Luck, (2) Chance, (3) Taking whatever is available	☐	☐
9. There are no sources on campus to get information on careers, universities or scholarships. You must GO off campus.	☐	☐
10. You can make a good career decision without much information or planning.	☐	☐

Choosing a Major

Choosing a major is a decision all college students must make. For some it can be a relatively easy decision. However, for many it is a difficult and often frustrating process. It is important to realize that having difficulty choosing a major is a very common concern for many college students. There are several factors that contribute to the indecision. First, students entering their freshman year in college do not always know what their strengths and interests encompass. Second, there are peer and parental influences. Some parents place unintentional pressure on their children by making suggestions such as "you would make a great doctor," or "you should be a lawyer." These may not be the professions which the student is interested in pursuing. Peer influences may also play a role. For example, a student may pursue a major just because many friends have decided on that major. A third factor making choosing a major difficult is if you are uncertain about your future plans; it is perhaps the most significant dilemma students have in choosing a major. As you enter college, your future plans may change several times before graduation. Initially some students may have graduate school in mind, others may want to pursue a particular career immediately following graduation, but these plans may change several times. Despite the high frequency of indecision, students still let these future plans have a significant impact on how they determine their major. Far too often students limit their options by seeking a major that will be directly related to what they may want to do in the future. This may cause some students to choose a major that they do not have much interest in over one that they may enjoy. It is essential to understand that although choosing a major is an important decision, it will not necessarily determine the course that the rest of your life will follow.

There are several important variables to consider when choosing a major. (Only a few are mentioned here; clearly everyone has unique circumstances.) The first variable to consider is personal satisfaction and enjoyment. It is important to choose a major that is related to your particular interests or strengths because this is likely to lead to higher performance. The second variable to consider is possible future plans. Many students are not able to determine their future plans early in their college careers; as a result deciding on a major is difficult. The most challenging aspect of choosing a major is understanding that a certain major will not limit future goals or plans.

Some students wish to pursue employment immediately following college. Therefore, they seek out "practical" majors such as Economics or Business and Accounting fields. The decision to pursue a business related major is great for the student who may have an interest in the field; unfortunately, some will dismiss other areas of interest to pursue what they feel is practical for employment. The net result of such a decision could be an unsatisfying major and academic performance below one's potential. This scenario is far too common because many students link particular majors to particular careers. Assuming that there is a direct correlation between any particular major and a certain profession is a common misconception. Other students make the decision to proceed directly to graduate school, and some of these students also limit themselves by making a direct link between major and graduate school plans. Some graduate schools, for example medical school, have certain prerequisites, but it is possible to fulfill the prerequisites and major in another area of interest.

From *The Essential Handbook for Academic Success* by The California University Regents. © 1998 by Kendall/ Hunt Publishing Company.

An undergraduate major does not limit future plans. It is important to recognize the qualities that employers and graduate schools desire in potential candidates. Employers are looking for students that have demonstrated the ability to learn and be trained. Graduate schools are looking for academic success, diversity, and extracurricular involvement. Few employers and few graduate schools indicate a preferential major; rather, they seek potential. Potential can be determined in several ways; a particular major is not one of them. Employers and graduate schools will use a student's Grade Point Average (GPA) to assess their competence and potential. Academic success reveals the student's ability to learn or be trained. In most cases, the GPA is the first aspect which is reviewed by employers and graduate schools. If the GPA is competitive, the next step is to determine if the student is well rounded. This can be determined by looking at work experience, internships, (essential for those seeking employment) or other activities outside of academics. This demonstrates desirable qualities such as: time management, organizational skills, the ability to work with others, and initiative. These qualities are very highly regarded amongst employers and graduate schools alike. Finally, the next item which is evaluated is the student's major. Clearly this demonstrates that the major is not the determining factor for future plans.

The above illustrates the hierarchy starting with GPA and ending with major. Since GPA is a considerable factor for employers and graduate schools, the importance of choosing a major that one enjoys becomes even more important. If you dislike the major you have chosen, it is difficult to perform to your maximum capabilities. It is also more difficult to exert the effort required to perform well, possibly resulting in a disappointing academic record. The final outcome could be four or more years of an unenjoyable major that you thought would help with your future plans, resulting in a less than competitive academic record. An alternative outcome would be choosing a major you enjoy, resulting in a more gratifying college career with higher academic achievements which would be favorably received by employers and graduate schools. Clearly, the latter outcome is what the student should strive to achieve.

One of the first steps in choosing a major is finding one which coincides with certain interests and strengths. For example, if working with numbers and problem solving is a particular strength, a major such as Math or the sciences should be explored further. Moreover, if reading and writing are preferred, majors such as English, Political Science, or History could be more of a match. It may help to write out some of your strengths and interests:

STRENGTHS:	INTERESTS:
1. _____	1. _____
2. _____	2. _____
3. _____	3. _____
4. _____	4. _____
5. _____	5. _____

Another way to determine your strengths and interests is to take a personality mosaic, such as the one that appears on the pages following this chapter. There are several different types of personality tests, and this is only one example. It is not accurate for everyone, but it is useful to assess which majors match which type of personality. After completing the personality mosaic, it is a good idea to explore the majors that match your personality as determined by the test. The majors listed may be ones that have not yet been considered or the test may simply reinforce what you were already aware of.

The next step is to determine if any majors can be linked to these strengths and interests. One method of learning about majors at a university is to review the school catalog. Using the results from the personality mosaic, look over the majors that interest you in the catalog. Take a closer look at some of the courses offered within that major. Read the course descriptions and requirements for the major and become familiar with any possible prerequisites. Some majors are "impacted" and therefore require a certain GPA and that certain courses are passed before entering the major. Also pay particular attention to sequential courses. Some majors have sequential courses; course 1A must be completed before 1B can be attempted. Some students may prefer more flexibility in their courses. Furthermore, examine the flexibility of the major; the amount and type of courses required to complete the major. If a particular major has many course requirements, it will be difficult to take courses outside the major. All of the above steps can be labeled as preliminary research. Hopefully the aforementioned steps will assist in narrowing potential majors.

The next step is active research. After studying the catalog, a few upper and lower division courses from possible majors should be noted. One method of actively researching a major is to take a course in that major. This can accomplish two important objectives. First, it can help you to gain exposure to the types of courses in that major. Second, if applicable, you can utilize the course to fulfill General Education (G.E.) requirements. Another method of active research is utilizing one of the largest resources on a college campus, other students. More often than not students are willing to share opinions regarding certain courses and certain professors, which may be helpful in determining what aspects of a major fit with your personality. Another step is to approach the department advisors of the majors you are interested in. Advisors can provide more detailed information about the prerequisites of a major, and can also recommend a professor or a course.

After you have completed the above steps, hopefully your list of possible majors will be a reasonable one. Ideally, this step should come sometime around the end of the second year of school, particularly for those who wish to complete their undergraduate education in four years. In addition to the above steps, students should closely monitor their academic progress with a Degree Progress Report (DPR). The DPR should be obtained at least once a quarter. It explains courses and units remaining in order to graduate, as well as courses already taken and your GPA. One useful tool of the DPR is that it can be obtained with any major. If you have completed several courses in two different subjects, you may obtain a DPR for each major. If you have taken many courses in two different areas of interest, it is possible to double major or to have a minor or specialization. Students may find that they enjoy and excel in two different majors and wish to attain a degree in both. A student wishing to double major must receive approval from both major departments. For those students who wish to graduate in four years, a double major may be difficult, but can be done.

There are always students who can't avoid the "practical" major. If this is the case, an alternative is to major in a subject where the student's strengths and interests lie, and specialize or minor in what may satisfy a practical desire. For example, you may feel that you can best use your talents as an English major, but at the same time may not feel that it is "practical" enough. A specialization or minor may be a solution. You can pursue English as a major and seek out a "practical" minor such as Business Administration or Accounting. Alternatively, if you feel this may not allow you to graduate in four years, you can take "practical" courses outside the English major. Both options will give you an opportunity to major in something you enjoy, enabling you to perform well academically, while at the same time minoring or taking other courses that will help prepare you for future plans.

In summary, there are several important things to remember:

1. It is okay to be undecided.

2. A particular major does NOT limit future plans.

3. It is important to take the time to explore different majors and narrow the choices down through informed decisions.

4. Remember to find a major that is enjoyable because the amount of interest in the subject matter will probably be reflected by the GPA.

5. Although GPA is important, it is not the only factor that employers and graduate schools consider; they prefer students who have shown initiative by working, taking relevant courses, interning, or by participating in extracurricular activities.

6. Double majoring or minoring/specializing are feasible options.

7. Consider if graduating in 4 years is a priority.

Choosing a major is not an easy decision, but it doesn't need to be a painful one either. Take the time to do the research and make the effort and the result will be worth it! Good luck!

■ Coming Alive from Nine to Five

Personality Mosaic

DIRECTIONS:
Circle the numbers of statements that clearly feel like something you might say or do or think—something that feels like you.

1. It's important for me to have a strong, agile body.

2. I need to understand things thoroughly.

3. Music, color, beauty of any kind can really affect my moods.

4. People enrich my life and give it meaning.

5. I have confidence in myself that I can make things happen.

6. I appreciate clear directions so I know exactly what to do.

7. I can usually carry/build/fix things myself.

8. I can get absorbed for hours in thinking something out.

9. I appreciate beautiful surroundings; color and design mean a lot to me.

10. I love company.

11. I enjoy competing.

12. I need to get my surroundings in order before I start a project.

13. I enjoy making things with my hands.

14. It's satisfying to explore new ideas.

15. I always seem to be looking for new ways to express my creativity.

16. I value being able to share personal concerns with people.

17. Being a key person in a group is very satisfying to me.

18. I take pride in being very careful about all the details of my work.

19. I don't mind getting my hands dirty.

20. I see education as a lifelong process of developing and sharpening my mind.

21. I love to dress in unusual ways, to try new colors and styles.

22. I can often sense when a person needs to talk to someone.

23. I enjoy getting people organized and on the move.

24. A good routine helps me get the job done.

25. I like to buy sensible things I can make or work on myself.

26. Sometimes I can sit for long periods of time and work on puzzles or read or just think about life.

Source: Adapted by UCLA Career Planning Center from *Coming Alive From Nine to Five* by B. N. Michelozzi, Mayfield Publishing Company.

27. I have a great imagination.

28. It makes me feel good to take care of people.

29. I like to have people rely on me to get the job done.

30. I'm satisfied knowing that I've done an assignment carefully and completely.

31. I'd rather be on my own doing practical, hands-on activities.

32. I'm eager to read about any subject that arouses my curiosity.

33. I love to try creative new ideas.

34. If I have a problem with someone, I prefer to talk it out and resolve it.

35. To be successful, it's important to aim high.

36. I prefer being in a position where I don't have to take responsibility for decisions.

37. I don't enjoy spending a lot of time discussing things. What's right is right.

38. I need to analyze a problem pretty thoroughly before I act on it.

39. I like to rearrange my surroundings to make them unique and different.

40. When I feel down, I find a friend to talk to.

41. After I suggest a plan, I prefer to let others take care of the details.

42. I'm usually content where I am.

43. It's invigorating to do things outdoors.

44. I keep asking why.

45. I like my work to be an expression of my moods and feelings.

46. I like to find ways to help people care more for each other.

47. It's exciting to take part in important decisions.

48. I'm always glad to have someone else take charge.

49. I like my surroundings to be plain and practical.

50. I need to stay with a problem until I figure out an answer.

51. The beauty of nature touches something deep inside me.

52. Close relationships are important to me.

53. Promotion and advancement are important to me.

54. Efficiency, for me, means doing a set amount carefully each day.

55. A strong system of law and order is important to prevent chaos.

56. Thought-provoking books always broaden my perspective.

57. I look forward to seeing art shows, plays, and good films.

58. I haven't seen you for so long; I'd love to know how you're doing.

59. It's exciting to influence people.

60. When I say I'll do it, I follow through on every detail.

61. Good, hard physical work never hurt anyone.

62. I'd like to learn all there is to know about subjects that interest me.

63. I don't want to be like everyone else; I like to do things differently.

64. Tell me how I can help you.

65. I'm willing to take some risks to get ahead.

66. I like exact directions and clear rules when I start something new.

67. The first thing I look for in a car is a well-built engine.

68. Those people are intellectually stimulating.

69. When I'm creating, I tend to let everything else go.

70. I feel concerned that so many people in our society need help.

71. It's fun to get ideas across to people.

72. I hate it when they keep changing the system just when I get it down.

73. I usually know how to take care of things in an emergency.

74. Just reading about those new discoveries is exciting.

75. I like to create happenings.

76. I often go out of my way to pay attention to people who seem lonely and friendless.

77. I love to bargain.

78. I don't like to do things unless I'm sure they're approved.

79. Sports are important in building strong bodies.

80. I've always been curious about the way nature works.

81. It's fun to be in a mood to try or do something unusual.

82. I believe that people are basically good.

83. If I don't make it the first time, I usually bounce back with energy and enthusiasm.

84. I appreciate knowing exactly what people expect of me.

85. I like to take things apart to see if I can fix them.

86. Don't get excited. We can think it out and plan the right move logically.

87. It would be hard to imagine my life without beauty around me.

88. People often seem to tell me their problems.

89. I can usually connect with people who get me in touch with a network of resources.

90. I don't need much to be happy.

■ How to Find a Major

Scoring Your Answers

To score, circle the same numbers below that you circled on the exercise:

R	I	A	S	E	C
1	2	3	4	5	6
7	8	9	10	11	12
13	14	15	16	17	18
19	20	21	22	23	24
25	26	27	28	29	30
31	32	33	34	35	36
37	38	39	40	41	42
43	44	45	46	47	48
49	50	51	52	53	54
55	56	57	58	59	60
61	62	63	64	65	66
67	68	69	70	71	72
73	74	75	76	77	78
79	80	81	82	83	84
85	86	87	88	89	90

Now add up the number of circles in each column:

R _____ I _____ A _____ S _____ E _____ C _____ TOTALS

Which are your three highest scores:

1st _____

2nd _____

3rd _____

■ Dimensional Analysis

Holland's Group	Characteristic Interests	Characteristic Personal Traits	Characteristic Occupations
Realistic (R)	Activities that involve the precise, ordered use of objects, tools, machines and animals and includes agricultural, electrical, manual, physical and mechanical things and activities. Example: Working on cars.	Present-Oriented Thing-Oriented (rather than people or data) Conforming Practical Shy	Engineering Skilled Trades Agricultural and Technical Occupations
Investigative (I)	Activities that involve the exploration and examination of physical, biological and cultural things to understand and control them: sometimes includes scientific and mathematical activities. Example: Reading fiction	Analytical and Abstract Rational Curious Intellectual Introverted	Scientific, Analytical and some Technical Occupations
Artistic (A)	Activities that involve the use of physical, verbal or human materials to create art forms or products; includes activities and things related to language, art, music, drama and writing Example: Listening to music	Creative Expressive Rely on Feelings Imagination Non-Conforming Idealistic	Musical Artistic Literary and Dramatic Occupations
Social (S)	Activities that involve interaction with other people for enjoyment or to inform, train, develop, cure and educate. Example: Entertaining guests	Sensitive to needs of others Friendly Outgoing Persuasive Tactful	Teaching Ministry Social Welfare and other "Helping People" Occupations
Enterprising (E)	Activities that involve interaction with other people to reach organizational goals or economic gain; leadership, interpersonal and persuasive activities included. Example: Working for a community action or political organization	Aggressive/ Assertive Self-Confident Ambitious Sociable Persuasive	Sales Supervisory and Leadership Occupations
Conventional (C)	Activities that involve the precise, ordered use of data, e.g., keeping records, filing materials, organizing numerical and written data, clerical, computational and business. Example: Working as a treasurer for a political campaign	Practical Conforming Efficient/Accurate Orderly Set in Ways	Accounting Computational Secretarial and Clerical Occupations